ALEXANDER'S EMPIRE – 323 B.C.

Aral Sea

KAZAKHSTAN

Oxus (Amu Darya)

UZBEKISTAN

CHINA

Jaxartes (Syr Darya)

Alexandria Eschate (Khojend)

TAJIKISTAN

SCYTHIANS

Maracanda (Samarkand)

SOGDIANA

TURKMENISTAN

Hyrcanum Sea (Caspian Sea)

MARGIANA (Turkmenistan)

Bactra (Balkh)

BACTRIA

Aornos

GANDHARA

Hindu Kush Mountains

Taxila

Bucephala

EDIA

HYRCANIA

Rhagae (Teheran)

PARTHIA

ARIA

Nicaea

Hydaspes (Jhelum)

Hydraotes (Ra

Caspian Gates

Alexandria Ariorum (Herat)

Ecbatana (Hamadan)

AFGHANISTAN

Sangala

Hyphasis (Beas)

IRAN

ARACHOSIA

usa

Uxian Mountains

SUSIANA

DRANGIANA

Alexandria Arachoton (Kandahar)

Alexandria Opiana

Indus

Pasargadae

Persepolis

CARMANIA

PAKISTAN

INDIA

PERSIA

GEDROSIA (Baluchistan, Pakistan)

Strait of Hormuz

Patala

Persian Gulf

Gulf of Oman

Arabian Sea

UNITED ARAB EMIRATES

OMAN

ALEXANDER THE GREAT'S

Art
of
Strategy

The Timeless Leadership Lessons
of History's Greatest Empire Builder

PARTHA BOSE

GOTHAM BOOKS

GOTHAM BOOKS
Published by Penguin Group (USA) Inc.

375 Hudson Street, New York, New York 10014, U.S.A.
Penguin Books Ltd, 80 Strand, London WC2R 0RL, England
Penguin Books Australia Ltd, 250 Camberwell Road, Camberwell, Victoria 3124, Australia
Penguin Books Canada Ltd, 10 Alcorn Avenue, Toronto, Ontario, Canada M4V 3B2
Penguin Books (N.Z.) Ltd, Cnr Rosedale and Airborne Roads, Albany, Auckland 1310,
New Zealand

Penguin Books Ltd, Registered Offices:
Harmondsworth, Middlesex, England

Published by Gotham Books, a division of Penguin Group (USA) Inc.

First printing, April 2003
1   3   5   7   9   10   8   6   4   2

Gotham Books and the skyscraper logo are trademarks of Penguin Group (USA) Inc.

LIBRARY OF CONGRESS CATALOGING-IN-PUBLICATION DATA

Bose, Partha Sarathi
Alexander the Great's art of strategy : the timeless leadership lessons of history's
greatest empire builder / by Partha Bose.
p. cm.
ISBN 1-59240-06-X (alk. paper)
1. Alexander, the Great, 356–323 B.C. 2. Strategic planning.
3. Leadership. I. Title.
DF234.2.B665 2003
658.4/012—dc21   2002041634

PRINTED IN THE UNITED STATES OF AMERICA

Set in Electra with Bauer Bodoni
Designed by Sabrina Bowers

This book is printed on acid-free paper. ♾

To Baba, Ma, Vinita, Priyanka, and Pranay

CONTENTS

ACKNOWLEDGMENTS

THIS BOOK IS BASED ON MANY YEARS OF STUDY AND RESEARCH, AND therefore many people have knowingly or unknowingly helped shape the content and writing of this book. Of these, nine people in particular deserve special mention for reading outlines, commenting on various drafts, and helping guide the development of this book with their suggestions. Nick Sullivan, who is an accomplished writer, editor, and publishing and public policy entrepreneur, read every word in the book, and though he began with little to no interest in Alexander, he has become quite an expert himself. My good friend from my business school days, Paul Zigman, tirelessly read what I can only describe as my early musings, and gave me precise, often tough, feedback on the direction and content of the book. Max Landsberg, who is one of the most successful and erudite authors and commentators on leadership and coaching I know, read many early chapters and shared with me his experiences of having written three books. Martin Liu provided constant guidance from the moment I had the idea for a book, and responded to my incessant queries about the publishing process with his usual cheerfulness and grace.

This book would never have been possible without the help and guidance of my friend and mentor Graham Sharman, who took time off his busy schedule as a university professor, board director, and strategy consultant to provide detailed chapter-by-chapter feedback. I feel privileged to have worked closely with Alan Kantrow, my friend, colleague, and mentor for over a dozen years; his insights and intelligence improved the content and direction of this book. Alan, the chief knowledge officer of the Monitor Group, has been extraordinarily generous with his time and highly supportive in the arduous task of writing this book. The encouragement, inspiration, and guidance of Mark Fuller, the chairman of the Monitor Group, have been pivotal. On several occasions in the course of my writing, I turned to Mark for help or guidance on some substantive issue or other, and he not only helped steer me in the right direction, but also his enthusiasm for, interest in, and knowledge of the topic inspired me to achieve a bar I know will only remain aspirational. I also owe a very special thanks to Joe Fuller, the CEO of Monitor Action Group, and Steve Jennings, a senior partner at Monitor, for their constant coaching, guidance, and mentorship, and most of all for their encouragement and friendship, which made possible the writing of this book.

Because this book has been "in the works" for several years—indeed, decades—friends and colleagues almost everywhere I have lived have in many ways contributed to it. Even at the risk of turning this into something resembling an Oscar-acceptance speech, I would like to acknowledge the contributions of some of them. From India, my friends J.R.S. Rathore and Vinayak Hazare have put up with and facilitated many visits to out-of-the-way bookshops and libraries. My engineering school buddies, Abhijit Chavan, Jay Chennat, Mukul Gala, Virender Jamwal, Krishna Kilambi, and Bryan Shah who generously put up with my interests in ancient history and covered for me on those many occasions when I should really have been calculating the frequency distribution of a cantilever beam or drawing the isometric view of a truss. I am grateful to my friend Raj Pillai, who has been my guide and buddy for twenty-five years. He and his wife, Sudha, have been there for every transition I have made—often facilitating a smooth one. I also owe a very special thanks to my dear friend from engineering school and now Silicon Valley venture capitalist, Ajmal Noorani, for his thoughts on and help with the book. I wish to thank my teachers in India—in particular, Ramesh Dewani and Rumi and Veena Mistry—for their constant enthusiasm, guidance, and encouragement of my various interests, as well as close family friends, Sanat Kumar Banerji and Haripada Mukherji, for their tireless support. My cousin Joydeep Ghosh I thank for scouring antiquarian bookshops in Mumbai for some out-of-print book on ancient India or the other.

There are many friends from my days as a journalist in New York City, who have been immensely thoughtful and helpful. Three of my fellow travelers as writers, Aseem Chhabra and Arthur and Betty Pais, have been constant sources of inspiration, and their counsel and guidance on this project especially and on many professional and personal quests in general, have been more helpful and beneficial than they will ever know. I also wish to thank Susan Qualtrough, who is not only one of the toughest and most demanding editors I ever worked with, but has also remained a beacon of encouragement to me for twenty years. The late Charles Emerson, my senior colleague at McGraw-Hill, provided advice and encouragement on life and journalism, and helped steer me toward my career in business. Jahar and Bharati Bhattacharya and Yatin and Shukla Ghosh remain pillars of support from my arrival in New York City twenty years ago.

Many friends in London have been very helpful to the book, especially Martin Giles, who heads *The Economist*'s new enterprise unit; Lucinda McNeile, who is one of the first editors to have expressed interest in the book; and my friend Roger Katz, who, as general manager of Hatchards, has created the most unique and interesting experiences that any book buyer could possibly have — anywhere in the world. I also wish to remember the late Gordon Lee, who for over thirty years as the defense and the surveys editor at *The Economist* not only shaped the editorial course of the publication, but also readily reached out to anyone he thought could benefit from his wise advice and counsel. I also owe Jhumur and Bhabanath Basu, Susan and Hamish Curran, and Angela and Roger Price a large dose of thanks for their enthusiastic cheerleading of the book. At McKinsey, my former senior colleagues and mentors, Ian Davis and Shyam Lal, and my former colleagues Allison Gallienne, Torsten Oltmanns, Ivan Hutnik, Michael Hersch, and Pom Somkabcharti have been ardent and relentless supporters of the book. All of them have provided invaluable advice throughout the course of planning and writing the book. Geoff Andersen, who worked with me on *The McKinsey Quarterly*, never ceases to amaze me with his innovative graphics design, which can take the most intricate, detailed, and convoluted set of facts and turn them into something that is clear, concise, and visually appealing.

Many friends in Boston have gone out of their way to provide help in all sorts of ways — not least by their kind understanding during my many months of social reclusion. Bob and Anne Eccles have not only been great friends and champions, they have been thoroughly helpful in frequently guiding me toward founts of knowledge that have proved especially helpful. So have Som and Subroto Bhattacharya, Steve and Marian Carlson, Tony and Swati Elavia, Vivek and Bhavini Joshi, Raman and Anju Mehra, as well as Harvard Business School professors Nitin Nohria (and his wife, Monica Chandra) and Pankaj Ghemawat. *Harvard Business*

Review senior editor Anand Raman has patiently read several chapters and offered incisive guidance that has benefited the book. At the Massachusetts Institute of Technology's Sloan School of Management, Professor S. P. Kothari has been an enthusiastic supporter every step of the way of writing this book; his wife, Dafni, who is of Greek origin, has been terrific at clarifying many of the subtle differences of the region. Among my Sloan friends, my classmate Shankar Suryanarayan, now at Roche in Basle, Switzerland, and his wife, Jayashri, have been relentless supporters. Finally, among friends in Boston, I would like to thank Tony and Jane Worcester, who have been great supporters and introduced me to their friend, Professor David Mitten, who teaches the hugely popular course on Alexander the Great at Harvard.

Several friends and colleagues at Monitor have been terrific at reading various chapters and commenting on them. I especially want to thank Jeron Paul and Stephanie Kehrer, who pointed me toward sources of knowledge and information that I would never have stumbled upon without their help, and for giving up their weekends to read early drafts of the book. Jeron's father, Charles Randall Paul, was gracious enough to go through the chapter on myths and offer several highly beneficial course-shifts and content suggestions drawn from his extensive academic work in the area at the University of Chicago. George Eliades, a historian by training, provided incisive comments on various chapters and made very useful connections for me to Harvard's history department, from where he had received his PhD. Similarly, Amy Hustad connected me up with her husband, Mark Kurtz at the Archeological Institute of America, who in turn introduced me to his teacher, Helmut Koester, professor emeritus at Harvard's Divinity School, from whom I got a better understanding of the role divinity played in the characterization of a hero in the ancient world. I am also grateful for the suggestions of and help provided by my colleague Dave Dyer, one of the finest business historians in the world. Dave's colleague at the Winthrop Group, Julia Heskel, who has studied and taught ancient Macedonian history at Harvard, Brown, and Yale, gave me several suggestions that helped improve the content of the book. I also thank Jon Pearson, Anne Lee, and Ervin Tu for the many rounds of discussions we had about the book. Several partners at Monitor, especially Chris Argyris, Bhaskar Chakravorti, Ralph Judah, David Levy, John Moore, Nikos Mourkogiannis, Fernando Musa, Jeffrey Rayport, Rajeev Singh-Molares, Mark Thomas, and Katsuyuki Tochimoto, were incredibly supportive and helpful in the writing of this book. My assistant, Fern

Fergus, watches over my calendar like a hawk, and I am indebted to her in ensuring that I did as little travel as possible over weekends, which is when this book got written.

My agent and friend Rafe Sagalyn has been a constant source of encouragement and strength throughout the conception and writing of this book. I would not have embarked on it without his help and support, and his endless wisdom about the publishing world and guidance through the publishing process have helped make the writing a much easier one than I know it is. Jennifer Graham at the Sagalyn Agency helped me to miraculously traipse through the complex world of foreign rights, and Antony Topping at Greene and Heaton masterfully negotiated the UK and Commonwealth rights. I am grateful to Bill Shinker, my publisher at Gotham Books, for his immense confidence in investing in the book, and his good humor and judgment throughout the process has made the writing process an absolute pleasure. I am constantly awed at Bill's insights and ideas on publishing a book. Lauren Marino, my editor, has spent many days and hours going through the book in great detail, providing lots of feedback, and being tough and demanding but also sensitive and kind all through the process. It has been a joy collaborating with her, and I am grateful for her guidance and suggestions that have miraculously turned my drafts into chapters of a real book. Brooke Capps, Lauren and Bill's highly efficient deputy, has put up with an incessant stream of minor inquiries, which she has always responded to with amazing grace and good humor. Finally, thanks to Mark Roy at Gotham for masterfully shepherding the manuscript through the publishing process and to Craig Schneider, who thoughtfully and marvelously copyedited the entire manuscript.

No one deserves more credit for this book than my family, who bore the entire brunt of many years of research and many months of writing. I had missed so many social functions that friends began to question my wife, Vinita, whether she was still married. Vinita cheerfully read many different drafts of every chapter, and her constantly positive feedback was hugely helpful in crafting the book. Without her encouragement, enthusiasm, and unwavering support, this book could never have been possible. My children, Priyanka and Pranay, put up with my continuous absence at soccer games, fencing bouts, parent-teacher meetings, and musical recitals, and beneath their cheerful exterior I know they sorely missed having Dad kick the ball around with them or go take in a movie. Priyanka, who is tiptoeing into classics herself, brought home many books from her library in the expectation that they might help Dad; and they invariably did. Pranay, I thought, had been bribed by my publishers, because he constantly checked on the progress of the book to see when we would return back to leading our lives as a normal family. I wish to thank my parents, Kali Krishna Bose and Sibani Bose, for always encouraging me to pursue my dreams and for going out of their way to help make them real. My brother, Suprotim; his wife, Lilian; my parents-in-law, Sharad and Nirmala Khandekar; my brother-in-law, Sunil Khandekar, and his wife, Swati; as well my nephew, Sujay, and nieces, Maya and Supriya, deserve thanks for their constant encouragement as well as for letting me off on important social occasions—so I could write the book. I am grateful to all of them.

ALEXANDER THE GREAT'S

Art

of

Strategy

INTRODUCTION

THE DOYENNE OF CLASSICISTS, EDITH HAMILTON, ONCE WROTE, "THERE is something breathtaking in Alexander the Great. Like everything stupendous—the pyramids, the Grand Canyon, Mount Everest—one can never get quite used to it. It drives us out beyond the everyday limits we set for ourselves of the possible."

Alexander's contributions span many endeavors—cut across many disciplines. Arguably the greatest military strategist, tactician, and ruler in world history, Alexander's achievements have influenced many military, political, and business leaders. In the ancient world he influenced the actions of such powerful Roman leaders as Pompey, Julius Caesar, and Mark Antony, as well as Rome's first emperor, Augustus Caesar, to Rome's nemesis, Carthage's Hannibal, to faraway India's Chandra Gupta Maurya and his wily prime minister, Chanakya.

During the Renaissance the Medicis of Italy and the Habsburgs of Austria studied him extensively. Indeed, Niccolò Machiavelli made a bit of a career interpreting and reinterpreting the military campaigns and the systems of rule of Alexander. It was common for Renaissance princes to hang, as the centerpiece of their art collections, tapestries depicting the life of Alexander. When the Habsburg emperor Frederick III arrived in Rome in 1452 for his coronation by the pope as sovereign of the Holy Roman Empire, it was the opulent tapestries detailing Alexander's exploits from the collection of Cardinal Francesco Gonzaga, the marquis of Mantua, that were singled out for depiction and praise.[1]

In the seventeenth, eighteenth, and nineteenth centuries, he was the model for the greatest generals of the era such as Frederick the Great, Prince Eugene, Napoleon Bonaparte, Horatio Nelson, the duke of Wellington, and Winston Churchill's forebear, the duke of Marlborough. America's great generals, George Washington (who, after his retirement tried unsuccessfully to procure a bust of Alexander the Great to adorn his Mount Vernon residence), Robert E. Lee, and Ulysses S. Grant attributed their military successes to Alexander's strategies and tactics. Leading generals and politicians in and since the Second World War, from Erwin Rommel and Bernard Montgomery to Norman Schwarzkopf, are said to have been inspired by the actions of Alexander.

Among business leaders Ted Turner, the founder of CNN, is reported to be an admirer of Alexander the Great.[2] Comparisons with his achievements are common. J. Pierpont Morgan, the financier who helped build such American industrial mainstays as General Electric, U.S. Steel, the railroads, and the eponymous financial institution now called J. P. Morgan Chase, and served as the unofficial central banker (the Federal Reserve was established a few months after he died), was compared to Alexander the Great by the Yale professor conferring a honorary degree on him. Not only are there many parents who name their children Alexander—after Alexander the Great—but some parents are even inspired by specific events from his life—as Ty Cobb's, the baseball great's, father was, when after reading about Alexander's siege of Tyre, named his son Tyrus.

My personal introduction to Alexander occured when I was seven years old, and my parents took me to see the ruins of Alexander's port city on the island of Failaka, just off the coast of Kuwait. The island was settled by Alexander on his return journey from India and, after his death, used by the Seleucid kings as a way station between the western end of their empire in today's Iraq and the eastern end in India. Failaka, which housed a museum showcasing a large cache of ancient Macedonian coins, and a relatively well-preserved ancient Greek temple, was unfortunately mined and looted by Saddam Hussein's invading Iraqi army in 1990.

Growing up in Kuwait in those formative years, it was difficult not to be exposed to the rich and varied heritage of ancient Mesopotamia (spanning modern Iraq all the way west to today's Turkey), Phoenicia (encompassing today's Lebanon), and Egypt because of friends, neighbors, and teachers for whom these cultures represented their heritage. The contribution of Alexander the Great to these civilizations was always a subject of much debate, as were such inanely competitive questions as did the Greeks learn more about astronomy from the Egyptians than the Egyptians from the

Greeks? Were the Greek residents of Alexandria—especially such famous residents as the mathematician Euclid—Greek or Egyptian? Or, what did the Egyptians learn about measuring their pyramids from the Greeks that they didn't already know themselves?

There was an even more personal connection to Alexander in that I was born in Patna, India—today a ramshackle city that epitomizes urban anomie, blight, decay, and penury. Patna also has the unique distinction of being India's only city with negative growth in the almost sixty years since India gained independence, which means its residents are worse off today than sixty years ago. At one time, however, the city reigned supreme: It was called Pataliputra, the capital of ancient India, which Alexander wanted to reach but never could. It was out of his base in Pataliputra that Chandra Gupta Maurya, India's first emperor, who befriended Alexander when he set foot in India, pushed Alexander's successor, Seleucus Nikator, out of India—but not before striking a negotiated settlement (which included marrying his daughter) between the Indian and the Seleucid empires. Much of the history of ancient Pataliputra (or India, for that matter) is to be found not in ancient Indian texts—unfortunately most have disappeared—but in Greek historical documents. Indeed, even the central historical text on Alexander, which was written by Arrian, is called the *Anabasis* [History] *of Alexander and India* [after India]. Like almost anyone curious about his place of birth, I, too, have had a long-term interest in Pataliputra, and the more I learned about it, the more I learned about Alexander.

It is also the case that no one attends school in India without exposure to Alexander. Every Indian child is told the story of Alexander's battle with the Indian king Porus, and every Indian child commits to memory a nursery rhyme about the valor of both men. No one grows up in India, or, for that matter, in any of the nations that fell under the Macedonians' reign, without local films, dances, and drama romanticizing the role of the Macedonian ruler. India has produced about as many films on Alexander (or Sikander, as he is known) as have been made in the English language. A black-and-white movie titled *Sikander*, made in Hindi and Urdu in 1941 by Sohrab Modi, even today attracts matinee audiences. Interestingly, Modi was a Parsee—a descendant of the Persian followers of Zoroaster. It was the Parsees whom Alexander defeated to conquer Persia, the greatest empire of the time; most Parsees today live in India.

It was as a student of and adviser on strategy that I realized how large a shadow he cast over the way we approach business, military, or political strategy today. Not only is there something, in Edith Hamilton's words, "breathtaking," there is also an element of timelessness about his actions. This became starkly clear in 1991, when a senior colleague and mentor, Graham Sharman, and I visited with the general leading the logistics of the multinational forces in the Gulf War, General William "Gus" Pagonis, and saw firsthand how Alexander's strategies and tactics had defined the way the U.S. was framing the strategies and tactics of a war on those same sands of Arabia that Alexander had crossed some 2,500 years back.

As an observer, participant, and writer of management ideas and trends, it has been a rather humbling experience for me to watch how many of the ideas and concepts we use today to make better sense of uncertainty, or to make decisions that craft our future, have their origins in him. It is no surprise, therefore, to frequently hear a chief executive or a senior manager exclaim, in the depths of a discussion about an intricate current problem, that the way to solve it might be to take the approach that Alexander once did. Nor is it not surprising, to walk into a top manager's office and see a set of books on Alexander staring from a shelf or to see a bust of his likeness perched on some pedestal to guide and inspire.

There is a simple reason why people look to Alexander for guidance. Take the area of management thinking, for example. Despite the strides made in the field of management in the last few decades, and a preponderance of so called "breakthroughs" and "big ideas," the reality remains that the ideas that fundamentally shaped and changed the practice of management were by and large adaptations of long-held beliefs and tried-and-tested approaches from other fields. Frederick Winslow Taylor, the father of scientific management, was a machinist and an inventor, without whose contributions mass production would have remained only a dream. Elton Mayo was an Australian-born psychologist, whose work on the importance of short breaks on worker motivation and productivity at Western Electric's Hawthorne plant near Chicago have done more for understanding employee behavior than all the tomes on organizational behavior put together. Mary Parker Follett was a political activist and social entrepreneur whose work on citizenship and other democratic values in the inner cities of Boston and London has done for collaboration and empowerment what today's ideas on teamwork can only aspire to achieve. W. Edwards Deming was a statistician whose work on the Japanese census after World War II was to provide the foundations of the quality movement. Jay Forrester, the father of system dynamics, invented the field by applying lessons from feedback control systems in electrical engineering.

The greatest of the management thinkers, Austrian-born Peter Drucker, spent much of his life working as a full-time journalist. These are some of the people whose ideas, despite passage of decades, remain central to the practice of management.

On the other hand, faddish ideas of the nineties like "reengineering," "core process redesign," and "core competencies" today carry about the same weight in business circles as the Ghanian cedi in foreign exchange. While these ideas of recent decades seem as phony as a three-dollar bill, the ideas of decades and centuries past still resonate loud and clear in the hearts and minds of people. Learning about the ideas and actions of Alexander the Great is an experience akin to drinking from the original fount of knowledge about strategy and tactics. He was in most ways not only the originator of today's strategic and tactical practices that nations use to win wars and businesses to defeat competitors, but in applying them he also changed the way generations for almost 2,500 years have viewed and interacted with the world.

Like most events characterized by fundamental change, Alexander came to power at a pivotal and worrisome moment in Macedonian history. His father, Philip II, had just been assassinated, the Greek city-states that Philip conquered were on the verge of rebelling, and the mighty Persian empire was on the spur of attacking Greece and Macedonia.

After prevailing in a succession battle, at the tender age of twenty, Alexander became king of Macedonia and Greece. Interestingly, so as not to give the impression to the Greeks that he was their ruler, he never styled himself "king of Macedonia and Greece," but simply King Alexander. Soon his empire stretched from the Balkans in Central Europe to Southern Europe, and from northern Africa, through all of Asia, up to northwest India. In his quest to rule the world from Greece to the land on "the other side of the Ocean," he conquered several great ancient empires and civilizations: Persia, which had ruled much of Asia for over three centuries, as well as Egypt, Babylon, Assyria, and India.

Alexander completely altered the face of battle. Until then, warfare had all been about a full-frontal assault, one side attacking another like moths hurling their tiny bodies against a streetlamp—till the larger army prevailed. Alexander was the first general to reveal how a smaller force could overwhelm a larger one through smart strategies and tactics—repeatedly. He showed how to overwhelm an opponent by attacking his most decisive position, demonstrating where that decisive point of an enemy's front or flank should be. Most important, perhaps, he revealed how the most decisive point is not necessarily the weakest as everyone had assumed. He showed what intelligence gathering was all about—not by torturing or paying off locals as the leaders of the Persian empire did, but triangulating from the insights offered by experts in a variety of fields, and synthesizing them.

What made Alexander so exceptional? Certainly one factor was that his father had arranged, when Alexander was just a teenager, for a noted scholar to come to Macedonia to tutor him. The teacher was Aristotle. Under Aristotle's guidance Alexander learned to be sensitive toward people and cultures in a way that no ruler before him and few rulers after him did. That quality stood him in good stead. None of his occupied lands ever rebelled. When he needed to double the size of his forces midway through his campaigns, thirty thousand Persian volunteers willingly joined his army.

He had an enviable quality to motivate his troops to take on the greatest challenges, against the toughest odds, such as in crossing the snow-covered Hindu Kush in Afghanistan and the Uxian Mountains in Iran in late winter and early spring, or marching across the Saharan and the Arabian desert on foot or horseback, or fighting enemies with armies four times the size of his. He always led from the front, never demanding of his troops anything that he wasn't willing to do first himself—the first to charge into battle, always in the thickest of the fight, ready always to come to the rescue of a fellow soldier, no matter what his rank.

When Alexander died in Babylon in 323 B.C., he left behind cities and cultures that exist even today. He epitomized empire building. He was what the best of the world's conquerors aspired to be and served as a model for many empire builders.

This book is written for anyone interested in Alexander the Great and who wishes to learn about the way he has inspired what we do today. It is not an encyclopedic record of all his achievements—that would be too large an undertaking, and many more qualified authors than I are better positioned to tackle that. Indeed this book is deliberately selective in the events and situations it chooses to highlight.

Thucydides, probably the greatest historian who ever lived, defined almost 2,500 years ago the target audience for his book, *The Peloponnesian Wars*: "those who want to understand clearly the events, which happened in the past, and which (human nature being what it is) will at some time or the other and in much the same ways be repeated in the future." The historical context of this book is much more modest: It is to remind ourselves of the events of the past, and realize how seldom what we often characterize as "breakthroughs" in thinking and approaches are genuinely new.

Finally, a goal of this book is to render for readers little snippets of Alexander's voice. Great leaders are known as much for what they said as for what they did. Few, outside of classicists and scholars, are acquainted with what Alexander said (or what got passed down from one generation to another as he supposedly said). Wherever possible I have tried to provide a brief glance into his voice in the hope that, despite the centuries between him and us, readers will hear brief echoes of his words waft through.

It was in 336 B.C., almost 2,500 years ago, that Alexander the Great ascended the throne of Macedonia after his father, King Philip II of Macedonia, was assassinated.

Philip was forty-six years old when he died. He began his rule over Macedonia in 359 B.C.—three years before Alexander was born. In the twenty-three years of his rule almost all of Greece had come together under his leadership, and his empire included the outer reaches of modern Turkey. He had taken a vast number of Greek city-states (or "polis") and brought them together as a unified force under his leadership. A couple were democracies, others were oligarchies in that power rested in the hands of an aristocratic elite, and the rest were totalitarian regimes. He never imposed his direct rule on them or positioned himself as king of all Greece. He died Philip, king of Macedonia, and "hegemon" or "captain general" of all Greece.

It was in his role as "captain general" that almost all of Greece came together under him. Although Persia had been soundly defeated by the Greeks at Marathon in 490 B.C., the Persians remained a menace: In 480 B.C. the Persian army under the Great King Xerxes ravaged Greece, destroyed its lands, and razed its greatest monuments—including the Temple of Athena on the Acropolis—to the ground. The Greeks again won that year in 480 B.C. in a naval battle in which the Athenians had snared the gullible Persians into the Gulf of Salamis, and then again next year when the landlubber Spartans led the Greeks in a land battle at Plataea.

Even though the city-states disliked and distrusted each other, and two coalitions of city-states fought each other in the twenty-seven-year-long

Peloponnesian War, between 431 and 404 B.C., Philip knew most would come together to battle Persia. So despite having conquered much of Greece, Philip, ever the politician, in 338 B.C. humbly asked the city-states to unite under him as "captain general" in a future holy battle against Persia to seek revenge for all the sacrilegious acts it had committed on its soil. Two years later he was dead.

Without a shadow of doubt Alexander could never have reigned over all Greece, conquered the Persians, marched as far away as India, and become known as Alexander the Great had it not been—literally and metaphorically speaking—for Philip, who was one of the finest tacticians of the ancient world. It was Philip who, inspired by the work of a Theban general named Epaminondas, put a conclusive stop to the senseless, full-frontal assault that was the tactic of choice for warring armies, regardless of size. On the other hand, Alexander was no mere undeserving benefici-ary of his father's legacy. Alexander was the greatest strategist and tactician who ever lived.

Building a Winning Army Organization

Philip brought thousands of troops together to function as a self-confident, disciplined, well-trained, and well-organized unit. He im-proved the organization of the Macedonian cavalry. While he was held as a hostage in Thebes (to ensure that his two older brothers behaved them-selves after his mother and brother-in-law had killed his father, King Amyntas) he had studied the Theban king Epaminondas' cavalry maneu-vers. He was in Thebes immediately after the Battle of Leuctra, where Epaminondas, considered one of the greatest generals of ancient times, led the Theban army in a blistering defeat of Sparta, and thereby ended Sparta's thirty-five-year totalitarian rule over the rest of Greece that had lasted since the Peloponnesian Wars.

Philip heard firsthand from Theban fighters about the way Epaminon-das had organized the Theban cavalry into a unit, and how the unit had charged into battle. Until Leuctra cavalry operated as a group of individu-als on horseback, who engaged enemy infantry or cavalry as individuals—never as a coordinated unit. Like Thebes, which had a long tradition of horse breeding and horsemanship, Macedonia, too, had a similar tradi-tion. Macedonian horses, fortuitously, were trained for control—to maneuver through the hilly local countryside—rather than for speed as the Persian horses were.

Philip was an ardent fan of the writings of Xenophon, a military historian, philosopher, and general, who had once led what is known in history as simply "the Ten Thousand." Xenophon's many contributions to warfare included the idea of planning for and conducting a retreat (See Chapter 2), and we shall read how Philip, and Alexander, used Xenophon's insights about retreat in the various battles they fought—especially the Battle of Chaeronea.

Xenophon also wrote two other books that deeply influenced Philip. One, *About Horsemanship*, detailed the breeding and care of horses, as well as providing a primer on dressage. The other was a book about the benefits of division of labor. Describing the workings of a Greek shoe factory, Xenophon wrote in 370 B.C.: "He who devotes himself to a very highly specialized line of work is bound to do it in the best possible way"[3]—more than 2,000 years before the Industrial Revolution would embrace the notion of division of labor wholeheartedly.

Bearing Xenophon's prescription in mind, Philip organized the cavalry into three discrete units, each specialized to perform a unique task. The highest order of the cavalry was the Companion unit. Like medieval European knights the Companions wore a horsehair-plumed bronze helmet, a fish-scalelike bronze cuirass or armor plate that covered them from neck to waist, and long greaves wrapped around from toe to knee. Each was equipped with a lightweight, hide-covered wooden shield, a long spear, and a Celtic sword. Horses were also covered with a headpiece and breastplate of armor. Although some of the Companion units were comprised of barons, who had been enfeoffed with provinces by Philip for services rendered to him, most members were either family members or professional cavalrymen in the service of the barons. Myths formed, resembling those of King Arthur's knights, about the courage, valor, and chivalry of the Companions.

Training the Elite Companion Forces

Each Companion was accompanied by a maximum of three pages. Philip had designed the structure of the Companion order to accommodate the pages as apprentices, who learned the craft of being a Companion from as young as seven years of age. Considering the legends that spread around the land, there were always many more applicants for pages than there were roles. A page would make squire when he had traveled with a Companion in battle as his shield bearer, and, after having achieved proficiency in military training and the arts of statecraft and diplomacy, would be designated as a Companion. All army commanders and generals, as well as civil administrators, in Macedonia, were selected from the Companion unit. There were about 2,000 Companions in all Macedonia at any given time, serving in eight squadrons of 250 each. The Companion's shock tactics decided the outcome of almost every one of Philip and Alexander's battles.[4]

The next order was the Thessalian cavalry unit. The royal family of Thessaly, a small nation just to the south of Macedonia, also traced its origins, like Macedonian royalty, to the Greek god Heracles, and the people of the nation considered themselves to be not-too-distant cousins of the Macedonians. Thessaly had a long track record of allying with Macedonia, and its heavy cavalry unit, which was about the size of the Companion unit, always served next to the Companions. The Thessalians in the unit were noblemen and their relatives, and equal in battlefield prowess to their Macedonian cousins.

The final order was the light cavalry. These horsemen were equipped only with a shield and a sword, and because they were lightly armored they could move swiftly. Both Philip and Alexander drew the light cavalrymen from allied nations or from bands of Greek mercenaries, who were willing to fight for anyone for the right price. They used them every now and then for a lightning charge across enemy lines to disorient—not necessarily maim—the ranks and frequently as a reserve to bolster or redirect an ongoing heavy cavalry action. Often, when a large military expedition was in progress, units of archers or lancers on horseback would accompany these light cavalrymen for the explicit purpose of disrupting the enemy's flank. For the first time in battle cavalry became a disruptive technology.

Following up any cavalry charge were light infantry troops called hypaspists ("shield bearers"), who would move in with swords and spears as they waited for the heavy infantry to arrive. Numbering about 3,000, these shield bearers were the squires, who were in training to become Companion cavalrymen. In Philip's—and Alexander's—mind, cavalry and infantry needed to act together in battle, and the transition from a cavalry to an infantry attack needed to be seamless. Hypaspists, because they had spent many years in training as pages to the Companions and knew what a cavalry charge was all about, were best positioned to coordinate the transition from a decisive "hammerlike" cavalry charge to a formidable, spear-bristling infantry attack. Because hypaspists knew what an infantry attack was all about, they would develop into better cavalrymen.

Philip's greatest organizational innovation was the phalanx formation, which would become the most respected and imitated formation in the history of infantry warfare. The Greek city-states had engaged in phalanx warfare for several centuries, but organizing a mass of men to hold their formation as a cluster, carry heavy equipment, protect their comrades, *and* strike the enemy was a combination of actions beyond the ability of most mortals to control and coordinate.

Philip simplified the purpose as well as the organization of the phalanx. In so doing he transformed the phalanx into an indomitable unit. Philip began the transformation by first getting rid of the heavy metal armor that the infantryman (hoplite) wore. He replaced the plate armor comprising a breastplate, tassel around the waist, and long greaves on the legs with lighter toughened leather and composite materials. The heavy bronze helmet, with its restrictive view, gave way to a leather helmet that covered the head but not the face. Philip then extended the length of the spear *(sarissa)* that every hoplite carried from eight to fourteen feet. The longer and heavier spear required both hands, so Philip also rid the infantrymen of the sword that they previously carried in one hand and introduced a small stabbing dagger, which hung from the waist.

In the past, phalanx members had been concerned about protecting their right side while moving forward. In their left hand they held their shield, in their right the spear. If a colleague on their right fell, it suddenly exposed their right side to an enemy attack. Philip totally changed the formation of the units so that all fighters had to concentrate on was forward motion. He decreased the diameter of the shield from three feet to two. Infantrymen hung these lighter leather shields around their necks—so they could move them to their left or right as they deemed fit. The smaller shield, and the slightly sideways shift of their body so they could hold the spear with both hands, meant that each unit could be packed more closely together. Now there were not only more bristling spears jutting out at the front of a phalanx, the longer length of the spear meant that at least the first five ranks of the phalanx—as opposed to the previous three—could strike the enemy at the first collision.[5]

Each phalanx column was a minimum of 8—and preferably 16—men deep, offering multiple touch points on the enemy. A column could be as wide as 128 soldiers. In motion they resembled a pack of centipedes moving sideways. As the first five rows of infantrymen dug their spears into the enemy, those behind, who typically held their spears up at an angle to-ward the sky, warding off attacks from archers, slingers, and javelin throw-ers, lowered their spears in the direction of the fallen enemy and finished off the job. The Greek historian Polybius wrote in the second century B.C. that an opposing army faced such a "storm of spears" that as many as ten spear points could be directed at each man. "Nothing can stand up to the phalanx," Polybius wrote. A Roman soldier with his sword, wrote Polybius, was helpless against the ten bristling spears that were at once rushing to-ward him. He could neither charge nor cut the spears down; the only op-tion for the Roman was to flee.

Once Philip got the basic orientation of the phalanx right, he then started to train soldiers to take on flexible formations while moving forward. In the past the phalanx moved forward only in a rectangular fashion. Philip often had the phalanx approach the enemy in an oblique formation, lead-ing from the left, say, which he reinforced with a deep column of troops. As soon as the enemy was struck, a reserve of men from the back of the pha-lanx would quickly run around on the enemy's right and squeeze the enemy troops from both the left and the right toward the center. Phalanx formations took concave and convex shapes as well. As soldiers moved, they had to adapt to situations on the fly. Should they stay in rectangular fash-ion, move diagonally, squeeze the sides in a pincer movement with the cen-ter falling back, or should the center thrust forward ahead of the sides?

One of the key elements in Philip's design of the Macedonian phalanx was that the infantrymen were not chosen for brute strength or speed but for courage and resolve. Holding up the sides and all of the back rows of the phalanx would be hardy, experienced men, who Philip knew would never flinch. It was their job to keep encouraging the relatively younger members of the phalanx not to lose their resolve in the face of an enemy onslaught. The phalanxes had a single objective—move forward in an of-fensive fashion. Philip delegated all decisions about how to achieve that objective to the phalanx officer.

Developing a Professional Army Cadre

Philip introduced the notion of a professional army whose soldiers served by choice, not conscription. No other nation had a voluntary standing army. Persia, for example, the most powerful nation of the era, called for volunteers or used its wealth to hire Greek mercenaries whenever there was a military threat or the Persians got ready for a military expedition, which was fairly often. Greek city-states such as Athens called up citizens for battle when needed; citizens elected whom they wanted as general, and leadership of the troops rotated from general to general. And Sparta decreed that all its citizens serve in the army from cradle to grave.

Philip invested heavily in the development of a professional Macedonian army. A page studying to become a Companion trained first in horsemanship. Because the stirrup still hadn't found its way to Greece from India, pages learned to ride by gripping their thighs against the horse and keeping one hand free to wield a weapon. As the pages grew up, they were trained to carry heavier and heavier equipment, preparing them to ride in full armor by the age of fourteen. Horses were simultaneously trained for control and endurance. It didn't matter whether a horse was the fastest; it was more important to be the fittest and most agile. It would take a minimum of five years to train a horse such that it was in harmony with its rider, responding to commands with precision. Horses were conditioned to support a fully armored rider over long distances—much of it through rough terrain.

Every Macedonian soldier was trained to withstand intense hardship. The infantry often took long marches—as much as forty miles—carrying full armor, arms, and additional weight equivalent to a month's rations. They traveled over ridge crests and valleys of Macedonia's verdant mountains and through marshy lands and shallow lakes as a way of building up their endurance for extreme hardship and toil. When they arrived at their destination some eight hours later, having marched at a rapid pace of five miles an hour, they were required to prepare their own food and make arrangements for rest. After a three-hour rest they often marched back to base in time for an early morning swim in the freezing waters of the River Helicon or the Thermaic Gulf, which flowed near the Macedonian capital city of Pella.

As the Macedonian soldiers marched, they were reminded of the experiences of great Greek victories and the acts of famous generals. The lead staff sergeant might yell to the contingent, "Who won Leuctra?"

And the chorus would ring out, "E-pa-mi-nondas!"

Philip had designed the training to instill in his soldiers deep respect for the exploits of great generals and a good understanding of all major battles. Interspersed within these lessons were recitations of the army's code of conduct, which he made certain every soldier knew and understood. Anyone breaking the code was swiftly, harshly, and publicly dealt with. When two officers were caught in flagrante delicto with a young fe-male lute player in the army camp one night, a practice that was strictly forbidden, Philip had them flogged before a crowd the next morning—not dissimilar from the public floggings George Washington had to carry out to instill discipline in the early days of the Continental Army.

The armies of the great Roman empire carefully studied Philip's ped-agogical approaches. In Rome, as in Sparta, there was no art superior to the conduct of war. They marched into battle with luggage, including spades, picks, shovels, trowels, and axes with which to dig trenches every night before retiring to sleep; they marched in peacetime with it. But compared to the Macedonians' forty, they could cover only twenty to twenty-five miles a day.

Rome's army could never achieve the speed of, say, Antigonus "the One Eyed"—one of Philip and Alexander's ablest generals. He once took a Macedonian force of 50,000 troops over 287 miles in seven days—cover-ing 41 miles a day. Not surprisingly, he totally astounded and defeated his foe. Or Alexander himself, who took a force of 50,000 over Afghanistan's snow-clad Hindu Kush in seventeen days and surprised his enemy, who never thought such a feat could ever be achieved.

At a time when leaders surrounded themselves with more men than would later surround a Renaissance prince, Philip's counselor retinue was incredibly thin. Even his army hierarchy, only seven levels deep, was de-signed to keep him in close touch with the troops at the lowest levels of the army ranks. His command structure consisted of himself as com-mander in chief, two deputy commanders in chief, and seven of the finest Companions, who served as generals. Under each general was a five-layer hierarchy that had control over the entire army. Rights, responsibilities, accountabilities, competencies, performance measures, and rewards and incentives for each layer were laid out in great detail. Although the com-mander in chief's word reigned supreme, due process on problematic is-sues was assured through the council of war, which adjudicated issues of a "political" nature. The generals were the members of this council.

Expansion Without Fighting

Philip, focused and resolute, allowed little to come between him and his ambitions—he wore his ambitions almost like a second skin. He was will-

ing to use whatever tactic would help him achieve his aims: The end jus-
tified the means.

As it won battles, Philip's Macedonian army gathered a mystical quality about it. Opposing forces had a tendency just to lay down their arms
when confronted by the Macedonians. Even when they fought, they were
constantly reminded that this was the invincible Macedonian army that
they were fighting against—as baseball teams do when they face the New
York Yankees. Despite his military prowess and the mystique of his army,
Philip didn't believe in fighting unless he had to. He abhorred senseless
bloodshed. Because of this men from all over Greece wanted to serve in
his army.

Rather, Philip deployed other tactics to expand Macedonia's rule: He
bribed the rulers of the neighboring nation to give up; he struck up an alliance in return for which he acquired their land; or he simply married
the nation's most eligible princess. At a time when nations would go to
war for the flimsiest reasons, Philip made battle the option of last resort.
In this regard he was clearly ahead of his times. Almost 2,000 years later
Philip's avoidance of unnecessary bloodshed would become the hallmark
of superior generals like Frederick the Great, Napoleon Bonaparte, and
John Churchill, the duke of Marlborough.

The Balkan nations that surrounded Philip's Macedonia to the north
had, as Herodotus wrote, a simple motto: "To be unoccupied is most pres-
tigious, to work the land most shameful; to live by warring and looting is
most honorable." These nations had fought against each other for so long
in the pursuit of their motto, that none of them could ever have created a
coalition that might save them from Philip's expansionist desires. To the
south of Philip's Macedonia were the Greek city-states for whom, then as
now, Macedonia didn't make a blind bit of difference. While the Greeks
led a life of leisurely walks on sandy beaches under the year-long, sun-
kissed, azure-blue-skies, Macedonians worked hard for their money.

In *Walden*, Henry David Thoreau wrote that the people of Massachusetts, and Americans in general "lead lives of quiet desperation." Macedonians, on the other hand, lead lives of *violent* desperation. Even today
when much of Greece spends its time snapping string bikinis and drinking cocktails with ice chips and little umbrellas in them, Macedonians
(especially the Northerners) fight ethnic wars and toil hard to eke out a
living. Long icy winters render many parts of Macedonia out of reach,
and the short summer spells make it difficult to produce enough food to
last through the winters.

Philip changed all that in the twenty-three years of his rule. He first conquered Macedonia's northern, eastern, and western neighbors, extending his country's borders to include everything from the Adriatic to the Aegean Seas—including today's Albania, Serbia, Montenegro, Bulgaria, and parts of Turkey. Then he moved south toward the Ionian Sea, capturing the Greek city-states. These nations were no pushovers. These were the mighty nations of Athens, Thebes, Thrace, and Thessaly, who had successfully staved off numerous incursions and occupations by the mighty Persian Achaemenid empire, the greatest empire of the time. But they all succumbed to the guile of Philip.

When war was the only alternative left to force the submission of a neighboring nation, Philip reluctantly waged war. But he made certain that the costs to the other side were high—to dissuade other nations from fighting him. He fought an army of 10,500 strong from Illyria (Albania), killing over 7,000 of them. The Illyrians had a formidable cavalry force. Philip plain ignored the Illyrian infantry and attacked the cavalry—actually decimated the cavalry. Once the cavalry had been destroyed, the morale of the troops went south, and they were easily routed.

But Philip never plundered or pillaged conquered lands or their people. He often created towns and cities, and made sure that the people participated in the growing wealth and rising prosperity of Macedonia. Neighboring kings were often under pressure from their subjects to ally with Philip. If they voluntarily struck an alliance, he left the ruler in place in return for complete obedience; they were forbidden to wage wars of their own and had to aid Philip in his.

So popular was Philip among the masses that even many Athenians secretly desired to be part of his efficient Macedonian monarchy rather than their chaotic democratic state. To Philip, too, Athens was a particularly prized possession. It was a democracy, adrift in a sea of oligarchies and monarchies. Being a democracy, however, there was never any consensus in Athens, least of all concerning the threat of an invasion from Macedonia.

Even Demosthenes, probably the finest orator who ever lived, was largely ignored when he walked around the streets of Athens warning of the Macedonian threat. His speeches soon began to sound like the vacuous thundering of an old warhorse—lots of emotions, but little substance. He castigated Philip thus: "Not only a Greek not related to the Greeks, but not even a barbarian from a land worth mentioning; no, he's a pestilence from Macedonia, a region where you can't even buy a slave worth his salt."[6] So vile and virulent were Demosthenes' protestations against Philip, that venomous and vehement rhetorical attacks and invectives are often called "philippics." Demosthenes' speeches won him awards for distinguished public service—nothing more.

Multiple Walks up the Aisle

If alliances and threats didn't work against his enemies, Philip investigated the possibility of marriage. Like Henry VIII, the sixteenth-century English Tudor king, Philip had a voracious marital—and sexual—appetite. If Philip had done nothing else than go through his eight wives and the numerous mistresses he kept, much as an Arab prince keeps a bevy of horses, he would have assured himself a prominent role in ancient history. Philip married often—and he married young, demure princesses of neighboring states. Unlike Henry's six marriages, which were undertaken in the quest for an heir, Philip's eight were for purely political or economic reasons—not for love's young dream, which he kept exclusively for his mistresses. The marriages were designed to stitch territorial alliances with neighboring states or to land a wealthy father-in-law to support his campaigns. Not surprisingly, all of Philip's marriages, except his last one, were to non-Macedonian princesses.

Philip married Olympias, Alexander's mother, when she was only sixteen. She was his third wife. Philip promised every one of his prospective brides that she and she alone would be the only swan in his pond—a promise he kept to Olympias for about a year. Olympias was a princess from the kingdom of Epirus, a small but powerful nation in western Greece that bordered the southern tip of today's Albania. The royal family of Epirus traced its lineage to Achilles, the Greek god and mythological hero, and the flotilla-launching Helen of Troy. Olympias was irreverently beautiful, though possessed of a volcanic temper. She had a persona that would at one moment make men want to crawl up the sides of a mountain on their bare hands and knees to get to her and at the very next, rush out of a room screaming, enter the priesthood, or wage wars to occupy themselves.

If ancient Macedonia had had a tradition of marriage licenses, Philip's would have expired in shorter time than most people's pet licenses. But no matter what the state of his marriage was, Philip always took care of his wives' families. They could be sure, as the Swedes say, that he wouldn't sell them a skin before the bear was shot. He was a reliable partner to them. In Epirus, for example, he intervened in support of Olympias' younger brother, also named Alexander, when the king of Epirus died, and her uncle made a play for the throne. Philip bolstered Alexander's hold over the throne by giving his daughter Cleopatra's hand in marriage. It was at the wedding of Alexander and Cleopatra that Philip was assassinated.

This nexus of marriages between Philip and the daughters of kings of neighboring states, together with wars that he had fought to conquer some states, and alliances that he had wrought with others, created an expanded Macedonia that was in size and power second only to Persia. Every citizen of this expanded empire, no matter how high his economic stature or how low his birth, enjoyed equal status: everyone was a Macedonian. The aristocracy that did exist was formed of people who had earned their station through personal qualities and actions, not because of their birth. "Although it is true that the Macedonians were accustomed to monarchy," wrote the Roman historian Quintus Curtius Rufus, "they lived in the shadow of liberty more than other races."[7]

Philip built new towns and cities, and improved the infrastructures of those that were already in existence. He built canals and waterways to facilitate irrigation and maritime commerce. Roads crisscrossed all over the expanded Macedonia, interconnecting all the villages, towns, and cities. Although Philip generally left the kings who had governed before his conquest of their land in place as governors of the provinces, he set all policies by which the provinces were governed in the capital at Pella. Philip's Macedonia is regarded as the first nation in Europe to feature centralized political, military, and administrative policy-setting and decentralized machinery for their execution.

It was into this world of rising Macedonian supremacy in Europe that Alexander was born. No longer universally and publicly derided as a "barbarian" nation by the Greek city-states, Macedonia under Philip had completely broken with its past to emerge as the next most powerful nation in the world after Persia. This is not to say that there was complete trust between Macedonia and the Greek city-states—there wasn't. Macedonia was feared for its power, revered for its efficiency, and respected for its economic and cultural prosperity.[8]

Each chapter of this book is organized around an important event in the life of Alexander, and the vignettes described are used to illustrate the

Macedonian ruler's approach to strategy—be it in winning wars, leading people, spinning myths, conquering new lands, carrying supplies, or bringing together different cultures into a unified global empire that spanned almost the entire known world. Each aspect of Alexander's life or approach is examined in the context of a modern-day setting or situation so that the connections to and similarities with what he did almost 2,500 years ago and what we do today are clear. Having said that, the eclectic choice of modern-day examples and personalities—drawn from business, politics, wars, sports, arts, and history—is mainly driven by personal experiences and circumstances of having lived in three different continents: Europe, Asia, and North America. It is also partly driven by a deeply held belief that strategy is too broad and too dynamic a subject area to be categorized narrowly and the more diverse the underlying experiences to draw from in framing strategies, the more effective the outcomes.

In each chapter I have tried to focus on contemporary issues, situations, or problems that we address, face, or wrestle with in our lives—be it in setting political, military, or business strategies or in the way we approach or view the world we live in. This is not, by any stretch of the imagination, a comprehensive history of Alexander the Great, nor is it by any means a complete treatise on everything we could possibly learn from his life. It is selective, it is judgmental, and strongly reveals my personal learning journey and biases. In return for this imposition I have tried to make it as interesting as possible a read; I hope in a very small way that I have succeeded.

The book begins with his birth and his early years, especially his years under Aristotle, and focus on those aspects of Aristotle's pedagogy, most of it derived from his writings, that we believe prepared Alexander as a ruler to conquer the world. We end the book with his death and the division of the spoils of his empire. The book therefore encompasses the entire life of Alexander. In between we try to follow a directionally chronological footprint, but when required we bring together different periods of his life—either because this further bolsters a point we may be making or because the events from two discrete time periods simply deserve to be assessed adjacent to each other.

The life and personality of Alexander were highly complex, and the sources documenting his life and achievements so far apart in quality and date of authorship that piecing together anything even remotely connected and unified is an impossible task. The chapters therefore may, now and then, have the feel of beads strung together on a string. Each of these distinct beads, however, is posited around real issues we confront today: How do we develop and train professionals? How do we think about basic issues in strategy such as where, when, and how to compete? How do we handle leadership transitions? How do leaders assert authority in their "First Hundred Days"? Why do leaders spin myths? What are the many styles of leadership a single person can possess in her quiver and which to choose where and when? How should we be thinking about convergence of cultures and divergence of social mores as we seek to expand the footprint of our influence? How does one think about what to carry and what not to carry on a campaign? What role does strategic deception play in competitive situations? Why is a leader's legacy such a delicately balanced equation that often totters on the verge of falling off a pedestal? These are the questions we focus on as we study the life of Alexander and many other leaders who have followed or emulated him or whose lives took a somewhat similar course to his.

CHAPTER 1

IN THE PRESENCE
OF GREATNESS

THE MEDITERRANEAN SEA HAD KICKED UP A STORM THAT NIGHT. GALE-force winds cut a wide path of destruction. Even the neighboring Aegean Sea churned, as the storm turned north and plowed inland over mainland Greece and Macedonia. In Macedonia's royal capital of Pella, as the palace walls were battered by the storm's powerful winds amid thunder and lightning, Queen Olympias gave birth to a baby boy in the wee hours of July 26, 356 B.C. The boy was named Alexander III. He would one day be given the sobriquet Alexander the Great.

In the first light of dawn the storm was gone, and Queen Olympias' husband, King Philip II, readied himself for a massive invasion of the Greek coastal city of Poteidaia on the Aegean Sea. Philip and his Macedonian troops had weathered the storm's powerful wallop all night as they readied themselves for the invasion. Along the coast the storm had downed trees, tossed boats, and buried houses under several feet of sand. But it had not shaken the resolve of the Macedonians. Despite a drenching from heavy horizontal rains the Macedonians were ready and in position to make the charge, and took the city within a matter of minutes. No Greek soldier in his right mind would take on an army so determined.

About the time Philip invaded Poteidaia that morning, north of Macedonia his top general, Parmenion, defeated the combined forces of Paeonians and Illyrians—two powerful nations in today's Serbia and Albania. As if these coincidences weren't enough, that same day, in southern Greece, in the little town of Olympia, Philip's horses handily won the first, and the most popular, event of the Panhellenic games (today's

Olympic Games)—the chariot race. This win was as momentous an event as Jesse Owens' winning the gold at the 1936 Olympics in Berlin before Adolf Hitler, because the Greeks had long castigated Macedonians as not entirely Greeks (and in those days the games were reserved only for Greeks), and Macedonia as a nation that had nothing to offer besides timber for their ships. By allowing Philip to participate the Greeks were willing to acknowledge Macedonians as Greeks. Of course, they had no other choice, since Philip's Macedonia had emerged as the strongest power in the world, next to the mighty Persians.

The Royal Birth

Days of such momentous portent were few and far between for the tiny nation of Macedonia in Greece's north. The military victories were important, the win at the games was exciting, but the reason why every Macedonian in the land walked with a smile and a spring in his step was that the birth of Alexander marked a clear line to the Macedonian throne. Although Philip was only twenty-seven when Alexander was born, begetting an heir to the throne was of utmost importance in a land where almost every one of its rulers had died violently and suddenly, with a blade between his ribs.

History had not been kind to Macedonia in recent decades. They had gone through three kings in ten years. First Philip's father, King Amyntas, was assassinated, then his oldest brother was assassinated, and finally his older brother had been killed in battle. Therefore, the events surrounding the birth of Alexander provided Macedonia's citizens with a rare ray of hope. The celebrations were a manifestation of their desire and will to survive the violent forces.

In Pella, even as citizens awaited the arrival of their king and their victorious army, they took to the streets to celebrate. Pella's tree-lined avenues ran north to south, connecting the royal palace to the agora, or city square, where the revelers stood. Streets crisscrossed the avenues east to west, carving the city into discrete blocks, each adorned with the trinkets and accoutrements of a royal celebration. Floats assembled in the agora represented the twelve Olympian gods that Macedonians, and all Greeks, held supreme. At each end of the agora was a sanctuary, adorned on top by a gilded cupola, from where courtiers served apple cider or high-alcohol wine.

Late that day Philip led his victorious army into Pella. As he rode up the avenue on horseback, his horsehair-plumed bronze helmet in one hand and the rein of his horse in the other, his subjects burst into rapturous congratulatory cheers. The setting sun gleamed over the lush green lawns that bisected the avenues in a mall, making them shimmer like a luxurious Aubusson carpet.

The birth of any royal baby sparks a string of rituals. Soon after Phillip reached the palace, set on top of a grassy knoll, he changed into his royal attire. Accompanied by his wife and with his baby in his arms, Philip confidently strode onto the torchlit palace veranda to present Alexander to his subjects. The cloud-streaked night sky disappeared behind the palace into the still waters of the Thermaic Gulf.

In a scene reminiscent of the *The Iliad* Philip raised his son skyward toward the distant peak of Mount Olympus and prayed to Zeus and the other gods. Like Hector praying to Zeus that he might grant his son the highest glory among all Trojans, make him brave and strong like himself, and rule over all Troy, Philip, too, prayed for Alexander's glory, might, and power—and his future rule over all Greece. And, like Hector, he prayed that all people might speak of his son as "a better man than his father."[1]

Macedonians believed their kings were direct descendants of the Greek gods who lived atop Mount Olympus, which on a clear day could be seen from Pella. The Temenid house of Macedonian monarchs was not indigenous to Macedonia, but had lived there since 650 B.C., when Perdiccas I arrived from the southern Greek city of Argos and launched the Argead reign. The Temenids traced their lineage directly to Heracles (Hercules, to Romans), son of Zeus. The foreign origins of the house set them apart from the petty wrangling of the various tribes within Macedonia, and their divine lineage set them above. Part of the reverence of Macedonians for their kings arose from a sense of admiration for their abilities and prowess as monarchs, but much of their devotion stemmed from their divine connections. Indeed, most treated their monarch as a living god.

Macedonian monarchs aggressively cultivated the myths surrounding their family origins. They seized upon and interpreted every omen to stress and advance their divine connections—and the hagiographers of the time were only too willing to comply with the wishes of their monarch. So that evening, as Philip stood high up on the veranda, supported by towering Ionic and Doric columns, he alluded to the razing of the temple of Artemis, the Greek goddess of childbirth, the night before. The temple, situated on a craggy mountaintop in the town of Ephesus in today's western Turkey, had been hit by lightning in the raging Mediterranean storm. The large wooden temple, considered one the wonders of the ancient world, quickly burned.

The temple's priests had run through the town proclaiming that the temple's burning signified the birth of *the* person who would bring down the Persian empire, then the greatest empire in the world and Greece's archenemy. Here in his hands was that person, Philip proudly proclaimed to the crowd, which broke into frenzied excitement. Later, even the historian Plutarch bought in to Phillip's propaganda of divine intervention. Plutarch wrote, "No wonder the temple of Artemis was destroyed, since the goddess was busy attending to the birth of Alexander."[2]

Alexander was thirteen when Philip decided that his son needed a much higher quality of education than was being provided by the usual run of linguists, grammarians, poets, and gymnasts who had been teaching him so far. Philip, having personally benefited from inspiring educational experiences under great teachers, while being held as a hostage in Thebes,[3] wanted a teacher for Alexander who would not just provide a good education but also train him to solve the problems he would encounter someday as a king. He didn't want Alexander just to learn rote answers to common problems; he wanted him to be equipped with a mental framework that would guide him forever in approaching and resolving the problems that surfaced. It was also important for Alexander to understand the limits to his own physical realities and mental abilities. As the Greek tragic playwright Sophocles would have put it, he needed a teacher who could provide the prince "the rudder's guidance and the curb's restraint."[4] Finally, he needed a teacher who could run circles around Alexander's mental prowess—a teacher who could see not just two sides of an issue faster than his son could, but maybe six.

Philip plucked Aristotle out of relative obscurity to be that teacher. Aristotle was a Macedonian, born on the island of Stagira. His family was well known to the Macedonian royal family; his father was a physician to Philip's father, Amyntas. Aristotle had been recently passed over for the top job at Plato's Academy of Athens, where he had studied and taught for over twenty years, and was living the good life on the intellectually barren island of Lesbos. Aristotle immediately accepted the offer.

It was into a Macedonia of cultural grace and literary elegance that Aristotle arrived. A palatial school had been built for him in the hilly resort of Mieza, just outside of the Macedonian capital of Pella. The school had, on one side, a stunning view of the Thermaic Gulf, where the spindly masts of the three-storied triremes could be seen bobbing up and down; on the other, of the verdant wilderness that surrounded it. Mieza on most days was a picture of sunny serenity, with cobbled pathways and shaded walkways where enclaves of students discussed Persian poetry or Greek plays. Botanical and zoological gardens had been built surrounding the school to entertain Aristotle's interests in the biological sciences.

Philip had already professionalized the Companion order of commanders and generals. The students at Mieza, he believed, were the pool from which to draw future generations of Companions. He therefore asked the Macedonian barons to send their sons of Alexander's age to study with him at Mieza. The school was designed as an institution of military as well as cultural and philosophical learning. But foremost, its function was to develop the professional military and ruling elite that would someday rule over Macedonia and its territories.

As future leaders of Macedonia these students needed to be prepared for solving complex, intricate, and unforeseen problems, whose solutions might not lie precisely in any well-defined subject area or specialty. They needed to be able to think on their feet, make tough choices, recognize patterns among different types of problems, search for facts to prove or disprove their hypotheses, draw on their knowledge and the knowledge of others, and work collaboratively with one another in imagining and then shaping the future of their country.

To ensure that they did not grow up with a narrow view of the world, he also invited teachers, poets, artists, and scientists from Egypt and those exiled from Persia to serve as visiting faculty at Mieza. Very little information survives about his time at Mieza, but we can imagine that Aristotle must have designed an academic program that would provide a deep immersion in his students' chosen field of specialization and, at the same time, provide a general exposure to other fields so Alexander and the others could address in an integrated way the issues of warfare, governance, public policy, and justice, which as future leaders of Macedonia they were bound to have to grapple with. The reason we can be confident of Alexander's having been exposed to multiple disciplines under Aristotle is that in his campaigns, he would demonstrate a prodigious interest in and understanding of many disciplines. We also know that it was Aristotle among the Athenian "schoolteachers" who had the most interest in a multitude of disciplines. Indeed, not mere interest, but deep understanding—he is credited with writing about 150 books on subjects as diverse as meteorology, metaphysics, physics, and politics. There is a famous line from the seventh-century Greek poet Archilocus that "the fox knoweth many things, the hedgehog one great thing."[5] Aristotle was considered to be a fox, indeed he is considered to be one of the greatest of all polymaths, opining on fields as diverse as politics and the interpretation of dreams, while his teacher, Plato, was regarded as a hedgehog with one massive, all-encompassing passion, which was rule by philosopher-kings.

Training the Mind to Think

Mieza was where Alexander's mind was trained to look for facts and patterns, and look for them in a variety of sources, places, and people so as to formulate a solution. One of Alexander's key skills as a general in battle was his ability to seek facts about a certain region from a diverse set of sources—say, from the meteorologist, agriculturalist, botanist, zoologist, civil engineer, hydrologist, historian, and even the odd sophist in his entourage—and then synthesize the facts in a way to arrive at a point of view as to the best time to invade the region, how many troops could be sustained in the region, and how this region might facilitate the next stage of his conquest.

Not only did he seek these facts from his experts so he could triangulate the information he got from them with what was in his head, he also deeply understood that no amount of sophisticated analysis would ever substitute for the local knowledge that resided in someone intimately connected to a region he was trying to invade or a problem he was trying to solve. He could overturn the advice of his experts about the best route to take his army over a mountaintop, for example, in favor of the directions received from a local shepherd boy, whose family might have been tending to his flocks there for decades and knew all the mountain's nooks, crannies, and pathways.

Related to this quest for strands of facts from various sources to arrive at a solution was a sense of humility that Aristotle, we can be certain, must have tried to inculcate in Alexander and the other students about the absence of a perfect answer to any problem. They were brought to believe that the world they would interact with, as rulers, governors, and generals, was a complex world of people, feelings, perspectives, assumptions, and biases. Given such a complex set of relationships underlying a problem—any problem—it would be incredibly difficult for them to arrive at a perfect solution. What they ought to strive for, Aristotle must have persuaded them, was the closest approximation of the perfect answer. As Charles Kingsfield, the character played by John Houseman in the film *The Paper Chase*,[6] reminded the first-year class on its first day at the Harvard Law School, "At times you may feel you have found the correct answer. I assure you that that is a total delusion on your part. You will never find the correct, absolute, and final answer."

The boys soon learned that figuring out the closest approximation wasn't going to be easy, however. Because they were going to operate in a world of people and politics, where their problem would be impacted not only by the set of complexities that underlie any problem but also by prior experiences and the moral and ethical positions they and others—individually or as a group—had or made about it, their judgment about solving problems was going to entail trade-offs. Not to forget fallacies in thinking, an issue that deeply interested Aristotle. They would therefore need to constantly test—and retest—that the choices they made were consistent with their personal and collaborative moral and ethical stances. Practice here would indeed make perfect. As generals and rulers they would need to make split-second decisions; having had the experience of going over and over through many problems in their head to improve their ability to make trade-offs would certainly help them make decision on the fly—decisions they would not later regret.

We can only imagine Aristotle using the rich set of experiences provided by Macedonia's involvement in a diverse set of political and military issues with its neighbors to train his students' minds to think. While the boys were at Mieza, the Amphictyonic Council, the supreme representative body of all Greek city-states, invited Philip to intervene and settle what the Greeks called the "First Sacred War." The Phocians, a warlike people in central Greece, had occupied the Greeks' most sacred temple, that of Apollo at Delphi, as well as the nearby pass of Thermopylae. If one were looking to thumb one's nose at anyone in Greece, no better way could be found than to occupy either—let alone both—of these sacred sites.

Delphi was at the heart of all Greek identity. Every city-state gave its geographic coordinates with Delphi at the center. Every Greek man, woman, and child held the Pass of Thermopylae sacred, and again much of Greek identity was intimately tied with the events at this pass in 480 B.C. when three hundred valiant Spartans, the head of their beloved King Leonidas impaled on a pole, their shields locked and spears drawn, vainly thwarted wave after wave of assault from 100,000 invading Persians—just so the Greek allies could retreat from the pass and prepare for a fight against the Persians on the plains. Although all the thirty or so ancient Greek city-states could—and did—endlessly fight among themselves, mention of the "hot pass" at Thermopylae immediately and magically coalesced them together as a group.

Philip marched in with his troops, and the Phocians summarily surrendered to him. Though the cause of the Phocians evoked as much sympathy as, say, the cause of the human flesh-eating Tonton Macoutes does among the beleaguered Haitian population of today, Philip, despite intense pressure from all the Greek city-states on the Amphictyonic Council, did not sell the Phocians into slavery or raze their towns and cities. These acts were not morally reprehensible to Philip, since he had done them to others. So why did Philip not punish the Phocians as requested by the Amphictyonic Council? What were the trade-offs that Philip had made in letting the Phocians go free? How did this gesture position him for broader control of the Amphictyonic Council, which was presumably what he was after? What can this mean? Aristotle, who, a few years after Mieza, would go on to found the science of logic, must have had a field day with these young minds.

One of the missions of Mieza was to teach the boys to work collaboratively with one another, and one can just imagine the forty-two-year-old Aristotle goading, prodding, and guiding the boys to work together to solve problems. On the campaigns we will learn about how Alexander and his colleagues learned to feed off one another's perspectives, gauged one another's moral standards, realized how one or another might view or solve a certain problem, integrated their various perspectives, and behaved like true colleagues who grew with and *on* one another. The collaborative interactions would build mutual trust and respect—bedrocks of professionalism. In their battles this trust and respect was to stand them in very good stead. Because they had always worked so closely together and knew one another's points of views so very clearly, they could make quick decisions and be confident that they would be carried out precisely the way they expected—we shall see this phenomenon over and over again. They had gotten so close that they could, literally and metaphorically speaking, finish one another's sentences.

Influence on Harvard Law, Harvard Business

There is very little, if any, precise record of what Aristotle actually taught Alexander, but we do know that those years Aristotle spent at Mieza were crucial in forming his point of view about a wide range of subjects, which have influenced and continue to influence the way we think about a great variety of subjects today. Aristotle's teaching methods are of importance because they are precisely the methods used today to instruct professionals in medicine, business, law, teaching, and the military arts, among other subjects.

Socrates was the first Athenian schoolteacher to engage his students through the use of dialogues. But there was nothing disciplined or rigorous about Socrates' methods. He would engage in a dialogue with anyone, anywhere—preferably at a gymnasium. Aristotle was among the first to take Socrates' method and apply it in a formal teaching context—in a disciplined, rigorous way. He brought discipline to the content of what was being discussed but retuned Socrates' approach to and method of discussion. It was common, for example, to see Aristotle come around a corner, leading a group of students deep in an intellectual dialogue (His followers, who also taught by walking around, were called peripatetic, and his approach the peripatetic style of teaching).

In 1870, in what is considered to be a revolution in the teaching of law, Aristotle's model became the foundation for the pedagogy of law when Christopher Columbus Langdell introduced the "elenctic"—or dialogue-oriented—method of teaching at the Harvard Law School. Using summaries of real legal cases to explain both the theoretical and the practical underpinnings of law, this approach is posited around someone in the class being "called on" to run down the facts of the case, present an analysis of the facts, and offer a course of action—filling the room with one's intelligence, as Charles Kingsfield said to his students.

A dialogue thereafter follows between the instructor and the students, with each student vying for airtime to build on or demolish the facts or the course of actions that have been advocated. To those unfamiliar with it, the process runs something like this: exposition of a problem, including a restatement of facts so as to view the problem with clarity; advocacy of a position; the refutation of the proposed position and the advocacy of a counterposition; and the advocacy of a continuous series of positions and counterpositions as the teacher tightens the noose around the key learning from the case.

In 1924 the Harvard Business School adopted the Harvard Law School approach, when it introduced the dialogue-oriented case method to help its students achieve the mythical state of "thinking like a chief executive." Every law and business school around the world, not to mention schools of medicine, journalism, education, and even theology, has now embraced this pedagogical approach—seminarians are now trained not only on delivering liturgies but also on the problems they are likely to encounter in their parishes.

While today the sight of a business-school teacher running all over an amphitheater-like business-school classroom, intently listening, questioning, or responding, is commonplace (ostensibly teasing out the wisdom that lies in knowledge, and the knowledge that lies in information—with apologies to T. S. Eliot)[7], the idea of a business school for training minds destined for the railroads, banks, and factories that were beginning to dot the American industrial landscape was not a shoo-in at Harvard, when its then president Charles W. Eliot first proposed the idea in the early 1900s, right after the business school was formed.

Plenty of professors at Harvard disagreed with Eliot, chief among them A. Lawrence Lowell, a professor of government who would later succeed Eliot as Harvard's president. "General business is a pretty vague thing," wrote Lowell, "for which it is probably impossible to give anything like a professional training." Eliot, however won out and the Harvard Business School opened its doors in 1908. But the debate about academic rigor and discipline in business continued.[8]

It wasn't until the school's second dean, Wallace B. Donham, was appointed in 1921 that the case method of teaching in business was seriously considered. Donham, a graduate of the Harvard Law School, had already been exposed to case method. His job was to instill a similar type of rigor when applying that teaching approach to business. Companies that hired the graduates welcomed the fact that their hires had been exposed to and were steeped in the complex nitty-gritties of running a business rather than on abstract and pompous ideas, frameworks, and concepts learned through theory and texts. Teachers, too, far from being shy of their affiliation with a field that had no theory, texts, or precepts, were actually un-abashed in their sense of pride that they were helping build the intellec-tual edifice for a new field of study. Instead of pursuing traditional research based on quantitative models and deductive reasoning, the teacher pur-sues "clinical research" in the real world that ends in lengthy cases that can be used to better comprehend senior management decision-making.

Building Character

Aristotle was the original optimist: he is credited with saying that those who act rightly are the ones who get the rewards and the good things in life.[9] One of the central themes of his book *Nichomachean Ethics* con-cerns the way we exercise character in situations where making the moral choice is not immediately obvious. Virtues such as mutual respect and ad-miration for each other through collaborative work could be taught, but how does one equip these Companions to make the right moral and ethi-cal judgments each time, every time? One only needs to cast an eye at the long list of today's insider traders, sexual predators, and balance-sheet ma-nipulators coming out of the immaculately maintained faux Georgian campuses of the nation's leading law and business schools to appreciate the permanence of this problem.

As in the works on ethics, Aristotle framed every problem in such a way that the moral implications were very clear to Alexander and the Companions. Characteristically, though, he did not seek or force moral absolutes. Aristotle believed there were no moral absolutes—practical decision-making could never offer the same certainty and conclusiveness as mathematics.[10] He also held that the adherence to moral virtues de-pended on the situation in which those virtues were being exercised—that it was impractical to demand the same level of adherence in every situation. He therefore encouraged people to seek "the mean"—a posi-tion somewhere in between. In matters of bravery, according to Aristotle, the mean lies somewhere in between the extremes of fear or cowardice and reckless confidence; in matters of victory, between magnanimity and ruthlessness.

To find their mean he forced his students to go through multiple rounds of self-inquiry, as he did when he taught at Plato's Academy in Athens, and thereby instilled in these young men a sense of where they tended to come out on issues of character—since their underlying values might not all be the same—so they could make necessary adjustments in the decisions they later made as rulers, commanders, and leaders so they would all come out at exactly the same place. Getting it wrong, Aristotle held, could happen in many ways but there was only one way to get something right, especially as it related to issues of moral virtues. Getting it right, each time, every time, was a matter of intense practice. Aristotle never tired, and like an acting coach forcing his young actors to get their lines just right, he rehearsed and rehearsed—much as the case method at business schools forces students to rehearse their positions over and over again.

Aristotle was a deep believer in the virtue of practice. "Moral virtue comes about as a result of practice," Aristotle wrote.[11] Just as a builder gets better by building and a lyre player improves by playing, "so, too, we become just by doing just acts, temperate by doing temperate acts, brave by doing brave acts."[12] Repeatedly. We shall see how Alexander's decision-making abilities would improve with time—the more decisions he made, the better decisions he made.

Aristotle knew that the more transformative the experiences he made for his students by designing truly arduous problem-solving engagements, the better the learning. The same underlying concept makes the first year of law and business schools, a doctor's residency period, a ballplayer's rookie year, the U.S. Army's basic training, or the Navy's boot camp such a rite of passage. This was truly in keeping with what the fifth-century-B.C. Chinese philosopher Lao-Tse once wrote: "If you tell me, I will listen. If you show me, I will see. But if you let me experience, I will learn."

Although Aristotle was clever enough to phrase every issue such that students were forced into considering the moral implications of their decisions, business and law-school case teaching, with its emphasis on making a decision at any cost (rather than simply walking away), frequently ignores the moral dimension and encourages the training of professionals who give ethical issues short shrift. The second drawback of the case method derives directly from its strength. Because of its bird's-eye, generalist, big-picture, senior-management point of view, the case method can often leave students ill prepared for the demands of jobs lower down the ladder.

To ensure the students at Mieza did not grow up with an entirely theoretical view of the world, small contingents of them were often taken into battle by Philip to observe firsthand how what they had learned in class could be put to use. Thereafter, they would be given minor commissions to prove themselves—even while they were at Mieza. During peacetime they would be invited to observe and participate in the decision making of the state. There was a mystique of invincibility that surrounded Macedonia's generals because of their record in battle. Working close to them and seeing them in action helped lift the mystique for the students. Importantly, it also revealed the way these great generals thought through the implications of their actions and prepared for the reactions their actions would entail.

It is very impressive that all through their conquests, the Companions from Mieza would demonstrate an uncanny ability to figure out exactly what kinds of reactions their actions would force. They would think through the implications of their actions three or four steps ahead, and could pinpoint with a fair degree of accuracy what the cascading effects their actions could bring. Unlike the Robert Redford character in *The Candidate*, who, after winning the elections to the U.S. Senate, asks himself, "What now?" the Companions had worked through the long-term system effects of everything they planned and did, so "What now?" would come naturally to them.

"The Companions" of the Second World War

The revolution in pedagogical approach that took place at the Harvard Law School and the Harvard Business School was also brought to bear on U.S. military officer training. It was in the late 1920s that George C. Marshall took over as head of instruction at the Infantry School at Fort Benning, Georgia, and began what has been called the "Benning Revolution" in military training.[13] Marshall's objective was to train officers through the creation of real, meaningful battle situations in which they had to make life-or-death decisions rather than provide training through books, manuals, and lectures. As the historian Barbara Tuchman wrote, "Tactics, as the heart of the military art, the area where a man must think on his feet, was the key faculty."[14] Marshall, a student of the campaigns of Alexander the Great, revolutionized the art of military training in a fashion that mirrored not too distantly the way Alexander and the Companions learned at Mieza.

Tuchman recounts the tale that when Marshall served in China with the 15th Infantry, he was infuriated to learn that an officer in his charge in a training exercise could not write an order to envelop a flank of the enemy because he had incomplete information about the terrain on which the exercise was being conducted. Marshall, according to Tuchman, was even further appalled to learn that the officer in question had stood first in his class at Benning. He couldn't wait to get his hands on the institution.

Marshall, also a student of the U.S. Civil War, was deeply aware of the way overplanning for action had stymied the ability of the Union troops under brilliant generals like Ulysses S. Grant, William T. Sherman, and Don Carlos Buell to exploit their victory—or at any rate a draw—against the Confederate troops at Shiloh (Pittsburgh Landing) and to secure decisive victories immediately after. It was mainly because generals like Henry Wager Halleck, who took over field command from Grant after Shiloh, dawdled on the way to Corinth, avoiding battle with the Confederates. Although the Union generals had many more men under their command, and a burgeoning military-industrial complex to support them, they could only secure either Pyrrhic or inconclusive victories against the South's mainly citizen-soldier army.

Part of the reason stemmed from these generals' reluctance to move until everything—supplies, men, and intelligence—was in place. Most of it was driven by their desire to wage war by the book. These were men who were steeped in the theory of war, but "their trouble was that the Civil War called on them for qualities which their studies had never revealed to them."[15] Military-strategy textbooks had long held, for example, that military campaigns are often won by not fighting—true if a Philip-like campaign of deceptive alliances and diplomacy is undertaken to thwart the campaign. These great generals, however, believed that a show of force alone could cow an enemy into submission. Unfortunately, the enemy here wasn't just the Confederate army; it was the entire population of the South, who, as historian Bruce Catton held, wouldn't be defeated unless it was completely and conclusively defeated so it could never fight again.

Even when the Union generals did fight, often they failed to pursue their foe after a victory to prevent their re-forming as an army ever again—one of the telling lessons from Alexander's campaigns. After Shiloh, for example, where Halleck's 125,000-man army was just more than twice the force Confederate general Pierre Gustave Toutant Beauregard had inherited from his superior, Albert Sidney Johnston, who died at Shiloh, Halleck went by the book and did not pursue the enemy to achieve complete "annihilation." Instead, Halleck, by the book, "undertook to occupy territory, dividing his army into detachments, leisurely setting to work to consolidate his advantages; he saw the map, and the things which a strategist ought to do on it, rather than the men who carried the opposing nation on the points of their bayonet."[16]

Going by the book, many historians believe, only prolonged the Civil War by another two years and destroyed the credibility—and will, as many in Washington claimed—of several otherwise brilliant Union generals. The war was to end only when generals like Ulysses S. Grant, with the resolve and guts to fight a forceful war, were given command.

When Marshall arrived at Fort Benning, the institution's faculty comprised a veritable *Who's Who* of future leaders of the U.S. armed forces, all of whom would become Marshall's protégés. These teachers would emerge as the great American generals of the Second World War: Dwight D. Eisenhower, who would become supreme commander of the Allied forces; George S. Patton, probably the ablest of U.S. generals and definitely the most feared by the Germans; Omar N. Bradley, Eisenhower's classmate at West Point and one of his most trusted and effective ground-war generals; General Walter Bedell Smith, who would serve Eisenhower as his chief of staff; General Joseph Lawton Collins, who commanded the ships on D-Day and whose guns blasted holes through Hitler's concrete Atlantic Wall large enough for thousands of men, trucks, and tanks to go through; and, among others, General Mathew Ridgeway, who commanded the 82nd Airborne, which parachuted thousands of men into occupied France. They all—about 170 military leaders of World War II—met at Fort Benning.

Only Alexander's class at Mieza could compare with Fort Benning in bringing together so many men who would one day change the course of the world. Alexander's classmates included: Ptolemy Soter, who would serve Alexander as a general and, after his death, set up the Ptolemaic empire in Egypt (it would end thirteen generations later with the death of the last Ptolemy, Cleopatra VII); Seleucus Nikator, who would also serve him as a general, and then launch the Seleucid empire that would rule over much of Asia, from Syria to the borders of India, for over 150 years; Perdiccas, who served Alexander all through the expedition as one of his ablest commanders, and to whom Alexander gave his signet ring when he died; and many others.

As soon as Marshall arrived at Fort Benning, he called Joseph Stilwell, whom Marshall had served with in Stilwell's many years leading the American involvement in China, to become his second-in-command. There was a reason why Marshall wanted Stilwell in that role. Stilwell, using his experiences fighting known and unknown enemies in the jungles of China, constructed realistic tactical exercises for the students in the dense pine forests of Georgia, where field telephones had been fiddled with to not work, messengers invariably got caught, intelligence reports were purposefully ill informed and misleading, maps had been redrawn to lie, and, no matter how well prepared the troops, the enemy always had a bagful of surprises—in strength, in maneuvers, in their line of attack, in where they would spring from. In their propensity for doing things that were either nonsensical from the theoretical point of view of conduct of war, or catatonically dim-witted, the enemy's actions were always, nevertheless, highly effective.

"Once in charge, Marshall threw out the book," Tuchman wrote, "in favor of realistic exercises that would train for initiative and judgment rather than for the correct solution."[17] Serving under General Pershing had taught him the value of short, clear orders from headquarters or a battalion command post and of leaving the execution of that order to the division- or company-level officer. Military training so far had relied on supplying detailed plans and accurate and complete intelligence reports on the enemy and the terrain, and depended on officers to follow highly detailed and prescriptive orders. Not only did Marshall throw out the theoretical aspects of war in favor of the practical, but he also persuaded his fellow instructors to focus their teaching on the first six months of a war, when supplies and men were lacking, rather than on the closing days when both these would be plentiful.[18] Marshall changed U.S. military training to force officers to think on their feet, and expanded the capacity of that training to develop officers who could lead.

Well over 2,000 years before Marshall, Aristotle knew that teaching Alexander to think on his feet could make the difference between failure and success, between life and death. Fast, clear thinking was a function of understanding one's environment and adapting to its conditions to achieve a goal. So Aristotle, the "facts" guy, would throw a continuous stream of facts and situations at Alexander to see how he framed, adapted, and solved a problem based on disparate, often conflicting, set of facts. He was taught to think about connections between facts, about soft points in the logic of an argument, and about what more information was needed—even as a fire hose of information already deluged him. Alexander and his peers soon became good at recognizing patterns, extrapolating, and making judgments based on intuition. The Nobel laureate psychologist Herbert Simon, who has studied human decision-making for several decades, calls intuition "analyses frozen into habit"—like those possessed by chess grandmasters, who are able to recognize some 50,000 patterns in which chess pieces can be positioned on a board.[19] Macedonia's success, especially in battle, would derive largely from this quality that Aristotle had nurtured in Alexander.

Asking Good Questions

Aristotle could often be seen sitting under the shade of a tree—as was his habit in Athens—pointedly asking questions of his students. Sometime there would be disgust or disdain in his voice, other times he would be terse and direct; generally he was pensive, thoughtful, and his voice had a kind, mellifluous timber. The differences in his tone were linked to the way he framed questions—each designed to elicit a certain response from his audience. Alexander studied Aristotle's subtle framing—the way he would phrase a question, the way he would elongate or emphasize certain words, where he would pause in the asking.

The ability to appropriately frame questions became a valuable skill for Alexander on his campaigns, when he had to rely on both the people he was leading, and also those he was conquering, for information, insight, and judgment. He could frame a question in a certain way and, based on the response he got, be persuaded whether he could trust the respondent or be wary of him. There would be several instances where, on such framing and responses, he would commit the fortunes of the entire Macedonian army to a young shepherd boy, a fisherman, or a seer he had just encountered. Other times he would probe and probe because he was convinced that the appearance of the situation didn't match its reality.

Aristotle, who had a deep interest in biology and spent all of his free time categorizing and segmenting different types of plants and animals, also applied his segmentation schemes to understanding the world of the intellect. He created a taxonomy for the types of questions people asked and imbued every one of his students with an instinct for asking good questions, where the tone, framing, and sequence of questions, and where to place the pauses and intonations for dramatic effect, mattered as much as the substance of the question itself.

The late Professor C. Roland Christensen, of the Harvard Business School, who did for the teaching of business—in particular the case

method in business—what Aristotle had done for the teaching and practice of philosophy and politics, once remarked that on the whole there are
only about six or eight basic types of questions that teachers can ask to
help students fully comprehend the complexities of a situation at hand.
There are dozens of subsets of questions underneath these six or eight
basic types; but at a high level of abstraction there are fundamentally
these few broad types.

The most important of these are questions of information, of interpretation, of extension, or questions simply hypothetical. "When do you per-
sonalize questions?" Christensen asked of teachers of business whom he
trained. "When do you lower the abstraction level? What questions are
most appropriate in the early part of the class, as opposed to the later part?
What's so special about a first question to a class?" Christensen has even
described the art of listening in case teaching—how does one distinguish
between listening for content versus listening for feeling? Finally, instructors, Christensen wrote, need to distinguish between a taxonomy of responses: "When do you say, 'Hmmm?' When do you put something on
the board? When do you paraphrase a student's comments?"[20]

Atmosphere of Irony

The Companions were risk takers, and risk taking was a trait that Mieza
encouraged in Macedonia's next generation of leaders. Key to risk taking
was an open atmosphere, where challenges to authority and ideas were
accepted. This suited Aristotle well. As a foreigner in Plato's Academy in
Athens he had felt stifled because he wasn't always free to speak his mind.
Although it was now some thirty years since the Athenians had poisoned
Socrates to death—an event that happened before Aristotle's arrival at
Plato's Academy in Athens—the killing of Socrates made philosophers
(especially foreigners like Aristotle) reluctant to vociferously express
strongly held sentiments. Not surprisingly, Aristotle, always a pragmatist,
kept largely to himself.

Aristotle did all he could to ensure that Alexander and the other students understood that everyone and everything was open to criticism.
Those who criticized were duly protected from those in the majority who
might hold a different point of view. No one and no institutions were beyond criticism—even the king, who among the Companions was primus

inter pares and ruled over them by virtue of his intellect and charisma rather than by the power of his bloodline or divine connections. No matter how ludicrously puerile or intimately vile the criticism might be, protecting an atmosphere of openness was a critical element of Mieza's educational environment.

The use of irony, especially Socratic irony, which involved the feigning of ignorance in an argument, was rampant. The boys were so deeply immersed in the Greek literary works—not only Homer's *Iliad* and *Odyssey*, but also the works of the major Greek tragic and comedic playwrights like Euripedes, Sophocles, and Aristophanes, as well as the lyric poet Pindar—that much of the conversation between them took the form of ironic interplay.

Couplets and quotes from the great works served as useful shorthand among the Companions to express their true feelings about something or about one another without broader audiences realizing what they were saying. One episode which we will read about in more detail in the next chapter, had Alexander reciting the popular "the father, bride, and bridegroom all at once" lines from Euripedes' *Medea* to obliquely suggest an assassination of his father, Philip, Philip's latest bride Cleopatra, and Cleopatra's guardian, Attalus. Or, at a royal dinner, where the Macedonian army's official historian, Callisthenes (who was also Aristotle's nephew) was singing the praises of the Macedonians, Alexander, quoting from Euripedes' *Bacchae*, "on noble subjects all men can speak well," urged Callisthenes to demonstrate the true power of his eloquence by being critical of the Macedonians. So steeped did the boys get in the Greek classics that even their actions in battle would resemble episodes from the great works. Alexander, for example, after conquering Gaza in Palestine, tied the ankles of the city's governor to the end of a chariot and ordered him to be dragged to death around the city—reminiscent of the fate meted out by Achilles to Hector at the end of the *The Iliad*.

Even Aristotle Not Spared

"Whoever undertakes to set himself up as a judge in the field of truth and knowledge," Albert Einstein said, "is shipwrecked by the laughter of the gods." Aristotle was determined to do everything in his power never to appear as an arbiter of truth and knowledge. He was, rather, resolute in his desire to do everything in his power to deny the gods that paroxysmal glee.

Of course, Alexander had a swell time with the openness—even skewering Aristotle at times. It had been a few years since Plato's *Republic* had been published, a book that, together with Aristotle's *Politics*, stands even today as one of the two most influential works of political philosophy. Plato's book argued the presence of three types of states, but his focus was on a utopian one, which he believed would be ruled by philosopher-kings. Such a state would be brought about by a revolution. Aristotle, while at Mieza, was formulating his refutation of Plato's ideas—importantly about the primacy of a revolution for bringing about change, the importance of communal versus private-property ownership, and concentration of power in the elite. There was bound to have been a lot of criticisms of Plato but, considering the way Alexander would assert his political philosophy through his campaigns, of Aristotle's positions as well.

Like university students who often serve as the early readers of their professor's draft chapters for a book, Alexander and the Companions were surely the guinea pigs for Aristotle. We can only imagine Alexander having a field day challenging Aristotle's ideas. Alexander was a deep believer in the importance of different cultures, not in the primacy of any single one, so we can be certain that he must have taken objection to Aristotle's strongly held beliefs about the supremacy of Greek culture and civilization over everything else and the inferior role of women in society. As we shall see, Alexander's life's work was dedicated to furthering beliefs just the opposite of Aristotle's in at least this regard.

The great relationship between Aristotle and Alexander would deteriorate toward the end of Alexander's campaigns, when, angry at Aristotle's nephew Callisthenes' criticisms of his embracing Persian social mores and culture, he had the official historian killed. He held Aristotle responsible for inspiring Callisthenes' outburst and sought revenge on his old teacher—to whom, throughout his campaign, he had written during almost every free moment he had, and whose personal copy of the *The Iliad* he read every night and tucked under his pillow.

It was an unfortunate falling-out between teacher and student. Alexander, too busy on his India campaigns, did not carry out his revenge. And Aristotle, said to have been gravely disappointed in his student, would be quoted as remarking that no one would willingly suffer the environment that Alexander had created. Unfortunately for Aristotle, his association with Alexander would prove costly after the latter's death. In the brief uprising in Greece against everything Macedonian, Aristotle would be forced to flee Athens and seek refuge in his birthplace, the island of Stagira, where in a couple of years, aged sixty-two, he would die. His life's work would cast a long shadow over every intellectual pursuit for the next two millennia.

In the three years of Alexander's training under Aristotle, Mieza was effective in creating a cadre or community of noblemen who were intellectually and physically ready to take on the world. Most of all Mieza gave Alexander, under the tutelage of Aristotle, a view of the world that was broader and more integrated than any other educational institution elsewhere could have provided. Mieza was also as much fraternity row as training institution. After-hours was as important as the curriculum. Socialization mattered. Who these children got to know among each other and how well they got to know them was almost as important as what they got to know. The boys would soon serve Alexander as peers, commanders, bodyguards, and confidants.

SUMMARY OF KEY THEMES

1. TRAINING THE MIND TO THINK.
Applying the Socratic method of teaching, Aristotle taught Alexander and the other Companions to look for facts and patterns among a variety of sources and integrate them in a systematic and insightful manner that was useful for solving the specific problem they were grappling with.

2. THE IMPORTANCE OF CHARACTER BUILDING.
To help them think through the moral implications of their decisions, Aristotle forced Alexander and the others to undergo multiple rounds of self-inquiry and instilled in them a moral purpose that would shape their role as empire builders, generals, and political leaders.

3. LESSONS FOR EMPIRE BUILDING.
At Mieza an impressive group of students learned how to make decisions that would enable them not only to conquer the entire then-known world, but also using what they had learned in there, to set up great empires such as the Ptolemaic in Egypt and the Seleucid in Asia.

4. A CULTURE OF RISK TAKING.

By cultivating qualities such as analytical reasoning, self-criticism, and intellectual honesty, a culture of critical thinking and risk taking was developed wherein everything and everyone was open to being challenged and questioned.

5. THE ART OF ASKING GOOD QUESTIONS.

Aristotle inculcated a taxonomy of questions, which these boys, as commanders and leaders, would use to triangulate information, get new information, and seek exactly the information they were after. As has been taught to teachers of the Harvard Business School, the art of asking good questions is often the most important element of managerial tasks.

CHAPTER 2

THE DAWN OF STRATEGY

AT AGE SIXTEEN, IN THE YEAR 340 B.C., ALEXANDER LEFT MIEZA TO JOIN his father in running the affairs of the rapidly expanding and increasingly powerful Macedonian state. He had been anxious in his Mieza days about the pace of his father's geographic expansion—not because he wasn't proud of it but because he worried that if Philip were to keep expanding the Macedonian empire at the speed at which he had been doing so far, there would be nothing left for him and his friends to conquer—a zeitgeist of impatience that has defined every generation since.

Aware of his son's desire for space to assert his authority, and of the potential threat he posed to the throne of Macedonia (Alexander's mother, Olympias, Philip was aware, had set her heart on securing the throne for her son), Philip would appoint Alexander regent of Macedonia whenever he went away on a long campaign. This way Philip took the heat out of what otherwise had every possibility of turning into a contentious father-son relationship. It was while he was on the campaign into the heart of Byzantium that Alexander first asserted his power as regent.

A tribal nation to the north of Macedonia, the Maedi, had risen up in revolt against Macedonian rule. Alexander, at the head of a small contingent of cavalry, quickly rode in and sacked the region. He disbanded the indigenous garrison that preserved security and replaced it with a multinational force from various Greek city-states. He also took over the largest city in the nation and invited immigrants from the neighboring states to settle in its most fertile and productive lands. He renamed the city Alexandroupolis, much as his father had done recently in Thrace, where he had sacked all of the important cities, changed one's name to Philippopolis (modern Plovdiv in Bulgaria), and stationed a force in the city drawn from various Greek city-states. As Philip marched back to Macedonia from his incursion into Byzantium, wondering how he was going to rehabilitate his reputation on the Amphictyonic Council, he was presented a fortuitous opportunity. It had been brought to the attention of the Council that the Locrians, who lived in the town of Amphissa in central Greece, were cultivating the land near the sacred Temple of Apollo at Delphi. This triggered the Second Sacred War. (The First Sacred War, discussed in the previous chapter, had been triggered by a similar incident when the Phocians of central Greece developed the land near Delphi.)

The Amphictyonic Council had requested that Athens and Thebes take care of this encroachment on their sacred land. Athens, too inwardly focused, and Thebes, chary after its disastrous role in the First Sacred War, both refused. The Council now turned to Philip. He not only agreed to intervene, but did so with alarming urgency. Philip was a great opportunist and a masterful diplomat, who clearly understood Greek values and motivations. To most erudite, self-styled readers of tea leaves he was an enigma. He wouldn't intervene in many calls for help—and then, suddenly, he would intervene in others. There was no discernible pattern or decipherable code to his actions. Yet they tried to read him as intently as a baseball batter tries to decipher the opposing pitcher. Except they always read him wrong—when they expected a change-up, they got a fastball; when they readied themselves for a knuckleball, they got a slider.

At times, with the stadium packed to its seams, all of Greece eagerly waiting for him to come out and save the game, Philip was quite capable of picking up his bat and simply heading home. This had happened in 346 B.C., only six years before these events, when Philip did not even react to a plea from one of Athens' greatest orators, Isocrates, to unite the four principal city-states of Athens, Argos, Sparta, and Thebes, in a crusade against Persia.[1]

Some historians have suspected that it was Philip himself, now that all of northern Greece was within his sphere of influence or under his direct control, who persuaded the Council to issue him the invite because he would have liked nothing better than to insert himself in the affairs of central and southern Greece. Moreover, helping clear the Greeks' most sacred Temple of Apollo at Delphi would be the kind of momentous act that would cause most Greeks to break plates in joy.

Philip, together with Alexander, marched the Macedonian army south toward central Greece; but as the army neared Amphissa, it turned east and occupied Elatea. This town was strategic because it was through here that people from the three most powerful states of Greece—Athens, Thebes, and Sparta, all located in central and southern Greece—had to pass to enter northern Greece. By capturing Elatea the Macedonians controlled passage to the north. This type of opportunistic capture of a town to prepare the ground for a broader objective—the defeat of the powerful Greek city-states—was unheard of in ancient times. It was adopted as a core element of Macedonian military strategy.

The other two elements were obviously the defeat of an enemy in battle, and the conquest of an enemy's capital to exert real or psychological pressure. These three remain the fundamental legs on which military strategies have largely rested right through the U.S. Civil War—and to some extent even today. The advance of technologically sophisticated mechanized and airborne attacks have added a few more degrees of freedom to the arsenal of the military strategist, but the fundamental tenets still remain the same. In the U.S. war against the Taliban and Al-Qaeda in Afghanistan, for example, despite the availability—and use—of advanced technologies to wage the war, at its very root the U.S. strategy has all been about the opportunistic capture of cities like Herat (interestingly, a city set up by Alexander as Alexandria-in-Areia) and Mazar-e-Sharif to position itself for a broader attack and engagement with the enemy in battle, and the capture of Kabul, the Afghan capital. All these maneuvers were designed to topple the Taliban from its stronghold of Kandahar (another of Alexander's cities in Afghanistan).

It was on a grim day in September 339 B.C. that the Athenian assembly heard how Philip and Alexander had moved the Macedonian army into Elatea, cutting off access to the north. The trumpeters sounded the alarm all morning, and rumor and fright quickly gripped the city. Even though the city elders came out and asked Athenians for their opinion as to what Athens should do next, no one was willing to speak his mind. Athens' population that day was so frightened that the city-state had the eerie silence of a pueblo during siesta. Some Athenians were genuinely fearful of the Macedonians. Others secretly hoped that the Macedonians would put an end to their democracy, which had lost its way; but because anyone who criticized the way Athens was run was immediately castigated by its city elders as being morally flawed, these people kept their opinions to themselves.

For almost a year Philip and Alexander did not attack. They could have launched an attack with Elatea as the base, but they were well aware that such an attack would stretch their communications and supply lines, and would force their troops to travel a long distance to meet the enemy (although this was not an issue that ever fazed the Macedonians, who could travel long distances at astonishing speeds).

At Elatea the Macedonians just sat tight and consolidated their hold. Harvard Business School professor Michael Porter, one of the leading thinkers on corporate strategy, once wrote, "The essence of strategy is choosing what not to do."[2] The Macedonians had chosen not to attack—for close to a year. Like President Abraham Lincoln, who amassed an army and made all the preparations for war during the early stages of the South's secession, but did not launch an attack, preferring a wait-and-see attitude (partly to get his ducks lined in a row), the Macedonians, too, waited to see whether the Greek city-states would cave in.

In some ways they seemed to be following the Chinese military philosopher Sun Tzu's insight on generalship: The highest form of generalship is to "balk" the enemy's efforts by strategy; the next highest form of generalship is to conquer the enemy by alliance or thwart the enemy's forming alliances with others not well predisposed to you; the still next highest form . . . is to conquer the enemy by waging a battle. The worst form of generalship is to conquer the enemy by besieging walled cities.[3] Sun Tzu's *The Art of War* did not find its way out of China for several centuries after Philip and Alexander, even though the book had been written in 450 B.C., a little more than a century before these events.

The Macedonians' move into Elatea, considering they had sewn up all of Greece's northern city-states and now controlled passage between the southern and central states to the north, was in keeping with Sun Tzu's advice on the highest form of generalship. But the Greek city-states didn't realize that they had been checkmated. Philip and Alexander then resorted to Sun Tzu's next option: conquer the enemy by alliances. Alexander led peace missions to all the three powerful city-states to seek alliances with them. These overtures were turned down. So the Macedonians resorted to Sun Tzu's third alternative: readied themselves for battle. They secretly planned for a war with two of them—Athens and Thebes; Sparta had been marginalized as a military and economic power by Thebes since its defeat at Leuctra in 371 B.C.

Athens' great orator, Demosthenes, was the only one to see through the Macedonians' peace overtures, and he went to Thebes and persuaded them to stand alongside Athens in a united front against the Macedonians.⁴ Athenians and Thebans were both persuaded by Demosthenes that they could not afford to be caught standing like ducks in thunder. There was just no way they could afford to trundle on with life as if nothing had changed.

Athens and Thebes, inveterate enemies with a long history of suspicion about each other, came together in the summer of 338 B.C., almost a year after the Macedonians' arrival in Elatea, under their statesman-generals, who were high on platitudinous moral rhetoric and low on strategic or tactical battle skills. The Macedonians, on the other hand, careful to not incur the wrath of either nation till they were ready, planned their moves in such a way as to be profound and strategically effective. They took small incremental steps to force these two city-states into a land battle on grassy plains large enough for the deployment of the Macedonian cavalry. Not only a land battle but also one that would be fought away from the walled cities of Athens and Thebes, from behind which they could have worn down the Macedonians in a long war of attrition, just as Sun Tzu had written. The Macedonians already had control of the Gulf of Corinth, which separated northern Greece from southern Greece, but they didn't move their navy into it. This way the Athenians, with their naval superiority, could not battle them at sea. The Macedonians knew how to maneuver in small steps, each of which would be viewed by their opponents as insignificant, but cumulatively would add up to a staggering threat.

Only when Philip and Alexander were ready to fight in the late summer of 338 B.C. did they reveal their intentions to wage battle. They made a lightning strike at night against the Locrian town of Amphissa and rid the town of the Greek garrison protecting it. The Locrians were the people against whom the Amphictyonic Council had originally requested Philip move to clear the sacred temple of Apollo at Delphi of any encroachments. The Macedonians captured Amphissa not to make good with the Council—indeed the Council had been rendered ineffective by their move into Elatea—but because it created a further bulwark against any movement of people or goods from central and southern Greece into the north. In so doing the Macedonians had set up the equivalent of two roadblocks—one on the right (Elatea), the other on the left (Amphissa). Even if anything got by Elatea, it could be stopped at Amphissa. Southern and central Greece was totally choked off. The Greek city-states still did not succumb.

The Battle of Chaeronea

The Greek city-states readied themselves for battle. Not sure if—and from where—an attack from the Macedonians might come, Athens and Thebes amassed an army as far north of their borders as possible. The place they chose was Chaeronea (modern Khairónia), in central Greece, on the main road that connected all the major Greek city-states to the nations in Greece's north. The town was just south of Elatea. As far as the city-states were concerned, such a site would keep the war away from the immediate vicinity of their territories, which they bolstered with stronger and higher walls in the hope that physical fortifications could keep an enemy out. A similar belief in the power of physical fortifications would lead Adolf Hitler to pour umpteen tons of concrete and steel into building bunkers, walls, and other defenses in an unsuccessful effort to keep the Allies out of his conquered territories in northwest Europe.

The choice of Chaeronea as the site of battle couldn't have served Philip and Alexander's purposes better. Chaeronea would mark the first time in recorded history where strategy, not tactics alone, would come into play in warfare. Philip focused where to attack such that it would provide his troops an advantage and possibly disadvantage the enemy; when to attack to preserve the greatest element of surprise; how to attack such that weaknesses in the enemy ranks were exposed early on and exploited; what deceptive ploys to engage to confuse the enemy about one's real intent; what ought to be the sequence of attacks, from which direction; who was going to lead which element of it, and how would each element be executed to fulfill the overall objective of completely and conclusively defeating the enemy; what precise outcomes were expected from each piece of the sequence—all critical dimensions of strategy. Also clearly delineated were the precise nature of the tactical elements: which pieces of the Macedonian lines would play a defensive role and when; which would play an offensive role and when; which would play both roles; and how would the individual pieces of the army (the phalanxes, the light cavalry, the heavy cavalry) interact with each other and against the enemy so as to lead to a quick, definitive victory—with a minimum of bloodshed on the Macedonian side. As we shall see in the battle description itself, the phalanx played initially an offensive role, then a defensive role, and then again a counteroffensive role, and the cavalry struck the decisive blow. Napoleon's dictum "The whole art of war consists in a well-reasoned and extremely circumspect defensive, followed by rapid and audacious attack"[5] could have been based on the Macedonian strategy. It probably was, considering how deeply Alexander's strategies and tactics influenced Napoleon.

Selecting "Where" to Battle

The grassy, expansive plains of Chaeronea were the kind of territory that would suit the Theban cavalry and the Athenian phalanxes. Only thirty years before Chaeronea the Thebans, under their great general Epaminondas, had defeated the much larger, better-trained Spartan army at Leuctra—putting an end to the corrupt and tyrannical thirty-five-year domination of Greece by Sparta, dating from its win in the Peloponnesian War. If Thebes' 6,000 troops could defeat an 11,000-strong Spartan army, the city-states' generals reasoned, the much larger joint army of the two Greek city-states could take on the Macedonians. Chaeronea, just north of Leuctra, had a similar physical terrain. Moreover, on the surface at least, the Macedonians didn't look as formidable as the Spartans, for whom warfare was the greatest art form. Spartans, from the age of eight, when they entered military training, to sixty, when they retired from military service, lived to fulfill the demands of the state. Individual freedom, responsibility, and initiative were suppressed, and the state took care of everything. Sparta was a model of the same sort of socialism that in recent times was to bring the Soviet Union down. The state's sole purpose was the conduct of war, nothing else. Every Spartan was trained to be fearless, hardy, and to follow orders—not to reason why. Many historians have written about the reasons underlying Sparta's autocratic rules. One of the most insightful was probably that of a visitor to Sparta who wrote that it finally dawned on him why Spartans were so willing to die—after he tasted Spartan food. Unfortunately for the Thebans and the Athenians, Chaeronea was also exactly the kind of territory that the Macedonians needed to roll their cavalry and phalanxes. Macedonians spies had reported back that the plains were largely flat surfaces, which meant that both the Macedonian cavalry and the phalanxes could operate at their optimum speed and maneuverability. Detailed information on the exact number and positions of the Thebans and the Athenians was also collected. This might not seem like a highly sophisticated operation in today's era of spy satellites and camera-fitted, unmanned drones. But in ancient times, when war was primarily conducted with two warring armies searching for each other (as we shall see later, often hundreds of thousands of men would pass each other like ships in the night less than a mile apart) and then attacking each other in a full-frontal assault, till the smaller gave way to the larger army, the Macedonians' analysis of their battleground in this fashion was a turning point in the history of warfare. Their strategies and tactics would put an end to the Hobbesian, state-of-nature challenge, where armies moved back and forth in a tug-of-war fashion till the smaller was run over by—or went over to—the larger.

We don't know whether it was Philip or Alexander who pushed for the information- and intelligence-gathering, but we do know that such detailed information-gathering about the opposing side was a hallmark of Alexander's military tactics. Much of that holistic orientation was derived from Aristotle's training at Mieza. Inspired by Alexander's success with information-gathering, many generals, who modeled their strategies and tactics on Alexander, like Hannibal, Julius Caesar, Augustus Caesar, Frederick the Great, and Napoleon, would also make information gathering a key milestone of their military careers—as evidenced by Caesar's famous observation "All of Gaul is divided into three parts," and references to Napoleon checking out all the books in the main Paris libraries pertaining to a nation he planned to conquer and assiduously studying each one of them.

Even two millennia later some of these basic information-gathering tactics remain valid. In the Second World War, for example, British submariners landed on the beaches of Normandy on New Year's Eve 1943 to collect soil samples from the beach because a Roman map of the area from two thousand years ago, when France came under Roman occupation at the end of the Gallic Wars, 58–50 B.C., seemed to indicate the presence of boggy peat fields.[6] If indeed the soil under the sandy beach were peaty, the Allied armies' plans for the Normandy invasion would need to be altered because such soil would bog down the tanks and trucks, which were crucial to the invasion. Or consider the broadcast by the BBC to its listeners shortly after the evacuation of the British Expeditionary Forces at Dunkirk to send in prewar picture postcards and family photographs of the Normandy coast.

So much intelligence—especially aerial photographs—had been collected after Germany's occupation of France that military planners in London needed to decipher German fortifications and reinforcements by comparing the postoccupation intelligence photographs with the preoccupation holiday snaps.[7] Even homing pigeons were used. These would be air dropped in the night in cages attached to parachutes. Detailed instructions for feeding these pigeons as well as little canisters in which to place intelligence information were also included. In the morning French farmers would write in the requisite information and release the pigeons, which would home back to intelligence posts in England.

It was partly her superior intelligence-gathering system that helped Britain, forlorn and dejected, keep Germany from invading her in that crucial year of 1940 when France fell. British prime minister Winston Churchill, knowing full well that he could not defeat Germany without help from the United States (the Roosevelt administration, though not willing to jump into the war then, was willing to provide Britain with material help), devised a three-pronged strategy to sabotage Germany. Intelligence-gathering by and infiltration of British secret agents into German occupied France, Poland, and even the fatherland itself; strategic bombing by the massive, four-engine, British-made Lancaster bombers of Germany's industrial and military assets; and a naval blockade in the seas by the British navy—which, since Elizabeth I's defeat of the Spanish Armada by her enigmatic admiral Sir Francis Drake, had remained the most powerful in the world.

Back in 338 B.C., while Thebes and Athens did not have any intelligence-gathering system in place, they had set up an information transmission system from the battlefield to the city-states. They had staked out their positions at Chaeronea with the mountains to the south as backdrops, and they had secured the mountain passes—not only to allow a retreat if needed but also to allow ongoing communication with their home city-states. A messenger service between the front line and the two city-states had been set up with riders in these passes. This relay-based information-transmission system could carry messages or results of a battle at a speed of up to 150 miles a day,[8] which meant that both city-states could receive updates on the battle in Chaeronea in less than two hours. To the east and to the west of their positions were impassable mountain ranges. The only way the Macedonians could approach was from the north, where the two allies had vacated the passes to facilitate just such an outcome. All other passes had been sealed off by the two Greek city-states, so there was no possibility of the Macedonians making an end run into Thebes or Athens around this plain.

The two Greek city-states stationed their armies between a citadel on

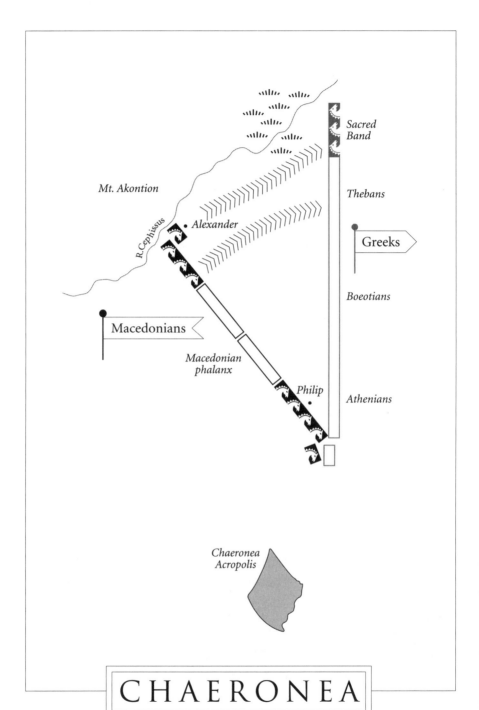

Sacred
Band

Thebans

Greeks

Boeotians

Mt. Akontion

R.Cephissus

Alexander

Macedonians

Macedonian
phalanx

Philip

Athenians

Chaeronea
Acropolis

CHAERONEA

their left, where they stored their supplies and equipment, and the River Cephissus, which flowed on their right just short of the mountain ranges.[9] They had stocked up enough supplies to last several months. The land on the south rose up as a shallow ridge, and it was on this ridge that the Athenian and Theban commanders decided to station as many of their troops as possible—to provide them momentum when they rushed to meet the Macedonian challenge. Thebes' 12,000 infantry and 800 cavalry occupied the right flank; Athens' 10,000 infantry and 600 cavalry bolstered the left. In between the armies of these two city-states stood another 14,000 infantry and 600 cavalry drawn from minor city-states and provinces friendly to the two powerful city-states. In all there were 36,000 infantry and 2,000 cavalry on the Athens-Thebes' side.[10]

Bikes, Snow Blowers, and Automobiles

While Chaeronea was one of the first example of armies making a strategic decision about *where* they wanted to fight the enemy in battle, the "where-to-compete" decision has become a core strategic issue for business, military, and political organizations today. The Allied forces' D-Day invasion of Normandy on June 6, 1944, is one of the finest manifestations of the where-to-compete decision. Hitler's units had spent over four years fortifying the beaches in and around Normandy by laying row after row of barbed wire in the shallow waters of the English Channel and mining it. The Germans believed that any invasion could be repelled from behind the massive concrete-and-steel bunkers and fortifications built along the Atlantic shore—like a Great Wall of China. The Atlantic Wall, the Germans thought, was impenetrable—it would throw any invading army back into the Channel.

The Allied forces' momentous landing at four beaches on Normandy, and their securing beachheads to lay the foundation for the invasion of France and the subsequent defeat of Hitler are now a part of popular history. The parachute drops all night, the bombardment of German positions, the minesweepers clearing a sea passage for the wave after wave of warships that followed, lowering thousands of assault boats and landing craft to take the almost 175,000 Allied troops successfully across the English Channel on the first day—a crossing previously achieved only by Julius Caesar and William the Conqueror, when they had invaded Britain about 2,000 and 1,000 years before respectively.

One of the best illustrations of a firm making the where-to-compete choice can be witnessed in Honda's securing a beachhead in the U.S. motorcycle market. Securing a beachhead is frequently the first step of a where-to-compete choice. It was in 1959 that a fifty-two-year-old former auto mechanic named Soichiro Honda, together with twelve junior colleagues, opened a small shop on 4077 Pico Boulevard in Los Angeles. Although Honda, and his business partner Takeo Fujisawa, had been running a fledgling motorcycle and moped manufacturing company in Japan for nearly eleven years, they had no international experience or presence. A Japanese Ministry of International Trade and Industry (MITI) study done recently had proposed that Honda's international foray ought to be somewhere closer to home, and recommended Indonesia as the nation to focus on. Indonesia had a large population, which would have provided a ready market for Honda's "breakthrough" moped: the Honda 50 SuperCub, which it had developed in 1959. For the first time in motorcycle and moped history riders had a reliable machine in that the 50cc, four-stroke, overhead-valve-engine SuperCub spent more time on the road than it did in a mechanic's garage—unlike other similar vehicles. The MITI study argued that focusing anywhere else could be deleterious to Honda's international plans.

Like the Macedonian army, which had had little experience (Philip had earlier defeated the Thracian king) at battling a tough competitor like Athens and Thebes but decided to take both on and, if need be, Sparta as well, Honda, which had had no previous experience at entering international markets, didn't heed the MITI advice and entered the U.S.—the largest and most competitive motorcycle market, already dominated by domestic producers like Harley-Davidson and British imports like Norton and Royal Enfield. Moreover, Honda's intention wasn't to sell the new Honda 50. Soichiro Honda and Takeo Fujisawa wanted to sell their 125cc, 250cc, and 305cc large (and therefore high-margin) motorcycles, and take on the leading players in the industry.

Honda employees tootled around the streets of Los Angeles on the SuperCub, lining up distributors for their motorcycles. This cross between a motorcycle and a Lambretta intrigued Angelinos so much that many started calling up Honda to find out where they could buy one. As reports seeped through about this virtually indestructible and totally utilitarian moped that quietly and efficiently reached a maximum speed of forty miles per hour, thousands rushed out to buy it. They couldn't find one at the motorcycle dealerships, who didn't want to erode their image as sellers of large, macho motorcycles. It was at Sears and at sporting-goods distributors that the SuperCub, which would soon be dubbed the Model T of the moped world, was sold. Honda directed its business processes, which had so far been focused on serving buyers of large motorcycles, to serve a customer segment for whom its campaign slogan, "You meet the nicest people on a Honda," meant something. These were the young and the old, men and women, who were using the SuperCub for all their basic transportation needs. The SuperCub has sold over 30 million units all over the world—and is still in production.

Once it had secured its beachhead in the U.S. moped—and thereafter motorcycle—markets, Honda turned its attention to cars. It went after the same customer segment with its cars as it had with its mopeds and, since its move into automotive manufacturing and assembly in the early 1960s, has emerged as a dominant force in the international market. Its deep understanding of its customer needs, and attention to serving these needs through innovative use and management of its dealer networks, has been a hallmark of Honda's success. Utility has been a major focus for Honda in its service of this market, as well as environmental friendliness. Although Honda today is one of the largest producers of automobiles in the United States—and the world—it hasn't given up its predominance in the moped business. Indeed, the technological beachhead it secured in small engines, with its mopeds, it has used to also expand or bolster its position in the motorcycle, lawn-mower, snow-blower, and Jet-Ski markets, among others.

What distinguishes Honda's success—as it does of many other firms, such as Wal-Mart in general merchandise retailing—is the firm's ability to identify *where* it wishes to compete. But once it has focused on a geographic segment or product market, it adopts a flexible stance on the strategic and tactical imperatives needed to succeed in that market—such as the desired customer segment; with which products, and through which customer channels, it wishes to compete (direct to customer, through intermediaries); and the precise pieces—and sequence—of its business system that it wants to control. In the U.S. it started off with its dealerships, and then moved into engines, and body assembly.

Similarly Wal-Mart, which in the early eighties was a small niche retailer with 250 stores based in the American South, grew within a span of a few years to surpass not only its much larger, and now bankrupt, competitor Kmart, with eight times as many stores, but also Sears, Roebuck and Company, which had pioneered over the course of a century the introduction of several retail formats (mail order, home delivery, own store brands). The key to Wal-Mart's success as the largest and most profitable retailer in the world lay in a simple logistical technique called "cross docking"—an inventory replenishment system whereby goods arrive from suppliers at Wal-Mart's regional warehouses, where they are sorted, repackaged, and shipped immediately to individual stores. This means that instead of goods sitting on warehouse shelves for several days, they can be shipped from a supplier and be on a Wal-Mart store rack in less than forty-eight hours.[11] The reason why Wal-Mart could replenish its racks in such a short time was because its stores were located away from large metropolitan cities, in small Sun Belt towns and cities with populations of about 100,000 or more. Not only were its stores sited in small towns, they were invariably situated in low-cost industrial parks, where operating its large fleet of delivery trucks on tight time schedules is a cinch.

Again, like Honda, Wal-Mart knew precisely which geographic regions it wanted to compete in, who its target customer segments were, and which parts of its business systems it wanted to tightly control—location and logistics initially and now supplier management and pricing. It is important not only to be thoughtful about the when, where, and how, but also be smart about the way the individual decisions about each one of these strategic criteria are combined or are sequenced to develop strategy. No two combinations of these individual decisions are ever the same. "The most important characteristic of a corporate pattern of decision that may properly be called strategic is its uniqueness," wrote Kenneth R. Andrews, a professor at the Harvard Business School, in his ground-breaking 1971 book, *The Concept of Corporate Strategy*. This is precisely the reason why Kmart's and Sears' attempt to copy Wal-Mart's pattern of decision making have failed: their strategies were not unique enough for their needs, indeed they were often a regurgitation of Wal-Mart's. Andrews advocated the clarification of the character, objectives, goals, and purpose of a company and tied these to everything it does. Competitive advantage in the marketplace could only result from a clear articulation and fierce pursuit of these differentiating characteristics, which gave each company's strategy its uniqueness. "In an industry where all companies seem to have the same strategy, we will find trouble for all but the leaders—as at various times American Motors Corporation, Chrysler Corporation, and Ford Motor Company have had different degrees of difficulty following General Motors Corporation, which got where it is by *not* following the previous industry leader, Henry Ford," Andrews wrote.[12]

When to Enter and When to Exit

Right up until dawn of August 2, 338 B.C., the commanders of the Greek city-states did not know for sure when, or even whether, the Macedonians were headed their way into Chaeronea. The Macedonians, for their part, even as they prepared for a battle against Thebes and Athens, sent diplomatic missions to each state to examine if either might join them in a battle against the other. To confuse the enemy they even sent a messenger with a dispatch of important battle plans to Pella in the hope that some Athenian or Theban garrison might capture him. That is exactly what happened. The plans outlined a fictitious march up north to Thrace—not unlike the fictitious, Scotland-based British Fourth Army's plans for invading Norway to launch the Allied armies' push against the Germans in the Second World War (See Chapter 9: The Art of Deceptive Strategy).

While the Athenians and the Thebans anxiously awaited them, the Macedonians were playing a purely proactive game of neutralizing potential allies of their enemy. Amphissa had been positively disposed toward Macedonia as well as toward Thebes. By moving in first the Macedonians ensured that the town was secured in their favor. Several of the Greek city-states were flummoxed by the Macedonians' capture of Amphissa. They thought maybe what the Macedonians were after was securing control of the Gulf of Corinth—the vital lifeblood of northern and central Greece though which the Macedonians could have received troops and supplies for their war effort. To destroy this source of advantage in the Macedonians' favor, the Thebans and the Athenians blocked all the passes through which people and goods had to travel to enter Greece if they arrived through the Gulf of Corinth.

Philip and Alexander did not use the Gulf of Corinth as a supply route. Their actions were partly oriented to confuse the enemy and were partly a series of well-executed moves to secure competitive advantage, because as an invading army they knew they would always be at a disadvantage. After all the scraps and brawls they had been in throughout Greece and elsewhere, they did not underestimate the resolve of an enemy fighting them on their own soil. They understood this lesson two millennia before the Russians were to teach it to Napoleon, the Afghans to the British and the Russians, and the Vietnamese to the Americans.

So even when the Thebans ousted the Macedonian garrison holding the symbolically important—and sacred—pass at Thermopylae, the Macedonians didn't take any punitive action against the Thebans. Thermopylae was too far to the east of their current theater of operations. Instead, they focused all their attention on freeing two passes that ran close to the critical pass at Parapotamii, which controlled access into the plains of Chaeronea. The mountain pass at Parapotamii was what the Cephissus River and the main road to Thebes ran through. If they seized control of the two neighboring passes, they rightly guessed, the allied armies would pull off their troops guarding Parapotamii. Seeing Macedonian troops take over the other two passes, the Theban garrison guarding Parapotamii was withdrawn. The Macedonians had secured open passage into Chaeronea, with all the regions and passes to Chaeronea's north under their complete control. They could now enter Chaeronea and, importantly, if need be stage a quick retreat as well.

The Macedonians' moves to secure an exit route were precisely in keeping with the writings of Xenophon, a fourth-century-B.C. historian and general, whose works rank in importance alongside those of other Greek historians such as Thucydides and Herodotus. Interestingly, the most prolific management guru of all times, Peter Drucker, also recommends the writings of Xenophon to those who wish to drink from the original spring of all management thinking. Xenophon had once led what is simply known as "the Ten Thousand"—a force of 10,000 Greek mercenaries who successfully marched into Persia in support of Cyrus the Younger, the second son of Persian emperor Darius II. The mercenaries had to retreat when Cyrus was killed in battle against his older brother, who commanded a force said to be twenty times larger than Cyrus'.

Philip and Alexander, both ardent fans of the writings of Xenophon, followed his advice closely. In their minds, *when to exit* was as important as *when to enter* Chaeronea. Xenophon's advice on the art of the strategic retreat remains one of the most practical guides on a key piece of strategic and tactical operations in battle. Interestingly, multinational corporations expanding globally have detailed plans and prepare for many months, if not years, for the when-to-enter decision, but few have any plans whatsoever for a when-to-exit decision. Not surprisingly, as the experiences of Coca-Cola and IBM in the seventies attest, when their operations were unexpectedly and forcibly shuttered by a few developing world governments, the when-to-exit decision remains the soft underbelly of global strategies.

In western military tradition, too, the when-to-exit decision did not hold much weight in relatively modern times. The historian Barbara

Tuchman recounts the way U.S. Army general Joseph Stilwell was caught unawares by the art of the strategic retreat. Stilwell, first arrived in China in 1911, a few weeks after the revolution began to transform the nation from a monarchy to a republic, and did several stints in the country as it went from control of the feuding warlords, to the domination of the Nationalists, and then the Communists, and through the Second World War. At West Point he had been trained on tactics and strategies related to offensive maneuvers—never on when and how to carry out a retreat. The Chinese, on the other hand, placed as much emphasis on backward movement as they did on the forward. They believed a calculated withdrawal gave them an option of a forward movement in the future. The need to strategically retreat, and the conduct of such retreat, was to remain a contentious issue between Stilwell and the great Chinese generals alongside whom he served. He could see their effectiveness, but in the context of his training at West Point under such great "offensive" strategy and tactics instructors as Dennis Hart Mahan, and the experience in serving in the American Expeditionary Force (AEF) under General John J. Pershing, they did not make much sense.

The AEF's role in the First World War was not only to help the Allies but also to persuade their leaders to abandon their trench-warfare orientation—that is, the pursuit of a limited set of objectives followed by rapid consolidation—in favor of the American military doctrine of maximum offensive penetration rather than consolidation.[13] Retreat had no role in such offensive doctrine. According to the Americans, as well as many European military historians who were largely ignored, the reason the Great War was so prolonged and costly was that both sides were battling a largely defensive war—a war of attrition where a limited offensive action was followed by months of digging in to secure positions.

Yamaha Wo Tsubusu

Henry Mintzberg, the Canadian management guru, has long observed about major strategic shifts that it is probably more important to be right about *when* to make the shifts than *how*. Delaying a shift till everyone onboard is equipped and comfortable making it can mean waiting till it's too late; making a shift too soon can sink the effort as well. The fight between Honda and Yamaha for supremacy of the Japanese motorcycle industry provides an interesting tale of appropriate timing.

Throughout the 1970s Honda, the largest motorcycle manufacturer in the world, watched with alarm the growing capacity and productivity of Yamaha. But at the end of the day Honda, too focused on building its automotive business, did not pay enough heed to the Yamaha threat up until 1981 when Yamaha signaled its intention to challenge Honda's supremacy in the motorcycle industry with a credible threat: They opened a new factory whose production output would have propelled Yamaha past Honda as the world's largest motorcycle producer.

Honda responded on a battle footing with the Japanese war cry *Yamaha wo tsubusu,* which roughly translates as "We will not only kill, squash, and bury you, but we will also be dancing on your graves." Honda, which had been focusing on automotive production, used the knowledge it had gained in Japanese flexible manufacturing techniques not only to replace the entire line of models it offered to customers but also to double the range. Yamaha, which also started off with about sixty models—same as Honda's—at the start of the war did not clearly understand when it ought to introduce new models to stem the defection of its customers to Honda's 120 new hot rods. It ended up replacing and introducing only half as many models as Honda.

Part of Honda's response was pure perception. It often used the same base machine but equipped it with enough customized accoutrements to make customers gawk longingly at showrooms. A lot of it was reality: Honda introduced many technological innovations, such as a much larger engine, which would be the same size as that on its automobiles, new composite materials, which made the bikes sturdier and lighter, and so on. But Honda understood the *when* of strategic maneuvering and did everything to get its timing right. Customers, tired of the old motorcycle models, were ready for a new range of "lifestyle" models that were new, fashionable, and stirred passions. To translate the passion into profits Honda supplemented its new model introductions with incentives, promotions, and advertising. Yamaha had been sunk. Not only was its president publically forced to cry uncle but the company was so laden with unsold inventory and losses that it took many years for it to recover.[14]

In the past two decades Harley-Davidson has made a remarkable and profitable comeback. The company has nearly gone under many times in its hundred-year history, since two twenty-year-olds, William Harley and Arthur Davidson, figured out a way to bolt an internal combustion engine between two oversized rubber tires. Realizing that its current customer profile of chunky, bald, or ponytailed, leather-jacketed, middle-aged male buyers (median age forty-six) might well put it out of business, Harley-

Davidson has once again—as it did after World War II—taken the step of designing and manufacturing hogs to appeal to young Americans and women. Making a break with its tradition of building large, heavy, lumbering machines with big back ends and a minimum of 650cc engine displacements, Harley-Davidson partnered with firms like the German car maker Porsche to design motorcycles that are hip, cool, light, and fast, while preserving the "potato-potato-potato" signature Harley rumble.

The Porsche-designed, liquid-cooled engine of the V-Rod not only marks a break with Harley's past of equipping its bikes with only air-cooled engines, but its adjustable-height seats and 360-pound weight opens up new market segments among women and young men—an important step for a company that has so far catered to Hell's Angels.[15] For Harley, which despite its profitability has been losing market share to light, fashionable Japanese motorcycles or their performance-oriented Teutonic cousins, the timing of its entry into the lighter-weight motorbikes couldn't be more propitious.

The How:
Leveraging Strengths, Shielding Weaknesses

As the sun arose over the eastern skies, the Theban and Athenian scouts on the mountain passes atop Mount Petrachos on the left and Mount Acontion on the right watched as 30,000 Macedonian infantrymen and 2,000 cavalry made their way through Parapotamii and its two neighboring passes in to the plains of Chaeronea. The buglers sounded the alarms, and a combined force of 38,000 Theban and Athenian troops (including small contigents from a few friendly city-states) took their predetermined positions atop a ridge bounded by Mount Petrachos and Mount Acontion. The Thebans took the right side of the mile-long front toward the river and the Athenians occupied the left on the side of the citadel. On the Macedonian side Philip occupied the right at the head of the Macedonian infantry, and Alexander commanded the left, at the head of the Thessalian horses. The Macedonian cavalry, in Parmenion's command, marched to Alexander's left. Positioned on top of the ridge was the famed 300-member Theban Sacred Band, which had struck the decisive blow to seize victory for Thebes (against Sparta) at Leuctra and at Mantinea. This cavalry unit of 150 couples, who lived together, trained together, and functioned as a tightly knit fighting unit, faced Alexander. In between the extremes both sides had stationed their phalanxes.

The Macedonians took their position on the battlefield, with Philip lined up against the Athenian left. The Macedonian front was arrayed at a forty-five-degree angle to the Greek city-states', so while Philip faced the Athenians eyeball-to-eyeball, there was a distance of several hundred yards between where Alexander commanded the Macedonian left wing and Thebes' Sacred Band. The right "thrown-forward" and the left "refused" formation was a regurgitation of a historically successful array: Thebes' general Epaminondas had twice won wars against larger enemies by deploying a similar "oblique" formation, and yet it was not the Thebans, or their allies, the Athenians, who had deployed themselves in this order, but the Macedonians.

The Macedonians were deeply aware of their strengths and weaknesses. Their strength lay in detailed planning for the battle, including of specific formations, which they had repeatedly practiced for several years. Their strength also lay in the maneuverability of their cavalry, the simplified nature of their phalanxes—whereby all the infantrymen had to focus on was moving forward or sideways or backward *and not* on protecting their right flank because their shields were on their left—and their longer and lighter (than those of the Greek city-states') fourteen-foot-long spears.

The Macedonians' weaknesses lay in that they were slightly outnumbered in troop size, in that the Athenian and the Thebans had arrived on the plains several days before and therefore had an intimate knowledge of the terrain (occupying the ridge was a clear indication of their willingness to take advantage of what the terrain offered), and finally, the Sacred Band was the finest heavy cavalry in all Greece.

The occupation of the ridge by the Thebans and Athenians at Chaeronea was an example of classic strategic positioning: The Thebans and the Athenians had found an advantageous position, they had dug in to defend—and attack from—this position, and they now awaited the arrival of the enemy to strike. Unfortunately, this is also an example of static strategic positioning. The Thebans and the Athenians had not planned for what would happen if the Macedonians were to charge in an unexpected manner.

In business-strategy terms their positioning was not sustainable. Not only because it depended on one particular approach by the Macedonians, but also because Athens and Thebes had not thought through the control and coordination issues related to two different types of armies—

one a standing professional army and the other an army of citizen-soldiers—which had been banded together in a loose alliance. In the business world Porter has held that the need for internal controls and co-ordination requires an organization to make trade-offs. Organizations "that try to be all things to all customers, in contrast, risk confusion in the trenches as employees attempt to make day-to-day operating decisions without a clear framework."[16]

Unfortunately, the Thebans and the Athenians had not made any trade-offs about either the right framework for engaging the Macedonians or about important control and coordination issues such as who was in overall control, how should they work together, how ought they back up each other in battle, etc. In addition, while Thebes had a formal leader-ship structure in its military, Athens, because it did not have a standing army, had no military leadership structure. Philip had once remarked that the Athenians seem to always suggest an endless trove of great generals to choose from, while in his entire life he had only found one great general in Macedonia—Parmenion.

Every Athenian citizen was expected to perform his or her duties in war. They couldn't be compulsorily drafted, but they were expected to do their duty. Their political leaders were rotated through senior military po-sitions, but these leaders could not make decisions, since all decisions had to be made by consensus. It was not surprising that an inexperienced and indecisive general found himself at the head of the Athenian entourage; even Demosthenes, who was a great orator, mediocre diplomat, poor politician, and pitiful soldier, by virtue of his political standing in Athens was given command of an Athenian contingent.

The Macedonians were aware of the lack of coordination and control between the Thebans and the Athenians. While that was going to be a huge advantage to them, they were also smart enough to recognize an inverse disadvantage—unpredictability. They recognized that their pro-fessional army was pitted against a combination of a professional army *and* an army comprised of citizen-soldiers. The Macedonians, especially Philip, considering his education in Thebes, had studied the strategies and tactics of the Thebans, and realized that outside of a few surprises the maneuvers of Thebes' professional army were predictable. As in a profes-sional American football coach's playbook Philip had prepared the Mace-donian army for and against a variety of offensive and defensive plays.

The maneuvers of citizen-soldiers, on the other hand, as the history of citizen-soldiers from ancient times to the present indicates, were largely unpredictable. In addition, while professional armies held a common notion of victory and defeat in battle, for citizen-soldiers, who often fought to preserve their way of life—which for the South in the U.S. Civil War meant the preservation of slavery—there was no single or common perspective on victory or defeat. The Macedonians therefore set about eliminating such unpredictability as it was in their control by concentrating on the planning and execution of attacks as well as the completeness and finality with which they decided to seek a resolution to the battle.

The Macedonians had very clearly detailed who was in control where. Philip was in overall charge, and he led the right wing; Alexander led the Macedonian left wing. Philip had surrounded Alexander with several experienced commanders, since this was Alexander's first command, and in case there was a need. Every member of the Macedonian army, whether infantryman or cavalryman, knew in a very precise fashion what was expected of him—what to attack, what to defend, and what to concede. In this way the Macedonians were in complete control of what in business would be described as an organization's "activity system."

Strategy, believes Porter, is "about *combining* activities."[17] Just like Southwest Airlines, which combines a whole host of activities—from rapid turnaround at airport gates through no-meal flights, no interline baggage transfers, and no seat assignments; to using only one type of aircraft (the Boeing 737) to deliver its high-convenience, low-cost proposition; and even the legend of its conception on the back of cocktail napkins—the Macedonians, too, combined an entire set of activities to create, in Porter's words, "strategic fit." Their troops could maneuver quickly through the use of lightweight armor, they gathered better information and intelligence than their opponents, they equipped their infantry with more effective spears than the other sides', each individual piece of their battalions was charged with achieving a predetermined objective, and they communicated through a combination of predetermined signals as well as messengers. In many ways, as in Porter's definition of business strategy, each activity mattered and reinforced every other to link together into the chain of Macedonian strategy, where the chain was as strong as its strongest link.

Deploying the Indirect Approach

One of the central tactical maneuvers of warfare is the indirect approach to an attack, whereby deception and guile are used to temporarily deflect an opponent's energies and strengthen one's own position. The Macedonians had already deployed the indirect approach when, instead of entering Amphissa, as requested by the Amphictyonic Council, they bypassed it and secured Elatea, then, many months later, in a surprise move, brought Amphissa under their control. They were to demonstrate use of the indirect approach on the battlefield at Chaeronea as well.

The natural advantage that the Athenians and Thebans had, standing atop the ridge in a defensive position, was an advantage that the Macedonians wanted to neutralize quickly, thus demoralizing their opponents. The battle began with Philip, at the head of a column of hypaspists (shield-bearing, light-armed infantrymen), rushing into a large contingent of well-armored Athenian heavy infantrymen. Seeing the Macedonians climb up the ridge, the heavier armed Athenians cheered and plunged down the ridge to attack them—their heavy equipment further revving their momentum. Just about the point where their spears would strike the Macedonians', Philip signaled a sudden, preplanned withdrawal. The Macedonians, lightly armed, retreated backward from the ridge, with their spears still pointed toward the charging Athenians. It was a ruse. The Athenians, overjoyed that the Macedonians were retreating, enthusiastically stepped up their charge at the Macedonian infantry, not realizing that they had given up their superior position on the ridge and that they had opened up gaps within their own front line. Philip, leading the lightly armed Macedonian contingent, like the Pied Piper of Hamelin had lured away a large force of heavily armored troops from their secure defensive positions. The Athenians had given up their strategic advantage. The retreating Macedonian infantry stopped, quickly organized themselves into an offensive formation, and charged into the Athenians.

The Athenians had not only given up their strategic *advantage*, by not thinking about what they were doing, they had also created a significant strategic *disadvantage* by opening up a gap in their lines. Now that the gap had been opened, Philip ordered his sixteen-person-deep phalanxes to move against the eight- and twelve-person Athenian and Theban phalanxes at the center.

At the other end of the Macedonian front the Thessalian heavy cavalry under Alexander charged the Theban phalanxes and the Sacred Band. Thanks to the melee that Philip had wrought, a wide gap had opened up between the Athenian and the Theban positions. The Thebans, however, within their position, stayed tightly knit. Into this opened gap, which exposed one end of the Theban front, charged Alexander, while Parmenion, leading the Macedonian light cavalry, went around the other end.

While the Athenian heavy infantry was being decimated, the much better trained Theban army tried to hold on to its position. But it was of no use. The Thessalian and the Macedonian cavalry thundered into the gaps opened up, and completely surrounded the Theban ranks. Mayhem and slaughter followed, including of the Sacred Band, which, unable to maneuver against the shoves and pushes of the completely surrounded Theban infantrymen, fell to the ground at exactly the spot where they had stood in formation. Only forty-six of the three hundred lived. Almost the entire Theban army, wishing to put up a fight, valiantly fell to the ground as swarms after swarm of bristling spear phalanxes and heavy cavalry descended upon them.

On the Athenian side the volunteer citizen soldiers had begun their retreat through the southern pass they had held again for exactly this eventuality. It wasn't a retreat so much as a mad dash for safety. Unfortunately very few escaped; most surrendered. The historian Plutarch, a Chaeronean by birth, recounts the tragic—or hilarious, depending on which side your allegiance lies—story of the retreating Demosthenes, languidly and sullenly limping away to safety. Whether the limp was brought about by the weight of the chip on his shoulder the size of all Greece or a genuine injury is not known. What is known is that his cloak became entangled in a bramble bush. As he tried to extricate it he watched, with terror in his eyes, the advancing gallop of the Macedonian cavalry. Demosthenes fell on his knees before the advancing Macedonians, and oblivious to the cries of pain from injured Athenians writhing on the battlefield like salted slugs, wept and begged to be taken alive. He didn't want to die. Over two thousand Athenian soldiers weren't so fortunate; nor were most of the Thebans. Their lives had been weeded out like dandelions.

MAGNANIMITY IN VICTORY

The armies of the great city-states of Thebes and Athens had been completely and humiliatingly routed on the plains of Chaeronea. Macedonia's victory was complete. Panic spread through both city-states as news arrived of their military defeat. But they had little to fear—especially Athens. The next morning after the battle, Alexander, accompanied by Parmenion, entered Athens at the front of a small cavalry unit, holding urns containing the ashes of the Athenian dead. Behind them marched the Athenian prisoners of war, which was virtually the entire Athenian army less the two thousand dead. The citizens of Athens watched in amazement as the Macedonian contingent rode up the hill to the main burial site of the city-state, followed by open carriages containing their dead — much as Athens' greatest general and leader, Pericles, had done with the Athenian dead in 431 B.C., the first year of the Peloponnesian War.

At the cemetery, which sat on top of a hill for every Athenian to see and remember their dead, in a grim and somber mood, with their heads bowed as if they were burying their own, Macedonian soldiers lined up the urns neatly along plots that were vacant. They then unshackled the chains of the prisoners and set them free. So moved were Athenians by this gesture, that afternoon in their Assembly, they voted Philip and Alexander citizens of Athens.

Philip and Alexander accepted their gesture and promised that no retributions would accrue to Athens as long as the Athenian Assembly was dissolved and Athens became a Macedonian ally. All Athenian troops — and most important, her ships — would from now on be at their command. With the Thebans they were not so lenient — partly because Philip, who as a hostage in Thebes had come to know and treat many Thebans as close friends, felt truly betrayed that they had joined Athens in a coalition against him. Much of this feeling of betrayal had to do with the stark fashion in which ancient Greeks and Macedonians viewed relationships. As the Gordon Gekko character played by Michael Douglas said in *Wall Street*, either you were completely in (as a friend) or you were out (as a foe).

The retribution that befell Thebes was partly driven by Philip's knowledge of how well trained the Thebans were. He did not want them to go back to Thebes and raise another army. All the Theban soldiers were sold into slavery; their commanders were summarily executed. To honor the fallen Sacred Band members, the Macedonians built a stone statue of a lion on top of the grounds where their bodies were interred. The statue not only stands today, next to a road that cuts across the plains, but recent excavations at the monument have revealed the remains of exactly the same number of bodies as the number of Sacred Band members who had died that day, almost 2,400 years ago.

The next year, 337 B.C., Philip convened the leaders of all the Greek city-states to Corinth, where the League of Corinth was created — just as the leaders of the nations fighting Germany in the First World War were convened at the Bourbon dynasty's magnificent palace at Versailles to create the League of Nations or the awe-inspiring presence of the Russian czar, the Austrian emperor, and the Prussian king, together with the regents and rulers of smaller nations, who met at the Congress of Vienna in September 1814 after Napoleon's first abdication.

At Corinth every Greek city-state swore—and repeatedly so—not to engage in war against one another; to not engage in a war against Philip or Alexander or their descendants; and that no citizen of any city-state was to sell his services to an outside nation without the explicit permission of the League—a move designed to discourage the Greek mercenary armies in the service of Persia.

Philip then rose up before the delegates and asked to be appointed "hegemon" or "captain general" or "supreme commander" of the League's combined armed forces. So completely in control of Greece was he that he could have asked them to elect him the ruler of all Greece—anyway, all of Greece was in his command. But he wanted their goodwill and their men, triremes, and wealth—he didn't care about their land.

Philip was a smart seller of dreams. He didn't want to become supreme commander just for the sake of it; he wanted it so he could lead all Greece into a battle against its archenemy, Persia. Even this wasn't offered as some generic proposition. He wanted to lead the Greeks in a battle against the Persians so they could seek revenge for the atrocities that the Persians, especially under their Great King Xerxes, had wrought on their towns, temples, and people. It was this sort of positioning of his efforts that Philip knew was sure to play well and rile every Greek into supporting him.

Although Xerxes was long since dead, Philip had named Xerxes, because it was his name that got all Greeks to vent spleen together—and his name evoked hope. Xerxes' attacks on Greece about 150 years before represented threat in that, of all the Persian emperors, his attacks on Greece had been the most vicious and sustained. Hope, in the sense that it was at Salamis, where the ruse of an Athenian general named Themistocles, and the doggedness of the Athenians, had defeated Xerxes' much larger naval fleet. The Persian threat needed to be met. United under him, Philip promised, they could, as Churchill said of the Second World War, fight the "Good War," and win. The League was unanimous in electing Philip supreme commander.

The eighteenth-century Prussian military philosopher Carl von Clausewitz defined strategy as the use of combat or force or the threat of combat or force for the realization or achievement of the military objectives or political purpose of the war. As Philip and Alexander demonstrated at Chaeronea, strategy is about the deployment of geographic, economic, social, interstate, political, and behavioral realities to achieve a broader set of objectives. For them it wasn't domination of Greece, it was domination for a purpose: to lead Macedonia and Greece together in a quest for domination over and subjugation of Persia. In geopolitics, too, we witness the application of a strategic mindset when nations conquer other nations not for purely tactical reasons but when it helps achieve broader strategic goals such as access to human or mineral resources or to ports and shipping lanes. Philip and Alexander had presented an old proposition, the defeat of Persia, which had existed as a goal since the end of the Persian Wars in 499 B.C., and they had bolstered their capacity to deliver that proposition in a unique fashion—by adding the might of Macedonia to that of the great city-states of Greece. It was a compelling proposition.

James Brian Quinn, professor emeritus at Dartmouth's Amos Tuck School of Business Administration, and one of the leading lights in business strategy, wrote in his highly influential book *Strategies for Change: Logical Incrementalism* that the "precepts" of the Battle of Chaeronea "were enduring and have constantly reappeared both in other successful 'grand' and 'battle' strategies and in the mainstreams of strategic thought over the next 2,300 years."[18] He went on to write: "Perhaps the most startling analogies of World War II lay in Patton's and Rommel's battle strategies, which were carbon copies of the Macedonians' concepts of planned concentration, rapid breakthrough, encirclement, and attack on the enemy's rear. Similar concepts still pervade well-conceived strategies—whether they are government, diplomatic, military, sports, or business strategies."[19]

SUMMARY OF KEY THEMES

I. END OF THE FULL-FRONTAL ASSAULT

Philip and Alexander's strategies and tactics demonstrated that wars need not be fought in the Hobbesian, state-of-nature fashion, but they also revealed how a smaller army could defeat a larger competitor.

2. THE APPLICATION OF STRATEGY, NOT TACTICS ALONE.

After capturing Elatea they sat tight for almost a year, planning, preparing, testing their next set of moves, but not attacking—demonstrating that in war, as in business and politics, "the essence of strategy" can be about "choosing what not to do."

3. THE IMPORTANCE OF CHOOSING PRECISELY "WHERE" TO BATTLE.

Like businesses deciding "where" to compete, the where-to-battle decision is revealed as a key underlying principle of Philip and Alexander's strategies and tactics. Focus on the "where" propeled Honda in the sixties from a small Japanese manufacturer of motorcycles to a position not only as the foremost motorcycle maker but as a prospective leader in the automobile industry.

4. "WHEN" TO ENTER AND WHEN TO EXIT.

When to push and when to pull back; and when to strike offensively and play defensively—are all revealed in the approaches and behaviors of the Macedonians. Honda's strike against Yamaha in the motorbike industry provides a relatively modern application of the Macedonians' insight.

5. THE "HOW" TO BATTLE OR COMPETE DECISION.

This pervades every move of the Macedonians from positioning to timing of attack, to feints and deceptions and other "indirect" ploys—all targeted at delivering the maximum damage on the enemy at the least cost to oneself—what magnanimity in victory is all about.

CHAPTER 3

THE MEN WHO COULD BE KING

I T WAS A TRULY FESTIVE OCCASION FOR KING PHILIP OF MACEDONIA when he walked his daughter, Cleopatra, up to the altar in October 336 B.C. After decades of war his country had emerged as the predominant power in southern Europe. Almost all of Greece was in Macedonian hands, under Philip's rule. As he walked, his head drooping with the touching sentimentality of a father coming to terms with the loss of his daughter to another man, he also visibly winced from the aches in his long, sturdy arms and the pain in his stocky shoulders. He had been injured so many times in battle that any long walk brought back the searing memories of those slashes, stabs, and bruises as if they had happened only yesterday. Even though he had to strain his one good eye to see, having lost the other in battle, he was a brilliant player of crowds. He returned every wave, clap, or cheer with the sincerity of an accomplished actor who can hide his true feelings and physical state behind a mask of well-rehearsed responses.

Cleopatra was going to wed her maternal uncle (Olympias' brother), who was also called Alexander. Philip had intervened in a succession struggle in Greece's northwestern neighbor of Epirus in favor of his brother-in-law, and the giving of his daughter's hand in marriage was meant to serve as a further signal of his enduring support. Philip was determined to walk up the temple steps to the altar without tripping over and causing an embarrassment. He had strategically placed bodyguards along the step to hold him upright lest his weak ankles should give way. He smiled warmly at his daughter and wanly at his subjects as he took the first few steps. Then he halted to regain his strength to clamber up the next few steps; but after a couple of them one of his ankles gave way and he fell forward into the arms of his closest bodyguard, who had been walking sideways up the steps alongside him.

As his daughter reached down to help him up, Philip's eye rolled skyward and he fell limp on the steps. Soon the white shirt he had worn turned crimson, and his daughter, who had knelt down to help him, let out a blood-curdling shriek and fainted. Philip lay in a pool of his own blood, which slowly spread over his clothes and down the steps like large swathes of thick paint. Philip's personal bodyguard, a nobleman by the name of Pausanias, whom he had trusted to hold him from falling, had run a dagger straight through his chest.

Philip was only forty-six years old when he died.

Successor Not Named

Philip had died without naming his son, Alexander, as his explicit successor, even though he had taken several steps (such as making him the next in command at Chaeronea) to signal just such intent. It happens often enough in political and business institutions. Forget lesser known institutions, even the venerable investment bank Goldman Sachs, which has a proud history of getting most things right, was left without a clear successor when its head, Gustave Lehmann Levy, died after suffering a stroke in October 1976. Although Levy had suggested the presence of successors, he had never named an heir apparent, and his death threw the firm into turmoil.[1]

Philip was proud of the abilities and acumen his son was displaying as a ruler of Macedonia in his absence. His heart had filled with joy and pride when on their military conquests, after a hard day's work, his commanders and generals sitting around a fire talked about Alexander as regent and Philip as *his* top general.

Of course, not everything was always ducky. Two events, had almost had the effect of air-brushing Alexander out of Macedonian power politics. The first had had to do with a marriage proposal that Philip received from a Persian governor for his illegitimate son Arrhidaeus by his Thessalian mistress. (Arrhidaeus was Philip's oldest son, and as we shall see in

Chapter 10, would make a return temporarily as regent of Macedonia after Alexander's death.)

As Plutarch recounts the story, the satrap (governor) of the Persian part of Thrace send an intermediary to propose to Philip that his oldest daughter be wed to Arrhidaeus. When word of this proposed match reached the royal palace, Queen Olympias is said to have persuaded Alexander that such a marriage would lead to a distribution of Philip's empire in Arrhidaeus' favor. She even enlisted the help and support of some of Alexander's closest friends, like Ptolemy, who would later emerge as one of his top generals and eventually the ruler of Egypt, to support her conclusion. Philip, they argued, would not be in a position to effect any other outcome because the might of the Persian empire would weigh heavily on his decision.

Alexander, once persuaded, decided to swing into action. He drafted a famous tragic actor who was performing in a Sophocles tragedy in Pella to torpedo the match out of the water. The actor, fully rehearsed by Alexander, traveled to the court of the Persian satrap in Thrace, and with the full force of a tragic hero's solemn gravitas and dignified and sorrowful concern suggested to the satrap that he was concerned about the match. With his puffy eyes and somber looks the actor slowly but convincingly nibbled away at Arrhidaeus' credibility. Arrhidaeus, he claimed, was not only dimwitted and mentally unstable, which he was, but also prone to violent epileptic attacks, which he also was—the content of the story was basically true, but the extent of Arrhidaeus' afflictions dramatically exaggerated. The next day the satrap quietly withdrew the marriage proposal. When word finally got around to Philip about what had happened, and who was behind it, he reportedly marched into Alexander's room in the palace and ordered him to leave Macedonia immediately—together with his friends who had been in on the plot. Alexander and his friends spent a few months in Epirus.

The other event that split them apart had to do with Philip's marriage to Cleopatra, the daughter of a Macedonian baron. Philip's daughter was also named Cleopatra (In ancient Greece the name Cleopatra for a girl was as common as Michelle is today).

Although Olympias and Philip's other wives had repeatedly railed against Philip's infidelities, they had come around to the conclusion that it was probably easier for a camel to walk through the eye of a needle than it was for Philip to remain faithful. But Philip had convinced them, and they had reluctantly concluded, that all of his marriages were ones of convenience—designed to expand Macedonia's territory or finance a military expedition. This is why all of his marriages had been to non-Macedonian princesses.

The one to Cleopatra, his eighth, was different. There was no territorial gain or treasure chest to be had—he already was the most powerful ruler after Persia's Great King. It also wasn't that Philip had hit his midlife crisis hard and needed to marry someone young, as so many men do. As a powerful man Philip had easy access to a sufficiently long line of women. The only conceivable reason for the marriage, many speculated, was that Philip wanted—or had been persuaded—to beget a fully pedigreed Macedonian heir. This reason obviously perturbed Alexander a great deal. But he maintained dignified silence on the topic—till the day of the wedding.

Although many barons had warned Philip that he might not be able to completely get away, in saying "I do," without some protests of "I object" from the attendees, the wedding had passed off rather well. All of Philip's wives, and their close relatives, had boycotted. At the wedding reception, however, Cleopatra's uncle, Attalus, a leading general in the Macedonian army, raised a toast to the couple—the forty-five-year-old groom and his sixteen-year-old bride. Attalus, seated next to the couple at the head table, called on the assembled guests to pray that the union of these two would result in a *legitimate* heir to the throne. As the guests raised their glasses, a bronze, drinking cup flew across the entire length of the palace's banquet hall and struck the toasting Attalus smack on his forehead. Alexander, from the back end of the room, where he was inconspicuously seated, had hurled the cup at Attalus. As blood trickled down Attalus' face, an enraged Alexander stood up on the table and shouted from the end of the room at Attalus, "Villain, do you take me for a bastard, then?"[2]—referring to his mixed descent from a Macedonian father and an Epirote mother.

As Attalus stood shaken and dumbfounded at this turn of events, Philip, enraged at his son's behavior, drew his Celtic sword and, brushing aside his bride, who tried to restrain him, took deliberate steps toward his son in a drunken stupor. Alexander, too, had unsheathed his sword from its scabbard, and leapt down from the table, to engage his father in a duel. Unfortunately Philip had had a bit too much to drink. After a few steps his knees wobbled, and he fell flat on his face on the banquet hall's stone floor. As guests tried to rush to Philip's aid, Alexander stepped forward and, brandishing his sword, moved everyone away from Philip. Then, standing next to the fallen Philip, he proclaimed to the assembled guests that here lay their king who wished to invade Asia. But he couldn't even move from one table to the next without losing his balance.[3]

He sheathed his sword back in the scabbard and, together with his friends, who were at his table at the celebrations, walked out of the palace. They rode toward Epirus, where Olympias was already in a self-imposed exile to get away from this wedding.

Within six months, however, Alexander was back in Macedonia, serving as Philip's deputy and leading the Macedonian cavalry in battle. He might have been a little hurt inside, but on the outside he displayed a disposition that suggested that the family imbroglio had been shrugged off like water off a duck's back.

Sense of Immortality

No other empire had as much trouble with succession as did the Macedonians. Britain's House of Tudor in the sixteenth century would come close, when, after the death of the oft-married Henry VIII, the crown would pass from sibling to sibling three consecutive times in just over a decade, ending with the forty-five-year-long rule of Elizabeth I. But even the Tudors didn't witness anything as violent or uncertain as the Macedonian succession. Most Macedonian monarchs had died a violent death, and Philip himself had been the beneficiary of a succession in which the crown had passed twice from sibling to sibling rather than from ruler to child.

Philip's failure to name Alexander successor might be due to a sense of his own immortality. Naming one's successor has often been compared to writing a will—it forces one to confront his or her mortality. Of course Philip was relatively young when he died, so his not naming a successor is to some degree understandable—only to some degree, though, considering Macedonia's violent history. There is little reason why the contemporary world of business and politics should be replete with the examples of CEOs and leaders who, despite advanced age and illness, have gone through life without an explicit succession plan. The succession difficulties of and with septuagenarian and octogenarian CEOs like Armand Hammer at Occidental Petroleum, Harold Geneen at ITT, and Harry Gray at United Technologies are the lore of succession planning courses at leading business schools—up there with such political examples as the

Palestine Liberation Organization's Yasser Arafat or Cuba's Fidel Castro, who have had established records of never cultivating lieutenants, protecting their power base by encouraging rivalries among people surrounding them, or, like Stalin, simply airbrushing anyone who is a potential threat into oblivion.

In the best of times, when companies have put in detailed succession plans, the transition to a new leader isn't easy—one only has to look at the teething troubles of GE's new CEO, Jeffrey Immelt, and IBM's Sam Palmisano, who were the beneficiaries of probably two of the finest succession processes ever conducted in corporate America. Neither CEO was prepared for, nor could they have foreseen, the changed expectations that shareholders had of public companies in the post-Enron environment.

There are also times when there is a succession plan, but the leader in charge, as if fearful he might spend the rest of his life like King Lear, restlessly pining for what was once his, refuses to share significant responsibilities with his chosen successor. Second-in-commands may therefore be relegated to doing whatever the leader *doesn't* want to do. Kevin Sharer, the CEO of biotechnology giant Amgen, describes the relationship that Larry Bossidy is alleged to have had with Jack Welch: "Jack gets to do whatever he wants and I get to do whatever is left." Ostensibly a lighthearted comment about Bossidy's role as COO at GE under CEO Jack Welch, it is nevertheless true that Bossidy left GE to run his own show as CEO of Allied Signal (now Honeywell).

Many vice presidents of the United States, too, have been relegated to cutting ribbons or attending the funerals of second-tier international leaders. It was well known that as William McKinley's vice president, Teddy Roosevelt was bored to a state of somnolence. If it hadn't been for the tragic assassination of McKinley, few would have known Roosevelt's resolve and drive as an individual and as a leader who, given rein, took the United States to unwavering greatness. Very few of us can name the forty-four vice presidents that the United States has had—with the possible exception of the fourteen who became president. John Adams, who, serving as the first vice president of the United States, was President George Washington's ridicule deflector—in that he frequently made himself the butt of jokes—once remarked of the office of the vice president as the "most insignificant office that ever the invention of man contrived or his imagination conceived."

Despite Adams's frequently taking the heat for Washington, the president and the vice president were never close, and Washington even maintained an "appreciable distance"[4] from Adams because the vice president's penchant for titles with which to address the president had made him hugely unpopular. While Washington kept a distance, some presidents were known to have been openly disdainful of their number twos. Even at the peak of the Second World War, Franklin Roosevelt, despite ill health, met only twice with Vice President Harry Truman after the FDR-Truman team won the elections. So much in the dark was Truman about the war efforts that only when he was sworn in as president after FDR's death did he find out about the "terrible weapon" the U.S. was developing. Truman would end the Second World War by issuing orders to drop the "terrible weapon" on Hiroshima and Nagasaki as well as steer the U.S. through the early phases of the Cold War. But Truman had been kept out of the information loop as vice president. If FDR had had his way, Truman would have been remembered as an unsuccessful haberdasher from Missouri and a former senator, who happened to have served Roosevelt as vice president.

Jockeying for Position

Although everything pointed toward Alexander as the successor, because there was no formal succession plan in Macedonia, it wasn't immediately or entirely obvious to everyone that Alexander, as Philip's oldest *legitimate* male offspring, was automatically in line for the throne. The sixty barons who ruled Macedonia wielded sufficient power and voice at Pella to influence a different outcome.

The slate of contenders had also been growing. Alexander's cousin Amyntas, son of his uncle Perdiccas, in whose name Philip had ruled Macedonia, obviously had a preexisting, and strong, claim to the throne. Amyntas had further ingratiated himself with Philip by marrying his daughter by his Illyrian (Albanian) mistress. Philip's newest bride, Cleopatra, had recently borne him a son, who was viewed by some as a blue-blooded Macedonian with a purer, and thereby greater, claim to the Macedonian throne than Alexander had. Attalus, Cleopatra's uncle, was influential enough to rally a few Macedonian barons behind this claim.

Then there were several unannounced bids that a few barons were investigating on behalf of the illegitimate children that Philip had fathered. There was a bid on behalf of Arrhidaeus, whose marriage to the daughter of a Persian satrap Alexander and his friends had managed to scupper. Arrhidaeus was older than Alexander, and a few barons were eager for him to rule. Of course if Arrhidaeus had won he would have ruled Macedonia as a puppet. There were also a few barons who thought Cleopatra, Philip's legitimate daughter (and older child), might have a greater claim to the throne than Alexander, since nowhere in Macedonia's laws was it decreed that the throne could only be occupied by a male heir.

Despite his young age Alexander was a practiced reader of tea leaves. He was aware of the intrigues under way in the back rooms of power to deny him the throne. Though they weren't a major threat, he wasn't one to take chances. At the same time he was unwilling to seize power and wrest control of the throne. The untimely death of Philip had cast a pall of gloom over Macedonia. There was already enough uncertainty and anxiety about which way this powerful nation might turn, now that it had lost its charismatic leader and nation builder. He didn't wish to add to the ambiguity. Indeed, he knew his task was to minimize the ambiguity and uncertainty. He planned a transition process designed to do just that.

He knew he enjoyed the love and respect of most Macedonians. He had already proven himself as a general at Chaeronea, leading the heavy cavalry charge against Thebes' Sacred Band, and thereby striking the blow that would make the Macedonians victorious. He had led several other successful military expeditions. He had ruled wisely and justly as regent in his father's absence, and even though he didn't enjoy a long track record as a ruler, he had displayed all the necessary qualities and acumen of a good ruler in those brief interludes as regent.

Most Macedonians were in love with the personality cult of their young prince. His physical stature was by no means imposing, but stocky and muscular. He had light brown hair and eyes of the same color, and historians have described him as rather good-looking. He was agile and fast, and was a fabulous rider even fully armored. He was a masterful swordsman and spear fighter, and the display of his personal courage in various wars and expeditions was the stuff of legends. Even myths: there were some who credited him with supernatural powers like running faster than a tiger, slaying dragons, or levitating in midair. As in any prince who has it all, there was a riotous side to him, too, but tales of the outrageous parties were sounding tamer by the year since he had begun to work alongside his father in running the nation.

Minimize Uncertainty and Ambiguity

Motivations in life are hard to determine; for Alexander, figuring out who would be loyal—and who wouldn't—wasn't going to be easy. Despite that, Alexander knew he had to design a highly transparent transition process. That was important for the nation at that time. He also realized that the longer it took to crown the next king the greater the uncertainty, and there was also the threat of backstabbing and throat slashing—literally. He wasn't one to lose any time.

Uncertainty and ambiguity over the process of passing the baton can be the single greatest determinant of political infighting within an organization, or even a nation. Take the example of Elizabeth I's accession to the throne of England. It was on an early, fog-ridden morning in November 1558, when England lost Queen Mary Tudor, who passed away peacefully in her sleep after a long illness. There were many potential successors to Mary, the oldest daughter of Henry VIII, by Henry's first wife, Catherine of Aragon. These possible successors included her sixteen-year-old niece and namesake, Mary Stuart, Queen of Scots, who had been in line for the English throne through her grandmother, Margaret, a sister of Henry VIII. Mary Stuart had already inherited the Scottish throne through her father, James V of Scotland. She had further bolstered her claim to the throne of England by marrying the son of the French king, Henry II. Mary Stuart was a Catholic, and at that time in England, being Catholic mattered a lot.

Catholicism had once again found a zealous home in England under the rule of Mary Tudor. It was as if Mary had wished to make amends to Rome for her father's hugely public battle with the Catholic Church, and therefore went overboard pushing Catholicism on the nation. Henry VIII had broken with Rome when it refused to grant him the divorce he needed from Catherine of Aragon to marry Anne Boleyn, the sister of one of his mistresses; Anne, the second of his six wives, was Elizabeth's mother.

Mary had not only reasserted the power of Rome in England, she had sought every means available to her to do so—zealotry, force, and even by her marriage to the ardently Catholic and immensely powerful King Philip II of Spain. England had once again reasserted itself as a Catholic nation, and Catholics in England wished for nothing better than for the crown to pass from Mary Tudor to her Catholic niece, Mary Stuart, and in the process bypass her sister, Elizabeth, whose religious leanings were fuzzy and therefore suspect.

Mary Stuart wasn't the only potential successor to the throne of England then. There were Elizabeth's cousins, whom her stepbrother, Edward VI (Henry VIII's son by his third wife, Jane Seymour) had willed as heirs to the throne. Edward was only ten years old when he had ascended the throne of England, after the death of Henry VIII, as his only son, but died six years later in 1533 without leaving any direct heirs. Indirectly, however, he had willed the granddaughters of his aunt Mary, the youngest sister of Henry VIII, as *his* heirs to the throne.

Elizabeth, Henry VIII's only surviving child that morning of Mary Tudor's death, not only had many potential rivals for the throne, but the deck couldn't be more stacked against her. To begin with, many in England, and powerful Catholic nations in Europe like France and Spain, considered her an illegitimate child of Henry's—because Henry was never issued a divorce from Rome, and so he couldn't have married her mother, Anne Boleyn.

Henry had broken with the Catholic Church to marry her mother. He was so incensed at Pope Clement VII's refusal to grant him a divorce from Catherine that he also introduced the Reformation in England by establishing the Anglican church and appointing himself as its head, only seventeen years after the leader of the Reformation, Martin Luther, had posted the Ninety-five Theses denouncing the abuses and perversions of the Catholic Church's teachings, on the door of All Saints Church in Wittenberg, Germany, on October 31, 1517.

The marriage to Elizabeth's mother, Anne Boleyn, unfortunately, didn't last long, and in a further sign that whatever Henry wants, Henry gets, the English Parliament acceded to Henry's request to invalidate his marriage to Anne—paving the way for the third of his six marriages. Henry didn't stop at invalidation—he had Anne beheaded at the Tower of London on trumped-up charges of adultery and treason. Elizabeth was only three years old. In the eyes of many, and especially England's entrenched Catholics, the lack of a divorce from Rome and the consequent invalidation of the marriage by Parliament meant that Elizabeth was an illegitimate child of Henry's—negating any claim she might have for the throne.

From Henry's perspective, however, nothing could be further from the truth. He treated all three of his children, Mary, Edward, and Elizabeth, the same; showered them all with love and affection; and, even as he led the nation to greatness, made certain that he spent sufficient time in his children's upbringing. Henry's ability to do the right things in most aspects of life and enter into the wrong marriages, for which he is probably best known in history today, was nothing short of genius. Indeed, the contradiction about Henry is probably best expressed in the words once applied to the Athenian general Themistocles, the brain behind Athens' victory at Salamis: "He was greater in genius than in character."

Henry died when Elizabeth was fourteen years old, and with his death ended the peaceful and privileged life of the young princess. Her ten-year-old stepbrother, Edward, with whom she was very close, ascended the throne. But Edward was the son of Henry and Jane Seymour, and the Seymour family did everything in their power to drive a wedge between brother and both sisters. They were so successful that were it not for the intervention of tuberculosis and troops loyal to the two sisters, Mary, as the elder of the two, would not have been crowned queen.

Mary and Elizabeth were never quite two peas in a pod, and their relationship rapidly deteriorated when Mary, who was ardently Catholic, pressured Elizabeth to embrace Rome. When Elizabeth refused, she was imprisoned by Mary in the Tower of London on charges of treason. But Mary fell ill, and during the months of her long illness Elizabeth, who had invested her income from her father's estate carefully and profitably, like a Mafia don running his business empire from within the confines of the clink, spent her allowance on consolidating and solidifying her support from inside the tower.

The non-Catholics in England were tired of the conspiracy-laden reigns of Edward VI and Mary Tudor. The nation was rife with cronyism and cliquery. Under Mary people also had to put up with Bible-thumping Catholic fanaticism and inquisitorial persecution unleashed by her on the nation. In addition, England had been humbled through a series of military misadventures against its historical archenemy, the French. The English yearned for the stable reign they had witnessed under Henry VIII, who had been not only a visible symbol of the English nation and the embodiment of monarchy but had also presided over the English Reformation and a return to the greatness that had once been England's.

Though Elizabeth, who, on Mary's death, would be the only remaining child of Henry VIII, was everyone's popular choice to replace Mary, she wasn't one to rest on her popularity and await the arrival of the crown. She knew, as the great Jimmy Durante once remarked, "everyone wants to get into the act." In those months when it was clear that Mary was slowly but surely losing her grip on life, Elizabeth had her supporters spread out all over the land raising grassroots support for her ascension to the throne. Like Alexander, who would rely on a couple of experienced and highly trustworthy advisers, she had convened a council of highly reputable, dedicated, and practical advisers, who had even set up a transition office (a relatively unknown measure in the politics of that time) at Brocket Hall in Hertfordshire, a couple of hours' ride from London. There people like William Cecil (later Lord Burghley), who was to serve her as her closest adviser for over forty years, Thomas Parry, her chief of staff, Nicholas Throckmorton, and Francis Walsingham, who organized and then ran a large spy network, planned strategy, played out scenarios, engaged friends, and neutralized foes of Elizabeth's accession. They even secretly amassed troops and stockpiled weapons throughout the country—just in case. Not only men, but also many women secretly joined the cause, persuading their husbands and friends to support Elizabeth's claim.[5]

Through all this Elizabeth maintained an impassive stance, holding her cards closely to her chest. Throughout her life her public persona would be a carefully managed and cultivated display of positions, stances, and appearances. No one knew where she stood on Roman Catholicism, for example. This deception not only led King Philip II of Spain to champion her cause, but also persuaded his wife—and *her* sister—Mary that Elizabeth was the successor best likely to protect and preserve Catholic interests. They were both to be proven wrong. England was to move in her reign from a Catholic into a staunchly Protestant nation and Philip's influence over England was to ebb not only into insignificance but intransigence—ending in the defeat of the mighty Spanish Armada by an emerging British navy under the command of Sir Francis Drake.

With all the groundwork she had laid, within six hours of Mary's death Elizabeth was firmly on the throne. There could be no doubt in anyone's mind as to who was in control, and which way the nation would now turn.

Managing the Transition Process

Recognizing that the threats to Macedonia's monarchy were huge, and many of the neighboring Greek city-states, which had been forced to become part of Macedonia, as well as Greece's archrival Persia, could move in an act of aggression against it, Alexander had several of his closest friends from Mieza, who were now senior commanders in the Companion ranks, secure the palace and the major border crossings. They had to visibly demonstrate that they were completely in charge. It was important for Alexander to have a coterie of people he could shorthand and rely on because he knew them and trusted them always to deliver whatever they had signed on to deliver. It was also important that he not be offered emotional and intellectual arsenic in these early days. It is common for a new leader to be fed pet projects or personal advice from one and all that are mostly self-serving. He needed to be completely buffered from them.

Once the palace and the borders had been secured, even before he could organize the funeral arrangements, he convened a meeting of his father's most trusted generals. Most had known him since the day he was born. At this meeting he proclaimed to all the barons that the last thing that he was going to push for Macedonia was a "vision thing" about leading Greece into a new direction. He held out the specter of Persia on its shores, and Macedonia—together with Greece—needed to prepare for a war immediately. Taking Greece and Macedonia in a new direction could come later, after the security threats had been ameliorated. As Lou Gerstner famously proclaimed on April Fool's Day, 1993, when he took over an ailing IBM on the verge of being split up thirteen different ways, the last thing the behemoth needed was another vision.

Alexander asked Antipater, one of the two most senior of Philip's generals, to lead the transition process. He informed the gathered generals that a messenger had arrived from Parmenion, the other most senior of Philip's generals, who was leading an expeditionary force of ten thousand troops into Asia Minor. Parmenion had not only pledged his complete support and allegiance but had also offered to come back to Macedonia, if needed. He wasn't going to call Parmenion back from Asia, but he was going to appoint Antipater and Parmenion (in absentia) as coleaders of the transition process.

The choice of Antipater and Parmenion met with strong approval of the assembled generals. Both were in their sixties, the veterans of many battles, among the richest barons in Macedonia, and commanded the greatest respect of the armed forces as well as the Macedonian populace. It was well known that neither had any interest in the throne. Most of their children were leading members of Macedonian society—their sons were generals; their daughters, wives of leading generals. Both had frequently talked about retiring to some secluded spot in greater Macedonia (preferably in the warmer climes of one of the southern Greek city-states) and tending to their fruit orchards. They dreamed of watching deer graze in their backyards, listening to the burble of a brook running through their estates, or gazing at a spouting fountain.

Antipater and Parmenion couldn't be more different from each other in background and personality. Antipater was an up-by-the-bootstraps, self-made general with a reputation as a consensus builder, while Parmenion, who had had a privileged upbringing, was brusque and quick to cut to the chase. Antipater was the consummate diplomat who smoothed ruffled feathers, while Parmenion was an operator. Despite their style differences both had a long history of effectively working with each other, and with Philip, and publicly portraying a highly amicable relationship so as not to allow daylight to come between them.

Persuading these two men to lead the transition process was a shrewd move on Alexander's part. Parmenion, for example, was not only a great general, but he had strong following in the army ranks. He had personally trained many of its senior officers, and almost every soldier in the Macedonian army had at some point served under his direct command—when not directly under Philip's. Parmenion represented the "institutional memory" of the Macedonian army. No one knew the skills, capabilities, and, most importantly, the weaknesses of each and every officer as well as Parmenion; and now that Philip had died, no one was more battle scarred than Parmenion.

Antipater was a great general and a terrific administrator. When Philip was appointed hegemon, or supreme commander, of all forces at Corinth, Antipater, together with Alexander and Parmenion, had worked alongside him to draw up secret plans for the invasion of Persia. No one else had been brought into the details of the plans, because it was imperative to retain the element of surprise against such a formidable enemy. While Philip had planned for Alexander to stay behind as regent while he led the early expeditions into Persia, Alexander wanted to find a suitable regent to stay behind as ruler of Macedonia while he led the forces. No one would be a better regent than Antipater. He had strong credibility in the baronial ranks. In addition, Antipater was the only baron who could resist his mother's seductive behavior. This was a crucial determinant of whom he selected as regent in his absence. Olympias was now only in her mid-thirties and highly capable of using her charms to get her way. She was still very attractive and knew how to make most men's brows sweat, knees wobble, and jaws gape. Except for Antipater, who was happily married and not prone to losing his composure under Olympias' charm offensives.

Clarity in Roles

The roles that Parmenion and Antipater played were what many chairmen and vice chairmen at corporations do to help a new CEO manage the succession *and* the transition process. An interesting example of a CEO appointing a successor, but also along with that a team with clearly defined roles for transition, can be witnessed at GE. Jack Welch, before naming Jeffrey Immelt to succeed him as CEO, had brought in Dennis Dammerman, who was then CEO of GE Capital, and Robert Wright, who ran NBC, as vice chairmen, who would help Immelt ease into his new position. Those who would be disappointed in not being named the new CEO or couldn't work with him were not considered for these roles by Welch. These roles need to be filled by those who, as *New York Times* executive editor Max Frankel once wrote of former defense secretary Robert McNamara, however great their brilliance, were comfortable being "not a sun but a reflecting planet."

Katharine Graham, who led the Washington Post Company as owner and president through a series of business and national crises—including the Kennedy assassination, the Pentagon Papers affair, and Watergate—described the important role that company chairman Frederick "Fritz" Beebe played in easing her transition from full-time mother to president of the company, when her husband, Philip L. Graham, suddenly died in August 1963. Beebe had arrived at the Washington Post Company, a couple of years prior to Phil's death, from the tony, white-shoe law firm of Cravath, Swaine and Moore. In her autobiography, *Personal History*, Kay Graham described how her father, the owner of the *Post*, had counseled her husband to seek a real partner to help with the operating responsibilities of the company—"not an employee who is your executive officer but a real partner." In Beebe, Phil Graham had found that partner.

As she stepped into the role of managing the company, which she also owned, one of the first things she did was have a conversation with Beebe about their respective roles. Beebe, who had held the company together, including the recently acquired *Newsweek*, through Phil Graham's manic depression, had offered to remain as chairman, with Kay succeeding Phil as president. "The titles themselves didn't bother me or even interest me," she wrote, "but I did see that this might entail his being boss and my being number two, and I wanted to be clear"[6] that the relationship be an equal partnership—just the way it had been between Beebe and Phil.

At first it wasn't clear how the relationship might work between an experienced businessman like Beebe and a neophyte like Kay Graham, who, despite her lack of business experience, was owner of the company, which her father had purchased from bankruptcy at an auction only three decades before. Approaching the relationship as a "business marriage" helped—they remained equal partners through the *Post's* many ups and downs, especially through the publication of what became known as "the Pentagon Papers" and the initial coverage of "Watergate" till Beebe died in 1972 a few months after the June 17 break in to and wiretap of Democratic party offices at the Watergate hotel by seven men directly or indirectly tied to President Richard Nixon's reelection committee.

Katharine Graham's legacy in the history of newspaper publishing isn't only that she steered the *Post* through several crisis. She was an inspiring leader who wasn't willing to negotiate editorial standards, pursuit of a story, or her commitment to the First Amendment rights accorded by the Constitution of the United States. She enjoyed the allegiance and loyalty of her reporters, editors, and other employees, who viewed her not as a money-grabbing newspaper baroness, which was and is the prevalent image of newspaper moguls, but as someone who built an institution with a moral purpose. In so doing she also made oodles of money for her shareholders and employees. Legendary investor Warren Buffett thanked her for the money her stewardship of *The Washington Post* had made for his company Berkshire Hathaway. The $10 million that Buffett invested in the company in 1973 was worth about $140 million in just over a decade. "So instead of thanks a million," Buffett wrote to her, "make it thanks anywhere from $65 to 110 million"[7]—the difference in yield had Buffett invested in any other media property.

Like Katharine Graham, who was unexpectedly thrust into the stage, Elizabeth I was twenty-five years old when she became the queen of England. Despite having spent much of her youth in prison or forced obscurity, away from political governance, she had apprised herself sufficiently about the running of the nation to make quick and decisive decisions. In the early days of her reign some of her counselors, behaving in a patronizing manner, tried to suggest to her exactly whom she should keep and whom she ought to replace in the new administration. They fully expected her to follow their advice to the letter. They were to be gravely disappointed.

Not only did she not delay the appointment of key positions in her administration, as had been suggested to her to allow for the dust surrounding her accession to settle, she did it in a very public way to signal to everyone the decisiveness with which she would act. She had been advised to move slowly against key members of her sister's administration, yet in the first couple of days of her reign, even before Mary's funeral had passed, she got rid of the deadwood. She even truncated the number of councilors in her administration, and like her father—and unlike her sister and brother—appointed them for proven experience and expertise and never for position or patronage. Despite the eminence of her councillors, she never left anyone in doubt as to who was the monkey and who the organ grinder.

Nor did she refrain from letting the nation know that she was fully in control. Only three weeks after her ascension to the throne of England, Parliament sent a delegation to her, requesting she take on a husband "who might relieve her of those labors which are only fit for men."[8] These men informed her that her remaining a "vestal virgin" would be inappropriate, even contrary to the wishes of her subjects. Hearing this, Elizabeth is said to have pointed toward her coronation ring and said, "I am already bound unto a husband, which is the kingdom of England," and that all of those assembled before her, as well as all other Englishmen, were her children.[9]

Elizabeth went on to unequivocally state that she was willing to leave the issue of a suitable successor to her in the hands of providence, and she had full faith that a successor fit enough to rule over England would materialize. As far as she was personally concerned, it would be sufficient "that a marble stone shall declare that a queen having reigned such a time, lived and died a virgin."[10] So began the legend and cult of the Virgin Queen. Importantly, from England's point of view, in these words and deeds emerged clarity about how she planned to rule and how much she was willing to hear from her advisers as well as her subjects. She was the ruler, and she was going to rule the nation *her* way.

Transparency

Aware that a lengthy succession process could lead to infighting among the barons, Alexander gave Antipater two days to accomplish the task.

Despite the support that some alternate candidates had, Antipater agreed with Alexander that unanimity of support was going to be an important signal to the conquered Greek city-states and to Persia that despite Philip's death, every one of the barons stood behind their new king. Unanimity would signal business as usual. There would be no ambiguity or uncertainty about who was in charge.

A further design principle was that the selection process be transparent to everyone outside it. Antipater went immediately to work. Before soliciting support from the barons, he, together with Alexander, went through an elaborate process of asking himself, as Margaret Thatcher would ask of her ministers before promoting them, "Is he one of us?" If a baron passed this test, he was immediately invited to a meeting where the next king of Macedonia would be selected and crowned; if the two weren't sure, then the baron was only invited after the desired outcome had been "prewired" through appropriate bribes, promises, or threats. The "prewiring" would begin with either Antipater simply asking a baron whether he was "in" with them or "out"? Very few of these fence-sitters had the temerity to refuse the great general when asked. In the instance of a small handful of barons, who the two felt were certainly not one of them, they were just plain not invited. Ultimately, there were only three such barons.

Consider this succession process against Jack Welch's predecessor at GE, Reginald Jones, who put his potential successors through his now infamous, and totally opaque, "airplane interviews." He would invite a potential candidate into his room for a chat and, when the candidate was least expecting it, abruptly inquire who he thought of the seven candidates on the short list was most qualified to become CEO of GE if the two of them—Jones and the candidate—were to die in an airplane crash. Jones took fourteen months to decide on his successor in what was an incredibly public horse race for the top slot at GE.

Not surprisingly, immediately after Jack Welch got the nod at the end of 1980, four of the seven candidates left GE. So bruised were they from the elbowing and politicking that had gone on for so long in this nontransparent succession process that there was no way they could have remained within GE. Along with them left a large number of their direct-reports and other senior managers who had, often publicly, aligned themselves with one of the seven potential candidates or the other.

The Crowning

When the barons arrived at Macedonia's royal palace in Pella for the succession meeting, they were surprised that the meeting wasn't being held in the palace itself but in a marquee on the palace grounds. The flag of Macedonia, as well as the flags of all of its conquered territories, flew at half-mast. An atmosphere of war footing was palpable in the air. After most of the generals had arrived and were seated, Alexander arrived with a large contingent of barons who were his personal friends and followers. Antipater sat at the head of the table.

Antipater briefly spoke about the succession process. For most of the younger barons this was the first succession they had witnessed in their lifetimes. Philip had ruled for twenty-three years, and only a few remembered how tense and uncertain that succession had been. After Antipater had finished speaking, one of the barons rose, put on the ceremonial coat of arms bearing the royal insignia of the Temenid house of Macedonia, and walked up a set of steps to a stage that had been erected for the purpose. He then announced his support for Alexander. One by one the barons got up and, unsheathing their swords as they walked up the steps, lightly tapped the baron's breastplate, signaling their personal support for Alexander.

The support was overwhelming: fifty-seven of Macedonia's sixty barons had weighed in favor of Alexander. Again, Antipater, rising up from his seat, his heavy frame occupying almost the entire side of a room, began to speak. He had such an imposing figure that, as one biographer wrote of George Washington, his body just did not occupy space; it organized the space around it.[11] Despite his imposing figure, Antipater was never a threatening presence. He looked into people's eyes when he spoke, he radiated confidence in his voice, and there was always something reassuring in what he said. He was also a very good and intent listener—even taciturn at times. When dealing with Alexander's mother, Olympias, his taciturnity would sometimes take the form of a resounding and, for Olympias, highly frustrating, silence. This time in the marquee when he spoke about Alexander as the new king of Macedonia, and pledged his everlasting support and loyalty in the service of the new king, he was a far cry from his reticent self. With those words he crowned Alexander king.

Alexander graciously accepted the crown. He then went around the room where the barons had gathered to select him, and individually thanked each one, always making it a point to allude to something that they had done or an experience they had shared before. Although it looked very spur of the moment, he had spent several hours preparing and practicing exactly what he was going to say to whom. This was Alexander's way of securing his personal bonds of friendship.

He also promised the assembled barons that now that he was king it was up to him to deal with his father's assassins as well as those barons who had not turned up for the meeting. Although Alexander had wanted to retaliate immediately against the bodyguard who had stabbed his father, Antipater had advised him to not do so but rather launch an "investigation" to identify who was behind the assassination and to turn the event of his father's death into much more than an occasion of national mourning. He needed to create an atmosphere of solidarity among all Macedonians and Greeks. To achieve that solidarity he needed to use the sympathy that the killing of a middle-aged father walking his daughter up the aisle—one of the happiest moments in a man's life—evokes in the hearts and minds of people, and funnel this tide of emotion toward the destruction of a single, common, and identifiable enemy.

Two days after being crowned king of Macedonia, Alexander rode his horse, Bucephalus, outside the palace walls and declared to the crowds that the rumors of five deaths that morning in Pella were indeed true. They included the bodyguard who had assassinated Philip, his cousin Amyntas, and three barons. All five, he said to the crowd, had been tried before a tribunal and found to have been in cahoots with the Persians. Not until Lady Godiva was to ride down the streets of the English city of Coventry wearing nothing but her blonde tresses would a gasp so loud erupt from a crowd.

Alexander, like rock stars, knew a thing or two about the control and release of emotions. He knew he had the crowd's attention. He now decided to play out the message, which he knew would bring them together as a nation. The Persians, whose fleet controlled much of Greece's waterways in the Ionian and Aegean Seas, he proclaimed to the crowd, were preparing for an attack on Greece. This was in keeping with what the forbears of the current emperor of Persia, Darius III, had done for over two hundred years. But each time they attacked, he reminded the crowd, the courage of the Greeks had repelled them. This time, too, it would be no different.

He promised the crowd that, while he had every intention to traipse along his father's pathways, he had no intentions of leaving small footprints on them. Philip, he told the crowd, had been preparing for an invasion of Persia. He would complete that task. He offered them the vision of an all-powerful Macedonia that would decisively and conclusively put an end to the Persian threat. There would be no more chasing chipmunks. Macedonia was ready to hunt lions. Alexander was a master at not only offering a grandiose vision but also of translating, into meaningful and tangible descriptors, what achieving that vision would mean to his subjects. The crowd hoofed its lungs out to the cries of "Alexander! Alexander!" He asked them who would enjoy the spoils that an invasion of Persia would certainly bring. "We would," they shouted.

Alexander realized he had sold the crowd steak that was a long time away. He needed to provide them some immediate sizzle. He therefore announced a tax moratorium for all Macedonians and Greeks, adding that he was confident that the riches of the Persian treasury would pay for everything Macedonia needed. The crowd was now uncontrollable. Like fans reaching out toward the stage to touch their favorite rock stars, the crowd pushed toward him, wanting to touch him to assure itself that what it was hearing was for real. Even though he had gone out by himself, together with his personal bodyguards, to address the crowd, a few of the barons who had stayed over at the palace for the postcrowning celebrations, seeing the melee outside now rode out with their bodyguards to draw him back inside the palace.

As they escorted him back, one of the barons inquired of him that, if the people were going to enjoy the spoils of the Persian invasion, what benefit would they reap for themselves?

"Our hopes," Alexander said.

SUMMARY OF KEY THEMES

1. MINIMIZE AMBIGUITY AND UNCERTAINTY.

Despite the number of potential contenders for the throne of Macedonia and threats to Macedonia from within and without, Alexander did everything possible to create the impression of "business as usual."

2. APPOINT VISIBLE LEADERS AS MANAGERS OF THE TRANSITION PROCESS.

Although he was active behind the scenes, he brought Antipater and Parmenion in to manage the transition process. To everyone outside the palace walls it was clear that the two people Macedonians respected most were in charge of the process.

3. SEEK CLARITY IN ROLES.

Just as Antipater and Parmenion were assigned—and had carried out—clear roles through the transition, it was clear who the boss was. The transition of Elizabeth I to the throne of England, Katherine Graham as CEO of *The Washington Post*, and the handoff from Welch to Immelt as CEO of GE are remarkable for the clarity with which people conducted their roles.

4. MAKE THE SUCCESSION PROCESS TRANSPARENT.

Alexander ensured that the succession process was transparent to everyone, so there would be no questions about back-room, Kremlinesque intrigue to secure the throne. GE's recent transparent succession process assured a smooth transfer, while its previous, opaque succession led many senior managers to rush for the exit door.

5. IMMEDIATELY SET THE TONE OF YOUR REIGN.

In all the cases of successful transitions, we notice that the leader does not dilly-dally in setting the new vision or objectives of her tenure. Not only Alexander the Great, but also the successful tenures of Elizabeth I and Katherine Graham had to do with their setting the tone immediately after taking the top job.

CHAPTER 4

SETTING THE TONE
OF HIS REIGN

THE MACEDONIA THAT ALEXANDER INHERITED FROM HIS FATHER WAS much larger than the one Philip had inherited from his brother, Perdiccas. Every one of the major Greek city-states—except Sparta—was under Macedonia's rule or direct influence. But none of the city-states wanted to be under Macedonia's rule, and almost all tried to secede on hearing the news of Philip's death. Moreover, several non-Greek citizens to the north, like the Illyrians, the Thracians, the Triballians, and the Paeonians, who lived in today's Albania, Bulgaria, and Romania, decided to cast off their Macedonian "yoke."[1] In Thessaly, just to the south of Macedonia, where the citizens considered themselves to be near relatives of the Macedonians, an anti-Macedonia party came into sway, and the Thessalians, whose cavalry Alexander had commanded at Chaeronea, deliberated whether they ought to defect.

In Athens the anti-Macedonian sentiments were even more vituperative in tone and content. Ever since Philip's death Demosthenes had taken to parading around the streets of Athens adorned in garlands. His speeches denouncing Macedonia, to use a phrase once attributed to President Richard Nixon, "really flicked the scabs off." His gallimaufry of invectives, now targeted at Alexander, beseeched Athenians to rebel against the Macedonians, since what threat could a twenty-year-old, wet-behind-the-ears ruler pose to them? Persuaded—no, worn out—by Demosthenes' whinging banalities and insufferable political rhetoric, the Athenian Assembly declared that Athens was now absolved of its rule from Macedonia, and it was going to rebuild its army and navy for the greatness that had once been theirs. Demosthenes' posturing, even after he, and Athens, had been humiliatingly defeated at Chaeronea, only revealed that you could spend a lifetime in intellectual pursuits but still turn out thick.

The Thebans, too, considered an overthrow of the Macedonians ruling over them. The mighty Thebans, who had lost the Battle of Chaeronea, and seen the army of their allies in war, Athens, fall apart, had already begun to raise and train another army. Demosthenes went to Thebes and urged them to raise the army more quickly and disassociate from Macedonia as soon as possible.

Swift Action, Clear Goals

Hardly ever in history had so much turmoil erupted on the first few days of a new leader's taking office. Franklin Delano Roosevelt's inaugural day as thirty-second president of the United States on March 4, 1933, at the height of the Great Depression, and Abraham Lincoln's, exactly seventy-two years prior to FDR's, are two instances in history that possibly come close to the predicament that Alexander faced in his first few days on the throne. When FDR was inaugurated, one in four Americans was out of work, the nation's banking system tottered on the verge of collapse, with over five thousand banks already having failed since the stock market crash of 1929, and most American families didn't know whether or from where their next meal might arrive.

In Lincoln's case, just six weeks after his election on November 6, 1860, as the sixteenth president of the United States, South Carolina decided to secede from the Union, and in another six weeks Alabama, Florida, Georgia, Louisiana, Mississippi, and Texas had followed South Carolina's lead. On February 4, a month before Lincoln's inauguration, all federal building, forts, and armament depots in the South had been occupied by the secessionists, who even set up an interim government called the Confederate States of America in Montgomery, Alabama, with Jefferson Davis as its first president.

Five weeks after Lincoln took office, on April 12, 1861, and promised in his inaugural address to do everything to "hold, occupy, and possess" all federal establishments in the South, the Confederates opened fire on the pentagon-shaped Fort Sumter in Charleston Harbor, South Carolina, threatening to blow it to smithereens. Although no lives were lost, this opening thirty-four-hour salvo on Fort Sumter marked the launch of the Civil War, which was to cost so many lives. Both Lincoln and FDR could have become enveloped in the pressing, demanding, day-to-day, short-term demands of the job. Instead, they decided to focus on how to achieve their long-term objectives.

Back in Macedonia, 2,200 years before Lincoln and almost 2,300 before FDR, there was tremendous pressure on the twenty-year-old Alexander to come to terms with the present. Several of Alexander's senior counselors advised him to let the nations around Macedonia secede from Macedonian control as a way of making peace with them. They suggested to him that his time would be better spent securing Macedonia by making sure that all the barons were loyal to him than worrying about the recently captured nations outside of Macedonia.

Alexander, on the other hand, chose to be focused on those priorities which would secure the long-term stability of Macedonia and help him achieve his objective of defeating Persia and conquering the world—not the short-term imperatives of seeking peace with his neighbors. Genius, J.F.C. Fuller wrote, can be baffling. It isn't a product of intelligence or learning or discipline or training—or Demosthenes would have been a genius. It is instead an intuitive and spontaneous display of a power that reasoning can never fathom.² In keeping with the inexplicable nature of the actions inspired by genius, Alexander, at the head of the entire Macedonian cavalry contingent of three thousand, rode toward Thessaly. He had taken the coastal road along the Aegean Sea, which required him to go through the Tempe Pass, behind which ran the only road over Mount Ossa that one would have to traverse to enter Thessaly.

Thessalian elders met him outside the pass and asked him to wait because the Thessalian leaders were deliberating whether or not to sever ties to Macedonia. Some Thessalian heavy cavalry had been stationed in and around the pass, but most of them waited on the mountain road behind, ready to strike if need be.

Alexander halted outside the pass. But in the middle of the night, as the road and the mountain behind were engulfed in darkness, Alexander's troops began scaling the rocky mountainside to get around the pass. A slip of the hand or the foot would send them careening into the rock formations below, which had been formed by the crashing of the waves of the Aegean Sea against the mountainside. No one had ever scaled the mountain before, but such was Alexander's determination, and so deep was the sense of loyalty to him, that most of the 3,000 cavalrymen managed the feat—some had been left behind at the pass to distract the Thessalians.

As dawn broke, the Thessalian cavalry found themselves cut off from the road to Thessaly and surrounded. They surrendered to Alexander, who, keen to ensure their loyalty, which he needed for his future conquests, made sure that they were treated like close friends who had temporarily lost their way rather than as prisoners. The Thessalian Assembly caved in as well and elected him head of the Thessalian League—an alliance of Thessaly and its friends.

Alexander next turned toward Thermopylae. Capturing this most sacred of all passes into central Greece was more than a symbolic victory. The Amphictyonic Council was in session nearby, and seeing Alexander advance at the head of Macedonian and Thessalian cavalry, the Council caved in and elected him hegemon—rendering him the same title that they had given to his father. Alexander marched onward toward Athens and Thebes. He encamped outside Thebes—next to Athens, the most vocal opponents of his reign.

Athens rushed ambassadors to mediate peace between Thebes and Macedonia, and even though Demosthenes continued his criticism of him, and Thebes posed a military threat, and Sparta, which had not participated in any of the deliberations so far, also was a major threat, Alexander accepted the peace overtures and turned back toward Macedonia. He left garrisons behind in central and southern Greece—a large one within Thebes—to stay on top of developments there and snuff out any potential threats. From his perspective he had achieved what he had set out to accomplish in his first hundred days: secure his position within Macedonia and in the Greek city-states, and be assured the same honor and support from the city-states as had been promised to his father in leading Macedonia and Greece against the Persians. As for Demosthenes, he ignored and dismissed him as a third-rate intellect, who seemed convinced of his own genius—if Demosthenes had indeed been a genius, Alexander would have paid greater attention to him.

The First Hundred Days

It was President Franklin D. Roosevelt who, on entering office in 1933, popularized the shibboleth "the First Hundred Days" when between March 9 (the first day of the seventy-third Congress) and June 16, 1933, he got a bushelful of bills through Congress to save an economy tottering on the verge of collapse. These bills saved the U.S. banking system, put millions of people back to work in federally sponsored jobs, and enacted such key legislation in the securities markets as the Glass-Steagall Banking Act, which even today forbids commercial banks from trading in securities. His bills saved many homeowners and small farm owners from foreclosures, created the Tennessee Valley Authority, which brought electricity to, and provided flood control in, Appalachia, and initiated the process for bringing about such mainstays of the American economy as the minimum wage, forty-hour workweek, and collective bargaining.[3]

Although the New Deal is largely associated with FDR, it was his bipartisan approach that secured the passage of so many initiatives through Congress. Indeed, Congress had adjourned a day before FDR was inaugurated and was not scheduled to meet till December. To stem the literal "run on the banks" by depositors eager to take their money out, and to calm the nerves of jittery citizens, FDR's first task on being sworn in as president on March 4 (a Saturday) was to declare a three-day bank holiday and call an emergency session of Congress. He timed it such that when people returned to work on March 9, Congress would be in session as well.

So demanding were the times, with daily bank failures and the aftereffects of three years of biting depression, that FDR knew it didn't matter to people what he was going to act on; he just needed to act fast and act big. And act he did, with such urgency and preparedness that Congress on its very first day rushed an emergency banking measure through introduction, debate, and passage in only eight hours. So quickly did Congress act that at times only a voice vote was taken.

Obviously many mistakes were made in the rush. The Supreme Court overturned the National Industrial Recovery Act, which tried to provide government greater control of the national economy, as well as the Agricultural Adjustment Act. These acts were reversed, not on the basis of a misguided, "horse-and-buggy" interpretation of the Constitution, as FDR charged, but because the acts had been passed in such haste that important technical deficiencies and errors remained in them.[4] Despite the deficiencies, FDR was aware of the need to act. Columnist Will Rogers wrote at the time that if FDR had done nothing in his first few days but set fire to the Capitol Building, people would be cheering because at least he got a fire started.

The bipartisan group of legislators who worked with the Democratic President to shape and enact important pieces of the New Deal included people like senators Bronson Cutting (R-NM), Bob La Follette Jr. (Progressive-WI), George W. Norris (R-NE), Robert F. Wagner (D-NY), Edward Costigan (D-CO), and representatives David Lewis (D-MD) and Sam Rayburn (D-TX), who later became the Speaker of the House. While the totally bipartisan—or "tripartite," if the Republican Party spin-out Progressives were to be counted as a separate party—group of legislators, Costigan, Cutting, La Follette, and Lewis, were the architects of FDR's policies to put the unemployed back to work, Wagner, a Democrat, wrote the legislation behind the industrial and labor policies, and Norris, a Republican, helped create the Tennessee Valley Authority.[5]

FDR was undoubtedly a great leader, or the nation would not have elected him four times to the presidency. But his genius lay in getting the smartest people in the land to work alongside him. Although the New Deal is largely associated with FDR, he himself was the author and initiator of only two pieces of legislation: the Economy Act, which cut back government spending largely by trimming the salaries and pension benefits of government employees, and which many contend did more harm than good, and the act creating the Civilian Conservation Corps, which placed over half a million people on much-needed conservation work.[6] The more enduring pieces of legislation were the brainchild of others, whose creative energies and dogged pursuit FDR could harness. Some legislation, which is closely associated with him, like Federal Deposit Insurance Corporation, which even today protects deposits in bank accounts, he actually opposed, but caved in when he realized that it would pass with or without him.[7]

No less venerated a journalist than Walter Lippmann, the *New York Herald* columnist, only fifteen months before FDR's inauguration had ravaged FDR thus: "Franklin Roosevelt is no crusader. He is no tribune of the people. He is no enemy of entrenched privilege. He is a pleasant man who, without any important qualifications for the office, would very much like to be president."[8] A few months later Lippmann swallowed this harsh judgment and wrote that FDR's first two weeks had revived the nation's sagging energy as nothing else had done since victory in the Second Battle of the Marne in the First World War.[9]

Besides FDR, only Lincoln, among U.S. Presidents, had such an effective start. But the Washington media and the political pundits were not used to counting presidential starts in terms of their first one hundred days, and therefore termed Lincoln's raising an army and waging war with the South to save the Union simply as the Long Doleful Spring that had followed the Terrible Secession Winter.[10]

What was even more admirable was that, unlike FDR, who called Congress into session, Lincoln had to work through the initial efforts by himself, because it would be a while after his inauguration before Congress would meet. As some today might contend, this was also Lincoln's advantage. He didn't call a special session of Congress till June, by which time he was well on his way to accomplishing his objective of protecting the Union.

Though every president since FDR—and many business CEOs— have been measured by their performance along this numerical yardstick of the "First Hundred Days," the phrase owes its origins not to any person or event in the United States, but to Napoleon's escape from exile in Elba in 1815, his return to Paris, and his second abdication following his defeat at Waterloo to St. Helena—a period of exactly 116 days.

The phrase's authorship has been traced to an obsequious French official, the prefect of Paris, Louis de Chabrol de Volvic. When greeting the returning French King Louis XVIII, he spun the king's flight from the French capital as "a hundred-day" vacation for the monarch. It was Raymond Moley, a Columbia University professor and chair of FDR's "Brain Trust" (a collection of leading academics and economists who advised the president), who used the term coined in France almost a century before to describe FDR's performance in his early days in office. Moley is also the author of such memorable phrases, attributed to FDR, as "The only thing we have to fear is fear itself" and "This generation of Americans has a rendezvous with destiny."[11]

Although many complain that the tradition of measuring the presidency, or any high-profile leadership, by use of this guidepost has turned into an empty ritual, devoid of any significance, it still remains the case that, like Alexander's first hundred days, many others,' too, can provide a valuable and prophetic glimpse of things to come. Mussolini announced a hundred-day program after coming to power to demonstrate the fierceness with which the Fascists would take over Italy. British prime minister Harold Wilson came to power in 1964 after the Labour party had spent thirteen years in political Siberia, pledging a "hundred days of dynamic action."[12] Indeed, some presidents, like Bill Clinton, even borrowed the measure, prospectively, before they were sworn in, to suggest what they hoped to accomplish.

Unfortunately Clinton's early economic program and health-care reforms, which he tried to push through in the first hundred days of his presidency, were stymied by his lack of knowledge about the workings of Washington and his getting mired in distractions like gays in the armed forces. At least Clinton could laugh at himself: At his first appearance at the White House Correspondents' Association dinner, he dryly observed that at least his own had been better than William Henry Harrison's. "As some of you may remember," he remarked, referring to the ninth president, who came down with pneumonia after walking through a rain-drenched inauguration parade along Pennsylvania Avenue, "by the time his first hundred days were over, he had already been dead for sixty-eight of them."[13]

Those of another popular president, John F. Kennedy, were no better. The eighty-seventh day of his presidency was marked by the Bay of Pigs, where Miami-based Cuban exiles, under CIA direction, attempted a disastrous invasion. What Kennedy did not realize was that the director of the CIA, who had worked with him on the plan for the invasion, had brought in only one part of the agency—covert operations to help lay the groundwork for the invasion. CIA analysts, who had better on-the-ground intelligence on Cuba's capabilities to thwart such action, were not told because they would have scoffed at the plan. Interestingly, even the Joint Chiefs, who had been shown the plan many times, had not uttered a word about it blowing up, because from their perspective it was a CIA operation—they wouldn't comment unless asked.[14] This is a common problem within business organizations, too, where division presidents often run their own fiefdoms and feel little need to work together with—or contribute to— each other's divisions to enhance whatever competitive opportunities might present themselves for the broader firm.

Many of Kennedy's and Clinton's and even President Carter's troubles in the First Hundred Days stemmed from their lack of knowledge about the workings of—and the dynamics between—the White House and the myriad agencies of the Executive Branches of government. But a lot was also due to their lack of preparedness during their first months on the job. It is generally accepted that any incoming president's first task is to fill the thirty pivotal jobs—comprising the cabinet and the White House staff—by Christmas Eve that will enable him to hit the ground running. Richard Nixon, for example, had picked his staff and his cabinet nominations before assuming office. On January 20, 1969, when he was sworn in, he sent his entire suite of cabinet nominations to the Senate for approval, where, barring one nomination, all were approved in a twenty-minute session.[15]

"An orderly transition," wrote Stephen Hess, "shows Americans a presidency predisposed for success."[16] In Clinton's case it would be mid-March before the critical position of attorney general, the chief law-enforcement officer in the country, was to be confirmed. The nominations of Clinton's prior choices for this position—of Zoë Baird and Kimba Wood—ran into turbulence over reports of their having had "nanny problems." Ronald Reagan's cabinet and White House staff, on the other hand, which some had expected would be comprised of "nine guys from California," was not only complete by December 22, but featured a list of exceptional candidates from all over the nation, many of whom he didn't know well except by their incredible professional reputations. They were all selected on the basis of their prior experience in the Executive Branch of government, and therefore, this was a president who was seen by people to have "hit the ground running."[17]

The Right Way, the Wrong Way, and the IBM Way

It is well known that in business organizations, too, getting the top senior management team right is one of the critical dimensions of a good transition, and yet this is exactly the task that takes the longest time—and the most energy. An incoming CEO needs the help and cooperation of the top team, while at the same time making choices about which ones in the top team they want to keep and which to replace. Not only are these issues tightly wrapped up in the history of the organization, the politics of the place, but also in the reality that making changes to the top team frequently requires board approval. Of course while all this is going on, the rest of the organization, as well as outside shareholders and analysts, are watching the moves that the new CEO makes to ascertain how strongly and/or quickly she wants to shape the organization in her own vision and in line with her aspirations.

What is less well known, however, are the kinds of intricate organizational decisions that CEOs often make early on and the types of issues they choose to focus on. Lou Gerstner's arrival at IBM on April Fools' Day, 1993, when one of the main icons of American industry was quickly slithering away into morbidity, provides a telling example. The firm was losing market share in the computer desktop market to nimble players like Compaq and Dell, and even people inside the firm had serious questions about the long-term potential of IBM's mainstay mainframe market. Its share price had tanked, it had become the poster child of what was ailing in U.S. industry, and no high-profile manager was willing to accept the top job at IBM. After turning down initial efforts to recruit him, Gerstner was persuaded to leave RJR Nabisco when the job was, it is rumored, presented to him not only as a chance of saving a company, but, considering IBM's influence in the world and to the U.S. economy, society as well.[18]

When Gerstner arrived at IBM the company was on the verge of being reorganized thirteen different ways. After famously asserting that the last thing that IBM needed at that point was a new vision, Gerstner set about the task of turning around the firm with a sense of urgency—not crisis. To make that sense of urgency palpable to all employees, he needed to pick a team that would also radiate that feeling, and get the firm away from its unique, highly congenial, good-news-only culture, where no drastic action got taken no matter how bad the situation. An old saying at IBM ran as follows: "There's the right way, the wrong way, and the IBM way."

On his first day at Big Blue, Gerstner spoke to his senior management group for twenty to thirty minutes and said, "I want to sit down in the next couple of weeks with each of you and review your business. I want you to tell me what it is you do, who are your competitors and customers, what are your strengths and weaknesses, what are your short-term and long-term challenges?"[19] It is said that Gerstner spent a lot of time talking to people—managers, staff, factory-floor workers, suppliers, and customers. It was reported that he often asked an employee for an off-the-cuff impression of her managers above. He gathered impressions of people from as many perspectives as was possible. He told people that he didn't care whether they were stars in the previous regime or were on their way out; as far as he was concerned they started on a clean slate with him.

When he met managers, he demanded a note setting the context of the meeting, a precise definition of the problem they would be discussing, with relevant context and facts. He had to force that focus of purpose in a culture where the operating principle was about sharing "good news only." There would be lots of meetings, but nothing ever got done—and as in many bureaucracies where people attend meetings because their rank or position demands they be there even if they have nothing to contribute, meetings at IBM, too, had unfortunately taken such a turn. Reportedly, there would be a lot of small talk, backslapping, and exchanges of pleasantries, but little real work got done.

Gerstner had a turnaround to achieve; he had little time for idle small talk. Turnarounds by their very nature are difficult, leading to layoffs and mass anguish. But cutting costs through an aggressive turnaround was the only immediate option for him; growing revenues would come later. At meetings he observed and sized up participants. He banned use of prepared charts and slides at these meetings in favor of direct conversation. He urged managers to be direct, focus on their customers, and describe efforts in terms that were meaningful to customers—not to themselves. Gerstner was especially careful of being fed what he described as "intellectual arsenic"—pet projects—by managers at these meetings, or ideas du jour.

Within weeks he was well on his way to forming a team. The team consisted mainly of managers who had been at IBM awhile; a few he brought in from the outside. Some of the outsiders he hadn't previously known—they came in through referrals and searches. But some were people he had worked with before at places like American Express. These included his senior communications and marketing people, his general counsel, and even his assistant. These individuals not only bolstered key areas that needed strengthening within the company, but, because of their past record with Gerstner, understood implicitly what he needed done and how. Importantly, they were also people in pivotal jobs, who knew how to work with one another. "Having done this three times," Gerstner said, "let me tell you, it's pretty lonely parachuting into a company all by yourself"[20]

Gerstner's efforts at reorganization had a deep impact on the business. While he didn't waste months figuring out a new vision for the company, he empowered the company's own managers to effect the kinds of changes they needed to, to make their businesses fly again. He recognized the importance of the personal computer division and moved its operations far away from the head office. The division head was given an exceptional degree of autonomy, whereby his people could go to any supplier for their needs and not be restricted to supplies from within IBM. To prevent engineers and managers at the division being interrupted, he decreed that all intracompany communications with the division be routed though the division head's office.

Gerstner also challenged many long-held assumptions about the business. Many at IBM believed that not only were they a leading hardware company but also the largest software company—which they were, but only because, as it turned out, they were writing—and using—a large part of the programming code for themselves. Not surprisingly, there were substantial layoffs at IBM. For any new CEO at a struggling company there are two options available: Grow revenues or cut costs. Before he gets around to figuring out ways to grow revenues, the only option he can act on is to cut costs.

When Failure Is Not an Option

On his way back to Macedonia from central Greece, Alexander stopped off at the Temple of Apollo at Delphi—the same temple that had caused the First and the Second Sacred Wars—to seek an oracle from the gods about his planned invasion of Persia. As the Macedonian army encamped outside the temple's compound, an emissary from the temple came out to meet Alexander and inform him that it was not a day for the temple's high priestess to prophesy. He ought to return another day.

The lack of cooperation from the temple—considering Macedonia's support and intervention in freeing the land around it in the First and the Second Sacred Wars—perturbed Alexander no end. Here he stood with the entire Macedonian army, which had been on the road for three months, and the high priestess refused to offer him an oracle because it wasn't her day. He had no idea when he might return; he had received reports that the tribesmen who lived up in the states neighboring the northern limits of greater Macedonia were massing for a showdown with him, and he really needed to launch the invasion of Persia. He had no plans then for a return to central Greece—although he would be surprised at how soon he *would* return.

Not one to waste time, Alexander jumped off Bucephalus and charged into the temple quarters of the high priestess—not far from the large conical stone that stood at the center of the temple, marking the "omphalos" (meaning the center or navel). This stone for ancient Greeks marked the center of the world, and all distances for Greeks were measured from this stone. A few minutes later, as the Macedonian troops watched in amazement at the resolution of their king, he came out carrying the yelling and screaming priestess draped around his broad shoulders. He carried her inside the temple, wherein, smelling the sacred vapors (the vapors were recently discovered to be from oil-covered bituminous limestone, which lay below a fissure underneath the temple[21]) emanating from the floors of the temple, she went into a trance and was quoted as saying. "You are invincible, my son." That is all Alexander wanted to hear. He presented to her the gifts that the Macedonians had brought with them and at the head of his troops marched back to Macedonia. Interestingly, the priestess' pronouncement on Alexander, in terms of famous oracles of Delphi, would rank up there with "You are the wisest of all men" that had been given to Socrates several decades before.

Immediately after his return to Macedonia, Alexander led a division to quell the northern rebellion. The rebellion was deeper and more violent than Alexander had anticipated, but with his usual cunning, smarts, and guile he put down a series of insurgencies along the Danube. It took him a few months to completely annihilate every pocket of resistance. While he was mopping up, news reached him that the Persian emperor Darius III had sent emissaries to all the leading Greek city-states with promises of financial and military support if they were to strike alliances with Persia— thus weakening, and hopefully forestalling, Macedonia's planned invasion of Persia. Only Sparta officially accepted Persia's largesse. The Athenians and the Thebans, worried about retribution from the Macedonians, refused any formal, official gifts.

Many of the leading politicians in both states "unofficially" did, so much so that their palms were dripping with grease from the bribes. Demosthenes had accepted the largest payoff, part of which he used to buy arms for some of the Theban exiles in Athens. To rouse the emotions of the Athenians and the Thebans, Demosthenes, with the bribes from Persia, expedited his efforts at rabble-rousing and spreading canards. He proclaimed to the Theban exiles and the Athenians that in the previous few weeks, the great Macedonian army had been routed in the battles it undertook to secure Macedonia's northern borders, and that Alexander was dead. He even produced a soldier on the streets of Athens who claimed that he had personally witnessed Alexander die in a battle.

A select group of exiles and senior Athenians under leadership of Demosthenes slipped one night into Thebes. They made the rounds of Thebes' leading politicians and generals, who had escaped slaughter at Chaeronea. A few days later Thebes' army laid siege on the Macedonian garrison in the city-state.

Alexander had barely crossed into the borders of greater Macedonia when news reached him of the Theban insurgency. He was sanguine he could deal with the Thebans, but his greater worry was that an alliance between Thebes and Athens and, God forbid, Sparta, might form, which would inevitably take up so much of his time and energies that he would have to put the invasion of Persia on a back burner. He needed to reach Thebes quickly and put down the insurrection. Unfortunately from where he was in northern Macedonia, Thebes was a full three hundred miles away, and the terrain through Macedonia and much of Thessaly so mountainous that it would normally take three weeks for an army to cover that distance.

Alexander's army, on the other hand, was no normal army. In a forced march—that is, at the double—over the mountains of Macedonia, the tired Macedonian army reached the borders of Thebes in only thirteen days. Alexander wanted to preserve the element of surprise, and so he took extreme steps to cover the distance. He avoided all well-traveled routes through Macedonia and Thessaly. This meant taking only the mountainous road. He even avoided many of the passes. The only one he needed to use to enter central Greece was the one at Thermopylae, which he entered not from the road leading up to it, but descended on it from the five-thousand-foot mountains that surrounded it. So swiftly and silently did the Macedonians move that even Theban outposts around the pass at Thermopylae never picked up the passage of the Macedonians through it. Only after the Macedonians were through the pass did the Theban spies pick up on their presence, but so swift was the Macedonians' march that the spies arrived at Thebes (traveling on the main road) at exactly the same time as the entire Macedonian army did.

Thebes was caught totally unawares.

His army stationed outside its high city walls, Alexander gave the Thebans a chance to surrender two of their leaders who had been especially vituperative in their attacks against him. Not only did they not deliver these people to him, they even slaughtered some members of the Macedonian garrison that had been besieged inside the city. That was the proverbial straw that broke the camel's back. Alexander moved in and, except for a few people whom he set free, razed the entire city to the ground, killing over 6,000 Thebans and taking over 30,000 prisoners, who were all sold into slavery. Those set free included Thebes' priests and priestesses, family and relatives of the lyric poet Pindar (whose work he had come to appreciate at Mieza), and Timoclaea, the wife of the Theban general who had led Thebes' army against the Macedonians at Chaeronea.

A Thracian commander with the Macedonian army had raped Timo-claea. He had then demanded to be led to the treasures that a woman of such high standing would have surely possessed. As Plutarch recounts the story, Timoclaea led him to a well, at the bottom of which, she told the Thracian, large amounts of gold and silver were hidden. As the Thracian commander peered into the well, Timoclaea yanked him into the well and dropped boulders in on top of him for good measure. When several hours passed and their commander didn't appear, Thracian troops forced their way into the house and dragged Timoclaea and her children before Alexander. Hearing her story, he set her and her children free. The seventeenth-century Baroque painter Domenico Zampieri (Il Domeni-chino) immortalized the meeting in a painting titled "Alexander and Timoclaea," which hangs at the Louvre in Paris.

The terrible act of destroying an entire culture and society like Thebes hung over Alexander all his life. He often expressed deep remorse for his actions, but at this point in time he had decided to set an example to the other Greek city-states of the retribution that a revolt, any kind of revolt, would bring to them. He also knew that people had divided loyalties to-ward Thebes, and therefore a destruction of Thebes, while it would serve as an example, would not cause the anguish that a destruction of any other city-state would surely cause.

The divided loyalties stemmed from Thebes' actions during the Per-sian wars, when it allowed its territories to be used as a launching pad for attacks against other Greek city-states; Thebes' destruction of the Greek city-state of Plataea, during a truce in the Peloponnesian Wars; and Thebes' posture at the end of the Peloponnesian Wars to encourage Sparta to destroy Athens. Though Thebes would ally with Athens to de-feat Sparta at Leuctra and thereby free all Greece from the harsh reign to which Sparta had subjected all the city-states since winning the Pelopon-nesian Wars, and with Athens in a joint force against the Macedonians at Chaeronea, the grievances against Thebes were long and deep.

Alexander knew when to lead by intimidation, which, while it can be demotivating, demoralizing, and often demeaning to those it was targeted against, he believed, could be highly effective in confronting dire situa-tions like Thebes' intransigence. By making an example of Thebes, Alexander attempted to put down other acts of intransigency and insurrec-tion that were being planned by the other city-states. It had the desired "shock" effect of making everyone stop in his or her tracks and abandon any secession plans.

There have been many times even in recent history when nations have had to resort to unnecessary mass destruction to end a fight that could go on forever. We are all aware of the dropping of the atomic bomb on Hiroshima and Nagasaki to end the Japanese war effort. But take the Allied forces' bombing of civilians and civic infrastructure in German cities like Dresden, Leipzig, Darmstadt, and Hamburg during the Second World War, which killed, by conservative estimates, upwards of 150,000 German civilians. What has concerned historians is why Dresden, eight hundred years old and an architectural treasure, which did not even hold any strategic significance to the German war effort, should be bombed so heavily other than to send a signal to the Germans about the extent of the retributions the Allies were willing to effect.

Even though he was in complete control of Thebes, Alexander, to further the patina of "liberty" and "autonomy" that despite being ruled by Macedonia, the Greek states thought they still enjoyed, referred the question about the future of Thebes to the representatives of the Amphictyonic Council. He knew that the Council would do nothing that would even remotely come in his way. And the council didn't. Indeed, it recommended harsh punishment for Thebes, and Thebes was further castigated and ostracized for the diplomatic relations it had with the Persians.

Once the issue of Thebes was settled, Alexander then turned his attention to Athens—only forty miles away from Thebes—and demanded that it hand over all the orators and the generals who had encouraged the Theban uprising. He didn't lay siege on Athens to get his way. His demands, like the distant drone of a modern B-52 bomber or the British Lancasters over Berlin during the Second World War, sent shivers down Athenians' spine. Fearing that a similar fate awaited them as had befallen Thebes, they dispatched Demosthenes to plead before the king.

Despite Demosthenes' opposition to both his and his father's rule, Alexander met with him and relented on his demand as long as one of the most vociferous orators, Charidemus, were exiled. Charidemus left Athens to join Persian emperor Darius, who in a few years had him executed for his outspokenness. The Athenians conferred on Alexander even higher honors than they had on Philip.

Carlyle wrote of Napoleon, "There was an eye to see in this man, and a soul to dare and do. He rose naturally to be King. All men saw that he was such." Exactly the same could have been written of Alexander. Despite unheard-of cruelty in certain circumstances, such as in the campaign against the Thebans, a sense of nobleness, chivalry, and kindness pervaded his entire twelve-year reign.

SUMMARY OF KEY THEMES

1. ACT SWIFTLY TO STAVE OFF REBELLIONS.

Several states under Macedonian control threatened to secede after Alexander was elected. His actions against them were swift and certain. In Thessaly the troops scaled the mountain to get around a pass that was preventing access south.

2. MAKE A STATEMENT IN THE "FIRST HUNDRED DAYS."

FDR's urgent actions to get the U.S. economy back on the rails within a few days of his being elected president of the United States, as well as Lincoln's efforts to seek a resolution to the impending Civil War, provide examples, of relatively recent date, for which Alexander had set the model 2,300 years before. Lou Gerstner's first few months on the job, and the steps he took to shift the way things got done at IBM to save that company, provide another example.

3. APPLY OVERPOWERING FORCE
TO SEND A SIGNAL OF YOUR SERIOUSNESS.

Thebes was destroyed to send a strong signal to all the other Greek city-states about the extent of the retribution that would befall them if they tried to rebel against Macedonia. The use of overwhelming force to deter an enemy continues on as a cornerstone of geopolitics.

CHAPTER 5

SACRED COWS, GILDED SHIELDS, AND A TURK'S-HEAD KNOT

NOW THAT HE HAD THE ATTENTION OF ALL OF GREECE, ALEXANDER turned his mind toward invading the Persian empire of Darius III, the greatest and most formidable in the world. Leaving behind an army of 12,000 infantry and 1,500 cavalry under the charge of Antipater in Macedonia, Alexander, with 36,000 troops astride 160 Macedonian and Greek triremes, crossed the deep blue waters of the Dardanelles into Asia Minor. As the ships set sail, Alexander, like Odysseus tied to the mast of his ship to avoid the temptations of the alluring sirens, took his position on the bow and looked straight at the opposite shore—oblivious to anything else. Midway across the strait he offered a sacrifice to Poseidon, the Greek god of the sea, by killing a large bull that had been tied up for the purpose, and poured its fresh blood in to the water.

As the Spanish conquistador Hernán Cortés would do almost a thousand years later when he overthrew the Aztecs and seized Mexico for the Spanish crown, Alexander burned his ships upon arrival (though it is now believed that Cortés did not burn the ships but grounded them on the sand and used their wood to build houses).[1] The army was nearly broke, and with their ships gone Alexander forced them into foraging through a life of conquests. Or in Cortés' words, the reason he grounded the ships was that the expedition "then had nothing to rely on, apart from their own hands, and the assurance that they would conquer and win the land, or die in the attempt."[2]

In addition, Alexander wanted to engage the Persians on his own terms. The Persians had the strongest naval fleet in the world then, and Alexander did not want to engage them in a battle at sea. He wanted to engage them on land, where the Macedonians had a better chance of victory.

Alexander was on the first ship that crossed the Dardanelles. And, like General Douglas MacArthur wading onto the shores of Leyte, in the Philippines, in October 1944, Alexander was the first to come ashore. Like MacArthur's return to the Philippines three years after being evacuated from that nation's Bataan Peninsula, where MacArthur and his troops had sought refuge, and where, before leaving, MacArthur had famously said, "I shall return," there was a purposefulness in Alexander's eyes. He flung his spear on to the sands, got down on his knees, and thanked the gods for granting him Asia as his "spear-won" territory.

Even though he exploited every opportunity to convey to his troops the assurance that Asia was theirs by divine intervention, he realized that the expedition was going to be very different from those he and his father had conducted in the Greek city-states within spitting distance of Macedonia. He had never faced the wrath of the entire Persian army, and he realized he needed to take them on if he was to seriously pursue the mantle of the "Ruler of the World." Despite his young age, and maybe because of it, he felt sufficiently prepared for the task, after his education under Aristotle's supervision from the age of thirteen. The recent victories against Macedonia's northern neighbors and the Greek city-states had also bolstered his confidence and conviction.

The New Trojan War

Alexander knew that he had to "spin" a meaningful vision to harness the full capabilities of his troops. In addition, the 36,000 men in his service, 32,000 infantry and 4,000 cavalry,[3] hailed from different nations and city-states. Although the bulk of the troops were of Macedonian origin, 7,000 infantrymen were from the northern neighbors of Macedonia like Triballia and Illyria; the cavalry was split into 1,800 Macedonians, 1,800 Thessalians, and the rest from the Greek city-states. The troops had very little in common with each other, hence the need for a meaningful, commonly held purpose.

Alexander decided to spin the invasion of Persia as a new Trojan War, which had been immortalized in Homer's *Iliad*. Here he was a few miles from Troy, whose young prince Paris had carried off the most beautiful woman in the world, Helen, wife of King Menelaus of Sparta. The mythic link was clear: Like the Greeks in *The Iliad* who resolved to burn Troy to ashes, and did so, with the help of Achilles, the almost invincible Greek warrior, the Macedonians and Greeks would seek vengeance on Persia for its 150 years of wars against Greece. Wars with Persia had destroyed Greek cities, plundered Greece's wealth, and subjugated Greeks to harsh regimes. Alexander positioned the invasion as a battle of the civilized (the Macedonians and Greeks) against the barbarians (the Persians), conveniently ignoring the reality that most Greeks considered Macedonians to be barbarians as well.

Alexander's spin was no different from how leaders today spin actions around crises. Every time the United States goes to war, it isn't only to subdue a recalcitrant nation but also to protect American's "unalienable right" to "life, liberty, and the pursuit of happiness." American political leaders often hark back to the heroic efforts of the Founding Fathers in shaping a response to a challenge that might seem at first blush to be intractable. Then there are the myths that define American identity— foremost of which is about being a frontier land that was found by Columbus sailing the wide-open seas and by William "Buffalo Bill" Cody and Davy Crockett conquering the Wild West.[4]

Similarly, myths about America's entrepreneurial spirit often involve garages—after the garage where David Packard and Bill Hewlett began their eponymous company, Hewlett-Packard. When Carly Fiorina took over as CEO of HP in 1999, to change the stodgy culture of the company, she harkened back to the image of the garage and what it stood for— collaboration, entrepreneurship, and risk taking. The company today has not only bought the one-car garage in Palo Alto where the two Stanford University electrical engineers built the "audio oscillator" in 1939 (their first commercial product), and, in the process, launched the high-tech revolution there that led to the region's being named Silicon Valley; but, in addition, "The Rules of the Garage" (which are about granting employees broad autonomy to make decisions and solve problems) today dominate the company's motto. So pervasive is the myth of the garage that former hedge-fund manager Jeff Bezos founded Amazon.com in a garage ostensibly to be able to say that the online bookseller had started out in one."[5]

In Troy, where the Trojan War had been fought, the Temple of Athena stood on a hill. Athena (to the Romans, Minerva), the goddess of battles, fierce and ruthless, was the favorite of Zeus. Athens was named after Athena, because she was also the goddess who represented civilization.

On reaching Troy, not far from where they had landed, Alexander climbed up the hill with a select group of commanders and a large band of troops, to reach the temple. Outside it stood a seer, next to a fractured bust of a Persian satrap named Ariobarzanes.[6] It is not known whether the Macedonian "advance team" under Parmenion had had anything to do with the breaking of the statue (some historians have claimed that it was actually wrecked by Persians themselves when Ariobarzanes was overthrown in a coup, twenty-five years before Alexander's arrival here), but it provided a useful omen.

The seer's prediction was even more ominous: Coming out to greet him, he proclaimed to Alexander that he was destined for great victories, especially in his battles within Phrygia (modern Turkey), and that very soon he would defeat a famous Persian general, and that the goddess Athena had said she would assist him in battle.[7] The constant subliminal or even direct connections to Homer's Iliad, which most of his troops would have read, were impressive. Achilles' final victory over the greatest of the Trojan warriors, Hector, in The Iliad was made possible only by the intervention and manipulation of the goddess Athena. The gathered troops cheered such portentous omens.

Alexander entered the temple, took off his armor, and offered it as a gift to the goddess. On the temple walls were a shield and armor that Achilles had reportedly worn. Alexander, with the utmost respect, peeled these and other accoutrements off the walls and handed them to a bodyguard to carry. Henceforth, these would always be carried into battle for him. At the Battle of Multan, in India, Achilles' shield would save his life.

As Alexander plotted his moves, Persian commanders in the area met to discuss the Macedonian threat. The Persians could have destroyed the flotilla of ships in midsea, but they did not take Alexander seriously.

Memnon of Rhodes was the supreme commander of all Persian forces in Phrygia, the mineral- and agriculturally rich territories on the western end of the Persian empire. Memnon came from a long line of generals and nobles. He had visited the Macedonian court several times with his wife, Barsine, who was considered to be one the most beautiful women in Persia, they had both come to know and like Alexander (indeed, Alexander had a major crush on Barsine), and Memnon couldn't believe that the inexperienced Alexander with such a small force was serious about conquering Persia. Memnon ordered his troops to scorch the soil and destroy the crops around Troy, but not directly engage the Macedonians. Even though he was destroying his own crops, Memnon's calculation was that once the Macedonians ran out of food completely—they were already short of rations—Alexander would beat a hasty retreat back to Macedonia.

Little did he know that Alexander would conquer Persia, conquer all of Asia, take Barsine as his mistress, and father a child with her, Heracles, who would one day be murdered in the distribution of his empire after his death.

Lincoln's Spin on the Civil War

Like Alexander the Great, who wanted to give a higher moral purpose to his invasion of Persia, Lincoln used the Gettysburg Address to elevate the purpose of the Civil War to something much more than a fight over slavery. As Garry Wills wrote in his highly readable and thoroughly engaging *Lincoln at Gettysburg,* Lincoln had succeeded in doing what he had set out to achieve. "The Civil War *is,* to most Americans, what Lincoln wanted it to *mean.* Words had to complete the work of the guns."

Between July 1 and 3, 1863, outside the small, prosperous town of Gettysburg, Pennsylvania, 23,000 Union troops and 20,000 Confederates either lost their lives, were seriously wounded, or went missing—about a quarter of each side's troop strength. The 5,000 or so horses and mules that died were quickly burned, and the bodies of the troops buried in hastily made burial sites—often with little information collected beyond who was buried where. The stench of so many rotting bodies under the summer sun made gathering of more information or of a more honorable burial nigh impossible.

On November 19, 1863, more than five months after that fateful battle, President Lincoln arrived in Gettysburg to conclude an important task: to dedicate the grounds as a national cemetery. Lincoln's brief, 272-word "Gettysburg Address," would go down in history as one of the most memorable speeches ever made.

Rising up to speak with only two sheets of paper in his hand, Lincoln spoke for less than three minutes. The story goes about the event's official photographer setting up his instruments to take a picture of the president

for all posterity, was shocked that Lincoln had ended his speech well before he had set up his camera.[8] His short speech had achieved what he
had set out to do.

Not only did Lincoln not once utter the word *slavery* or *property rights*
or anything even remotely near the contentious words the war was being
fought over—indeed up until 1862, the Union's objective was solely "to re-
unite the country to its antebellum status."[9] But by his words "Four score
and seven years ago our fathers brought forth on this continent, a new nation, conceived in Liberty and dedicated to the proposition that all men
are created equal," Lincoln was, according to Wills, committing "the
most daring acts of open-air sleight-of-hand ever witnessed by the unsus-
pecting. Everyone in that vast throng of thousands was having his or her
intellectual pocket picked."[10]

The crowds left Gettysburg after Lincoln's address with a new conception of what it was that the Civil War was being fought for. The idea of
equality, which had been influenced by the ideas of the seventeenth century English political philosopher John Locke, lay in the Declaration of
Independence—not in the Constitution till the Thirteenth Amendment
was passed after the war. But like a lot of really effective political leaders,
Lincoln was, in effect, altering or at the very least preparing the ground
for altering the Constitution of the United States, which, as President, he
had sworn to protect.

By making the Civil War a battle for that fundamental tenet of "equality," an egalitarian purpose that, many leading newspapers were quick to
point out, the Constitution did not mention, Lincoln had successfully
shifted the purpose that the troops had died for—from preserving the
Union to a higher purpose of defending equality. Lincoln's oratory at Gettysburg ranks there with that of Pericles—given at the Athenian cemetery
specially built to honor the dead from the first year of the Peloponnesian
Wars almost 2,300 years before Lincoln—in setting the bar that all political leaders have tried to reach.

First Taste of Victory

Philip and Alexander had received equal credit for the Macedonian victory at Chaeronea. Alexander was soon to taste victory that was totally his
doing.

A few weeks after his arrival in Phrygia, Macedonian scouts reported back to him that a large Persian force was gathering about fifty miles northeast of their current location. The Macedonians had used their lightning speed to frustrate the scorched-earth policy of the Persians, getting to lush fields and foraging the land before the Persians had a chance to destroy them. Seeing their efforts not having the desired effect, despite huge costs and sacrifices to themselves, a large portion of the Persian leadership demanded the scorched earth policy immediately stop.

Memnon now decided that a showdown with Alexander was in order, indeed the only alternative left, and organized an army of 39,000 crack Persian troops, which included over 20,000 Greek mercenaries (most of whom served as infantry), to take on the Macedonians. Despite his past fondness for him, he ordered his troops to kill Alexander. Memnon had reached the conclusion that if they could achieve that objective, the Macedonian threat would immediately die down.

The Persians gathered along the craggy banks of the raging River Granicus (today's Kocabas River in Turkey, which flows into the Sea of Marmara) to meet the Macedonians. The mountains where the river originated were in the background, and little hills dotted the flow of the almost hundred-foot-wide river. The Persians figured they had nature on their side: The river's width and the strong currents would pose enough of a challenge for any army to cross it; leave aside crossing and *then* battling the greatest army in the world.

The Persians positioned themselves defensively, occupying every ridge and hilltop along the 1.5-mile-wide front and placing thousands of archers and spear throwers on them. Five thousand cavalrymen sat on their horses before the archers and the spearmen, ready to charge at anything or anyone that dared to raise its head over the water. The infantry stood behind the cavalry. This would prove to be a big mistake for the Persians.

It took 18,000 Macedonians three days to travel to the battle site; the rest had been left behind to reconnoiter for any other threats to the Macedonian army. As Alexander neared the river, he slowed down, waiting in anticipation for a Persian crossing from the other bank and an offensive cavalry charge. But none came. The Macedonians were tired after their three-day slog through the sweltering Turkish summer days and the cold nights. Seeing the tired faces of the troops, Parmenion rode up to Alexander and suggested they rest for the night before embarking on a crossing of the raging waters of the Granicus. But Alexander would have none of it.

"What challenge does a small stream like the Granicus pose to those who crossed the wild seas of the Hellespont?"[11] he inquired of Parmenion. According to the historian Arrian, he further admonished Parmenion for even broaching the idea, for it would both diminish his personal reputation for dealing with dangers as well as question the pride of the Macedonian army, which was beginning to get a reputation for its fearlessness.

Realizing that the Persians wouldn't attack, Alexander put on his shiny white-plumed helmet as a sign for the Macedonians that battle was near. He asked Parmenion to lead the left wing of the Macedonian front, where the Thessalian horses occupied the lead. He took command of the right wing, in front of the Macedonian cavalry, and lurched into the water. The Macedonian phalanx occupied the center between Alexander and Parmenion. The Persians had been watching him intently, convinced by his sharp attire and the level of constant activity around him that he was Alexander.

The rest of the Macedonians also entered the water, with Parmenion leading the left flank. Alexander had planned to go as far as he could across the water without the fear of a volley of arrows or spears raining down on him, and then allow his horse and himself to be carried slightly downstream with the river's current. The rest of the troops followed him into the water, and as soon as they hit the current they allowed themselves to be carried downstream even as they kept crossing the river. A natural oblique order opened up with the right flank thrown forward and the left refused.

The Persians had not been ready for this ploy—indeed they had never seen any such formation before. They watched mesmerized as the Macedonian formation began to take shape diagonally across the riverbanks. They pushed and shoved each other to follow the line of the Macedonian front. It was at this point that Alexander asked one of his commanders to lead a small band of cavalry across the river so they could get a taste for the nature and virulence of the Persian attack. No sooner had this entourage gone forward toward the Persian bank than volleys of spears, arrows, and javelins showered down on them. It was a literal bloodbath, as the water near where this small band of Macedonians stood suddenly turned crimson with the blood of the falling cavalrymen. So jubilant were the Persians, and so eager were they to charge and destroy this small contingent, that they failed to realize they had just revealed their defensive tactic. Not only that: In their glee and urgency to deal with the Macedonian threat, they had opened up gaps in

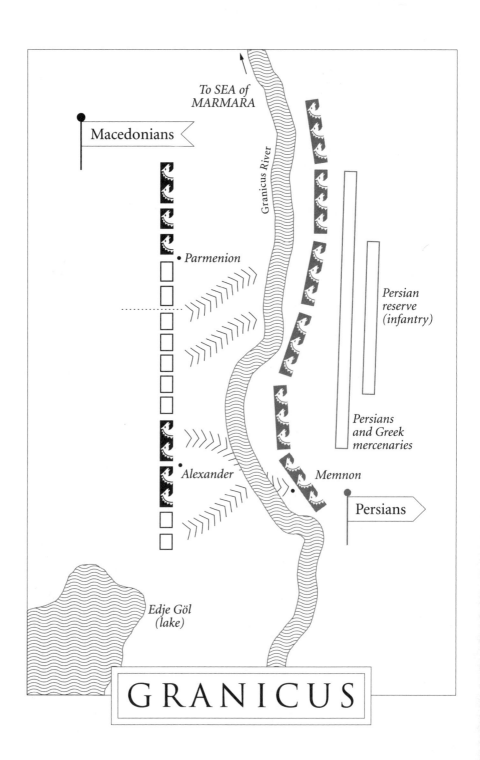

To SEA of
MARMARA

Macedonians

Granicus River

• Parmenion

Persian
reserve
(infantry)

Persians
and Greek
mercenaries

• Alexander

Memnon

Persians

Edje Göl
(lake)

GRANICUS

their concentrated positions, which they did not rush back to refill. They had also exposed their flanks.

Into the exposed flank Alexander charged, leading the cavalry against the flow of the river's current. They clambered ashore without being forced back into the water by the Persians. Parmenion, too, secured a foothold on the bank, and the Macedonians and the Persians were soon engaged in a fight where they pushed and fought against each other mano a mano. Wave after wave of Macedonian cavalry hauled themselves onto the riverbank, pushing the Persian cavalry back from their positions. This was the first time that cavalry had fought so closely with cavalry in battle. The Macedonian infantry was still making its way across the river when the Persian cavalry began to collapse under the weight of the Macedonian cavalry "wedge" that was barreling through their ranks.

There was a major incident as the Macedonians battled the Persians hand-to-hand—the Macedonians with their Celtic swords and the Persians with their curved scimitars. As per Memnon's instructions the Persians had surrounded Alexander, and while he closely battled one of Persian king Darius' commanders, staving off the others as far as he could, one surreptitiously came up from behind and struck his head with a battle-ax. The ax penetrated his helmet, splitting it in two, cleaved away the plumes, and almost went through the headpiece, which was the final protection before hitting the head. Alexander's attention was still focused on battling the first commander. As this second commander, who had scored a hit, readied himself for another blow with the ax at Alexander's now exposed head, Cleitus "the Black," a senior Macedonian commander, came to his rescue and struck the Persian commander dead with a long spear that went right through his leather breastplate. Philip's innovations in spear technology helped save his son.

Granicus was the first time in the history of warfare where the cavalry had been used as a "disruptive" technology. At Chaeronea the cavalry had been used to make a break in the opposite front, and then to "clean up" the battle, but Granicus was the first time that cavalry was the entire focus of the battle. It marked a turning point in the history of warfare just as the introduction of tanks as the dominant weapon in the Battle of Cambrai did in the First World War, when the British Third Army used them to break through German defenses in northern France, the introduction of the aircraft carrier at Taranto, which sank the Italian fleet, and the use of amphibious warfare by the Marine Corps to circumvent the Japanese defenses in the Second World War. Other examples of disruptive technologies include the aircraft-destroying Stinger missiles, which were used by the Afghan mujahadeen to defeat the Soviet invasion, and the naval-ship-sinking Exocet missiles, used by the Argentineans in the Falkland War. While the Afghans won, the Argentineans lost their battle for the Falklands against Great Britain—a useful reminder that the possession of a disruptive technology alone is no guarantee of victory.

Watching their commanders die (three of the seven Persian commanders fell in battle, and one committed suicide immediately after) and unable to withstand the successive waves of Macedonian cavalry onslaughts, the Persian cavalry made a quick retreat. Much of their light infantry, mainly comprised of men of Persian origin, also escaped, but their 20,000-strong heavy infantry of hired Greek mercenaries stood haplessly on the plains as the Macedonian cavalry and infantry descended on them. Partly it was their pride and partly it was the weight of their heavy armor that made retreat impossible. Alexander had little appetite for going after the retreating Persians, but he dealt with the Greek mercenaries immediately and forcefully. Long branded by their countrymen as traitors, several thousand mercenaries were slaughtered by the Macedonian troops right where they stood. About 2,000 were arrested and sent back to Greece as indentured agricultural labor—to serve as an example to any Greek of the fate that would befall him if he were to turn against his own nation.

Compared to only 25 Companions slain on the Macedonian side, close to 1,000 Persian cavalry lay dead (though some historians have placed the Persian toll as high as 20,000). Alexander had the Macedonian, the Greek, and the Persian dead buried with full funeral honors. He visited the Macedonian wounded, and wrote to the families of the dead about the valor their sons, husbands, and fathers had displayed in battle. Some historians have questioned whether the low fatalities among the Macedonians as compared to those of the Persians might just have been propaganda. One only has to look at relatively more recent battles of the fourteenth and fifteenth centuries for which detailed and accurate records were kept to conclude that it is indeed possible for much smaller armies to defeat much larger ones and score similar differences in casualties between victors and the vanquished.

Toward the early part of the Hundred Years' War, for example, the English suffered a handful of casualties at the Battle of Crécy (1346) versus the French losses of 1,500 knights and 10,000 foot soldiers, and toward the close of that war, at the Battle of Agincourt (1415), the English army of fewer than 6,000 under the command of King Henry V won against a French army of 40,000—losing fewer than 500 men as against the French death toll of nearly 10,000.[12] Crécy and Agincourt, together with Blenheim and Waterloo, are the battles that have shaped British identity and the mystique of Britain's invincibility. Churchill repeatedly used the achievement of these wars during the Second World War to shape Britain's bulldog spirit.

Granicus was where Alexander's mystique for invincibility began to take hold. In battles ahead it wouldn't be uncommon for well-defended and well-provided armies to surrender to a much smaller unit of Macedonians. Like Napoleon's presence on the battlefield, which Wellington surmised must have been worth at least 40,000 troops, Alexander alone would make up for 50,000 to 100,000 men in battle—such electrifying fear his presence would instill in fighting men of the opposite side.

To complete his victory Alexander sent three hundred Persian suits of armor back to Athens to be put up in honor of the goddess Athena at the ruins of the Acropolis. The Persian emperor Xerxes had destroyed the Acropolis, Athens' most sacred shrine and monument, in 480 b.c.— almost 150 years prior to these events at the Granicus. So shocked and dumbfounded were the Athenians that they had left the ruins alone for thirty years as a testament and reminder to all Greece of the nature and extent of Persian savagery. Then, under their leader and general Pericles, using what they could retrieve from the ashes of their destroyed monument, Athenians built the Parthenon on the site of the ruins of the Acropolis—which stands even today.

The armor sent from the Battle of Granicus was hung over the ruins of the temple of Athena with an inscription from Alexander, which, according to Arrian, read, "Alexander, son of Philip and all of Greece, except the Spartans, hereby presents these gifts won from the barbarians in Asia." There was not a mention of him as king; just a humble son of his father and Greece. The message implied Greece's revenge against Persia for centuries of past crimes had begun. All of Greece and Macedonia rejoiced at Alexander's victory.

Yankee Mystique and Tiger Stripes

There are several interesting parallels in the world of sports to Alexander's mystique of invincibility and its power to subdue opponents. Take the New York Yankees in baseball and Tiger Woods in golf.

For eighty years the New York Yankees have had a mystique about them, winning a total of 26 world championships—once five consecutively between 1949 and 1953, once four in a row, 1936–39, and most recently three in a row, 1998–2000. No other baseball team has come anywhere near the winning record of the men in their distinctive blue pinstriped uniform. It isn't surprising that the pinstripes intimidate the opposing team.

The club and its admirers have cultivated the mystique surrounding them. The hallowed grounds of Yankee Stadium honor the greats who have played there: Joe DiMaggio, Lou Gehrig, Reggie Jackson, Mickey Mantle, Roger Maris, Phil Rizzuto, Babe Ruth, among others. Today's players rub their palms against the busts in Monument Park for good luck as they run out to take their positions on the field. Commentators and record keepers fuel the mystique by debates about the best individual season: Was it the 1929 season, with Murderers' Row? Was it 1939 with Joe DiMaggio and Bill Dickey but also the sad and rapid decline of Lou Gehrig to the disease that now bears his name? Was it 1956 with Mickey Mantle, 1961 with Roger Maris, or 1980 with Reggie Jackson?

Behind the Yankees' "magic," most observers believe, is their players' ability to combine exceptional talent with focus and a drive to win. Sportswriters and commentators believe that behind the magic is an uncanny and innate ability of the Yankees to slow the game down to its elemental levels. According to them, while other players might be thinking of hitting a double, a good Yankees' hitter like outfielder Bernie Williams will be thinking: *Okay, I want to get a fastball in this situation. And if it's not a fastball, I'm not going to swing.*[13] It's that confidence of playing the way one always has that helps the Yankees win. Consistently.

The Yankees don't always have the best players in baseball. But the Yankees mostly do wonders with what they have—a mix of a few great and a lot of good players. The mystique that they have created, however, is that they have a lot of great players playing for them. It's a wonderful transformation that they go through between summer and fall, when they go from being just another team to a great team. And that's because while others begin to lose their heads in the postseason, the Yankees know just how to keep theirs on.

Individuals have mystique too.

Take Tiger Woods, for example. Everywhere he plays, records fall like pins in a bowling alley. He's not only won the U.S. Open, the British Open, the PGA, the Master's, and held these titles simultaneously, becoming the first in history to do so (four others scored a career grand slam) but also set a record in winning each (his Master's score of 270, 18 under par, for example, is a record for that tournament, as is his 19-under 269 at the British Open). Each time he plays, he does something that might have previously been thought of as unimaginable: drives of 350 yards that turn a par 5 to a midlength par 4 or hitting 218 yards with a six iron right at the pin, for example.

He is the first African American and the first Asian American (he is as racially mixed as the Californian working-class neighborhoods that he comes from) as well the first Generation Y'er to succeed in a sport until recently dominated by white, wealthy, and older men. Indeed, not only did he win the sixty-first Master's at Augusta, which had for years been a national symbol of segregation, but he did so only two days before the U.S. was about to celebrate the fiftieth anniversary of Jackie Robinson's debut with the Brooklyn Dodgers as the first African American to play major-league baseball, which was a civil rights milestone.

After winning the Master's—Woods, who has always studied and respected history, and never lost sight of what golf has given him, talked about the influence that African-American golfing greats like Lee Elders and their efforts to get over the bias in the game had had on him. Elders was only invited to play in the Master's in 1973—after several years of lobbying by others on his behalf—though he didn't play till 1975.

Yet, even as he breaks down records and barriers of color, race, and privilege like there is no tomorrow, and brings millions of new viewers and players to the game, as Michael Jordan did for basketball, he is also quick to point out that his sights are set on a world where no one thinks about his color—just as the greatest golfer who ever lived. As he pursues Jack Nicklaus' record of eighteen major titles, he is a sight to behold on the golf course: all grace and concentration. Like a medium in a haunted house, he sees more than others do, and his game is pure precision: his drives are exquisite, and his putts plain magnificent. His eyes are pure concentration, his mind switched on to every shot he makes till he finishes the last hole. And he practices religiously; coming into the U.S. Open at Pebble Beach recently, having won the previous tournament hands-down, he could be seen putting for two and half hours the evening before the match.

Despite all the records he has been breaking since he was three, all the accolades heaped on him, and the sounds of shattered glass ceilings that accompany him wherever he goes, it is as a sportsman with a fierce thirst and ability to win and impeccable manners on and off the course that he has secured a place in the pantheon of invincible sporting greats like Pele and Muhammad Ali. It is also this aura of invincibility that sends his opponents into a scramble for second place when he just shows up to play the nine hundred-year-old game of golf.

Cutting the Gordian Knot

Alexander secured the neighboring towns and cities in Phrygia around the Granicus River. As he neared established Persian cities in Phrygia, the satraps (governors) and military commanders surrendered to him. Alexander mopped up all of the Persian strongholds and moved farther east toward Gordium (modern Bela-Hissar), the ancient capital of Phrygia, near today's Turkish city of Ankara. As he moved through the towns and cities, he abolished the offices of the Persian oligarchs and introduced a democratic form of government in their place. In many cases he did not replace the Persian satraps if popular opinion was positively disposed toward them, but was quick to replace where it wasn't. He became very popular among the populace because now they had a say in who ruled over them. He kept the taxes the same, but instead of paying the Persians, now they were paid to his administration. He also made a special effort to promise his protection over those inhabitants from the land who had left their homes and fled during the Battle of the Granicus.

One of the hallmarks of Alexander's tactics, which would prove to be highly effective in fighting disparate tribes in Afghanistan, was that he divided his army into various divisions, each headed by a senior commander from the Companion ranks, which would go through the entire countryside to mop up any semblance of resistance. Gordium was where all the Macedonians met up in May 333 B.C.

The city was named after a Macedonian named Gordius (reputedly the father of King Midas), who had left his home country to settle down in Gordium, and eventually had become the ruler of all Asia. This was several centuries before Alexander. According to the local myth Gordius had arrived there in a wagon, which still stood in the Temple of Zeus, set in a citadel in the city's center. The wooden farm wagon featured a strange knot that held it to its yoke. Anyone who could untie the knot, the myth ran, would become the lord of all Asia.

Alexander had an immediate yearning to see if he could untie the knot. He went up to the temple in the citadel, near which ran the only trade route connecting Troy to the ancient city of Antioch in today's Syria. The knot, made of cornel bark, was highly complex in nature and it wasn't clear, according to Arrian, where the knot's beginnings were and where lay its ends.[14] It is what is popularly called a Turk's-head knot.[15] According to Arrian, Alexander, after observing the knot for a while, pulled the pin that ran through the knot, holding the yoke of the wagon to the shaft. Others say he drew his sword and hacked the knot in two—creating the metaphor "cutting the Gordian knot." Whatever it was, even Arrian was unsure other than that it definitely helped propagate the myth that Alexander had cut the knot. Thunder and lightning that night was immediately interpreted as a sign of pleasure from the gods, helping create a myth about his divine origins. He managed to create a cult following around him by seeking external corroboration for his divinity or by demonstrating, as at Gordium, that no problem was beyond him. When he started off he was still a young, unproven leader. The more external validation he could receive for his role in the world, as well as for his leadership and intellectual prowess, the more likely it was that people were going to get over any lingering hesitation to follow him in this campaign.

Two years after the incident at Gordium, Alexander would head south into the Saharan desert in today's Egypt and Libya in search of the oracle of Zeus-Ammon at Siwah. Greeks and Egyptians both venerated the temple of Zeus-Ammon, and Siwah, an oasis surrounded by the Libyan Desert, was believed to be the abode of the Egyptian gods, just as Mt. Olympus was for the Greek gods. Alexander's visit to Siwah is an important theme that all historians have focused on and deliberated about for over two thousand years. According to some he went to Siwah to trace his genesis; others say it was to gain political recognition; some believe he went there to seek forgiveness for the murder of his father, in which many suspected his hand; and, finally, some believe he went there purely in search of "glory" to emulate Greek heroes Perseus and Heracles, who had both been there.

The last reason is important. Glory in the ancient world, unlike the modern day where it stands for fame, fortune, or power, was tied to apotheosis—the process of becoming immortal like the gods. There were three ways to becoming immortal: one was through achievements so remarkable that one lived on through the tales of bards; second, more Judaic in tone, was to live on vicariously through one's children; and finally, to best the greatest of the divine heroes. We believe Alexander was following the final way to assuring his divinity. The Greeks kept their religious mysteries quiet, but as scholars like Werner Burkert have written,[16] their myths and dramas pointed toward the Egyptian desert, from which many of their heroes had come, and where they had achieved immortality. Cutting the Gordian knot had furthered Alexander's divine aspirations and helped him strongly position himself for the conquest of Asia, but Egypt might grant him a spot on Mount Olympus.

Whatever the real reasons, it was an arduous, two-hundred-mile journey from the vast tract of sand where Alexander would soon found Alexandria-in-Egypt through the inhospitable desert. By day four of their eight-day journey they had run out of water, only to be saved by a sudden rainstorm. They lost their way, only to be saved by the flight of two crows that had been spotted. When they reached Siwah, a priest is said to have led all of the troops to an antechamber, where they were asked to change their clothes before they could visit the oracle. Alexander, on the other hand, was taken directly to visit with the oracle. The high priest, who met him to lead him into the sanctum of the oracle, is alleged to have greeted him as the "son of Zeus-Ammon." Historians have again debated whether the priest said "my son," or "son of Zeus-Ammon," or "son of God," or if it was just a slip in translation. We shall never know. Suffice it to say, Alexander used it to full effect, and from that day on Macedonian spinmeisters stressed his divine roots.

Later, he would persuade his troops to invade India by telling them that their god Dionysus (also known as Bacchus), the Greek god of wine and ecstasy, had come through the country. He would even name one of the first towns he would visit Nysa, after the imaginary hamlet where the Greek god Hermes is said to have brought Dionysus for his upbringing. He would motivate his troops to climb the snowcapped Hindu Kush mountain, separating India from Afghanistan, by leading them to believe that, just on the other side of the mountain, was the cave where the Titan Prometheus was chained, for the eagle to fly in and feed on his liver—till Heracles was to arrive and set him free.

Alexander constantly sought symbols to suggest a sense of urgency. Several of the symbols were celebratory in nature. The sight of ivy vines growing along the slopes of the Hindu Kush mountain was regarded as another sign that Dionysus indeed had been here. His troops celebrated the event by wearing ivy crowns on their heads and dancing by torchlight, singing "Euoi, Euoi"—the traditional Bacchante celebratory rite.

Men in Kilts

In the sixties when Paris was rife with the coffeehouse culture that led to the comingling of leading French intellectuals who gave the world everything from the New Wave movement in cinema to the literature of Jean-Paul Sartre, Albert Camus, and Simone de Beauvoir, a French philosopher at the Sorbonne published an important book titled *Structural Anthropology*. Claude Lévi-Strauss defined the purpose of myth as providing a logical model capable of overcoming an inherent contradiction, and suggested several rational explanations to account for surviving myths as Freud had once done with dreams. Structuralism became a fashionable lens through which many enduring cultural and historical myths were examined, and many were revealed to be nothing more than useful means for explaining or clinging on to ways of life that the modern age had long passed by.

Ever since myths began to be created, they have been questioned. Historians over 2,500 years ago questioned Athens' vaunted democracy, for example, and many have revealed that *after* the Age of Pericles the city was nothing more than a citadel of chauvinism, double-talk, and graft. Myths about the American South, especially the legend of Dixie with its associated images of an idyllic antebellum culture, are now considered an inventive creation to provide the post–Civil War Southerners a set of images and symbols of their past to hang on to as the reconstruction of the South took place.

Many enduring myths have fallen by the wayside. Take the myth of the Highland culture and tradition of Scotland, which is a "retrospective invention."[17] The Cambridge historian Hugh Trevor-Roper revealed that the Highland tradition, with its "outward badges" of the distinctive kilt and the bagpipe, was an eighteenth- and nineteenth-century creation and did not come down from medieval times as the Scots had often claimed.[18] The origins of the kilt go back to Ireland, from where the Scottish Highlanders had migrated over the years. Once in the mountainous regions of Scotland, these settlers adapted the Irish long shirt that they had worn in the "old country." These shirts were suited to the needs of skipping over

rocks and bog and lying on the peaty soil of Scotland. In Scotland the settlers, for convenience, introduced a belt and shortened the length of the
shirt, so that below the belt the shirt had the distinctive look of a skirt.

In the early eighteenth century an English Quaker named Thomas
Rawlinson came up to the Highlands and leased a large tract of land near
Inverness, where he built a furnace to smelt iron ore that he had shipped
up from Lancashire. Seeing the impracticality of the dress his workers
wore as they felled the trees for wood to fuel the furnace, according to
Trevor-Roper, Rawlinson hired a tailor in the service of the local English
military regiment in Inverness to design a two-piece dress to replace the
one-piece shirt. This further innovation to the Irish long shirt resulted in
the kilt, which was fashioned after a pleated skirt.

So popular did the kilt become that people all across the Highlands
took to wearing it in any tartan color or pattern. But after the great rebellion of 1745, when the English defeated the Scottish clans at Culloden,
the English not only disarmed the clan members but also put an end to
the wearing of kilts, plaids, bagpipes, tartans, or anything else remotely
evocative of the Highland way of life. Even Boswell and Johnson, when
they made their celebrated tour of the region in 1773, were hard pressed to
see any sartorial remnants of what they otherwise considered the "peculiar" and "antiquated" life of the Highlanders.

In 1820, much to the surprise of everyone, a society to promote Highland culture was set up with Sir Walter Scott, a Lowlander, as a charter
member. The society owed its origins to the enterprising work of Scott,
who, in an effort to help the economically depressed Scottish weavers, set
about recreating Highland life for the visit of George IV to Edinburgh. It
was Scott's idea to dress up each clan in their own clan tartars, and the
Scottish weavers, who had lost their clients for kilts after Culloden, came
forward with recommendations for distinctive colors and patterns for each
clan; so far the only way to differentiate clan allegiance was by the cock-
ade in a Highlander's bonnet.

Trevor-Roper recounts how one weaver, William Wilson and Sons of
Bannockburn, came forward with a "Key Pattern Book," where the previously labeled tartan "No. 155," which had also been labeled "Kidd," to supply a Mr. Kidd enough cloth to dress his West Indian slaves, was relabeled
"Macpherson" and sold in enough quantity to dress the Macpherson clan.
So began the myth of clan colors, which almost two hundred years later
not only survives as a tradition, but also has a large industry devoted to promoting it—not least by the so called "Tartan Army," the not always tartan

clad but always hard drinking and generally good-natured followers of Scotland's rugby and football, who trot the world advancing the myth.

Many similar myths dominate our lives. Take the evacuation of the British Expeditionary Force at Dunkirk during the early stages of the Second World War, when in ten fateful days between May 26 and June 4, 1940, almost 350,000 men retreating from heavy German fire and air attack were evacuated from the port and beach town of Dunkirk, France. To position the conflicts as a people's war, Prime Minister Churchill and other British political and military leaders talked up the role played by private pleasure and fishing boats in the evacuation—leading up to Churchill's famous defiant speech to prepare the British nation and inform the Germans of a tough fight ahead: "We shall fight on the beaches, we shall fight on the landing grounds, we shall fight in the fields and in the streets, we shall fight in the hills; we shall never surrender."[19]

Reality, however, as recent reports from the British Public Record Office indicate,[20] was very different: Not only were most of the troops evacuated by the British Royal Navy, of the close to seven hundred private boats that helped in the rescue, especially from the beaches, most were actually commandeered by Royal Navy reservists and volunteers—not the general public. The image of tugboats, paddle boats, little steamers, and lifeboats sailing or even being oared out across the English Channel to save the troops, which has lasted for more than sixty years after the events, was a myth created by Churchill in an effort to make the war a "people's war." It had been created to provide the British with a national purpose and a generosity of individual spirit—and, most important, shake a nation that had not been invaded since 1066 out of a state of somnolence about the seriousness of the German threat.

Alexander, too, constantly spun his expedition as one for the benefit of the common folks back home in Greece and Macedonia. After his initial military successes he even enlarged the supposed beneficiaries of his campaigns to include the people he was conquering. We also don't know if Alexander really and truly believed in his divine origins—or was using a self-conscious myth to make his followers believe in him and his expedition. We do know that in ancient Greece, ascribing to humans divine powers and glory was a common practice. Greek heroes, therefore, were frequently viewed as possessing divine powers. If he didn't at first believe in his divinity, he likely did as his successes mounted and his followers began to spread the word. But the truth hardly matters, for Alexander was creating his own truths and myths to fulfill his huge ambitions.

SUMMARY OF KEY THEMES

1. POSITIONING THE WAR AGAINST PERSIA AS A NEW TROJAN WAR.
Alexander spun the war as a new Trojan War. By elevating the purpose of the war he ensured that all of Greece got behind the expedition. Lincoln's spin of the Civil War followed a similar pattern.

2. USE OF CAVALRY AS A "DISRUPTIVE" TECHNOLOGY AT THE GRANICUS.
Alexander defeated the much larger Persian army under command of Memnon of Rhodes by using cavalry as the strike force for the first time in the history of warfare—much like the use of tanks at Cambrai in World War I and the aircraft carrier at Taranto in World War II.

3. MANAGING THE MYSTIQUE OF INVINCIBILITY.
Like Tiger Woods in golf and the New York Yankees in baseball, the Macedonian army created—and managed—a mystique of invincibility about it, which led many opposing armies and garrisons to surrender rather than fight the Macedonians.

4. CREATING THE MYTH OF HIS ROLE AND THE WARS AS DIVINELY ORDAINED.
Like myths contrived for the people of Great Britain about the Highland tradition and World War II being a "people's war," Alexander created a myth about his divine origins and the role of the Macedonians in battle as divinely ordained.

CHAPTER 6

SEVEN DISTINCT
LEADERSHIP STYLES

IN THE MONTHS AFTER ALEXANDER'S VICTORY AT THE GRANICUS, MEM-
non of Rhodes, the greatest of the Persian generals, died of natural
causes. Memnon, just before he died, had consolidated the Persian navy,
and arm-twisted the Phoenicians, the Cypriots, and the Rhodians to cobble together a major fleet. Ostensibly, it could be a threat to Greece and
Macedonia as well as to the Greek and Macedonian army on the expedition with Alexander.

Realizing the looming naval threat, Alexander, who had burned his
ships after the crossing of the Hellespont, requested Antipater, his regent
back home, to send him a small flotilla of ships, mainly to carry his supplies and siege engines. Antipater quickly assembled a fleet, with twenty
Athenian merchant ships that carried grain from Asia to the city-state
(Athens, like many other city-states, had given up growing its own grain in
favor of the more lucrative olives and grapes, and therefore had to rely on
importing its grain). The Athenians subsequently never ceased to complain about their ships—as well as about the fate of the Athenians among
the captured Greek mercenaries who had been sent into hard labor—but
Alexander just ignored their protests. He knew that as long as he had their
ships and men working for him, the Athenians wouldn't pose any threat to
Macedonia.

Alexander's way of dealing with the naval threat posed by the Persians
was to analyze the threat as a complex problem. His understanding of the
ingratitude that the Persians had expressed toward the Cypriots, the Rhodians, as well as to the Phoenicians (all except those from the city of Tyre)

suggested that none of the naval contingents from these occupied territories of Persia would go out of their way to fight Persia's battles. So the Persian fleet wasn't as great a threat as it first appeared—except for the Tyrians, whose prowess at naval warfare and reputation at sea resembled those of the British navy in the seventeenth, eighteenth, and nineteenth centuries, after it had pulverized the numerically superior Spanish Armada in 1588. Second, the Persian ships needed docking at a port once a day for repairs and supplies. Alexander's tactic was to shutter every port in Asia Minor he could find and command Antipater to do the same back home in Greece. Finally, Memnon's death had rendered a further setback to Persia's naval aspirations, and ameliorated the threat posed by the large fleet.

Without the benefit of Memnon's advice Persian emperor Darius III was to make several major mistakes, which would cause him to lose his entire kingdom to Alexander. The first of these mistakes was made at the Battle of Issus in today's Turkey in late fall, 333 B.C. Darius was persuaded by his generals to go on the offensive against Alexander. In Babylon, in today's Iraq, where the royal council met to evaluate military options, the Athenian Charidemus, the fractious orator whom Alexander had exiled after razing Thebes, pleaded to the emperor that the only way Alexander could be defeated was if Darius were to raise an army of 100,000 trained soldiers, most of them Greek mercenaries, to fight the Macedonians. The Persian army or its generals, argued Charidemus, were not up to the task of fighting the Macedonians.

Darius followed Charidemus' advice but had him executed for his criticism of the Persian army. Criticism of the Persian royalty was impermissible. Indeed, so harsh was the Persian rule that subjects had to cover their mouths and noses when the Persian royalty was near because they didn't want to breathe the air that their subjects had breathed. Then, with an army estimated by some historians at 600,000 troops (including approximately 100,000 mercenaries), Darius set out west from Babylon (toward today's Northern Iraq where the Kurds live) in search of Alexander. He marched up the great Arabian Desert toward today's Syria. For a while he set up camp in the open plains of Sochi, the exact location of which has not yet been discovered, awaiting Alexander's arrival. The open plains were just what he needed to roll the Persian cavalry and chariots.

But the Macedonians were nowhere to be seen. Alexander had fallen seriously ill.

Trusting Style

Alexander had taken sick as he and his army were making their way through the mountain passes in southeastern Turkey near the town of Issus (not far from Turkey's current border with Syria). It was a hot day in October when Alexander, crossing through the mountains, saw a fast-flowing river. He had not realized that the water was freezing cold, and plunged into the river for a respite from the heat. The sudden drop in temperatures brought about an attack of such severe cramps that his body went into convulsions. Pulled out from the river, he lay on the banks with a raging fever, chills, and shakes. (Some modern medical practitioners, analyzing the written evidence, have reached the conclusion that Alexander was suffering from malaria; not only does this part of Turkey where Alexander was have a high incidence of malaria but Macedonia also, up until the early twentieth century, was one of the most malarious nations outside of the tropics.)[1] Doctors worried for his life—except for Philip of Acarnania, a childhood friend of his, who served as his personal physician. Philip concocted a potion, which he asked Alexander to take. He also warned Alexander that the potion would bring about a temporary state of coma out of which, he was certain, Alexander, given his general state of health, would surely recover.

As Alexander took the potion, he handed Philip a note that he had received from Parmenion. In the note Parmenion urged Alexander to beware of Philip, because he had reliable information that Philip had been bribed to poison him with medicine.[2] Alexander had already swallowed the dose, before Philip finished reading the note. Such was his trust in his closest friends—especially those he had grown up with. Alexander completely recovered in a few days. (Interestingly, nine years later, when his closest friend, Hephaistion, died of a fever in Ecbatana, Alexander had the physician treating him crucified.)

Alexander's trusting leadership style evoked fierce loyalty from those around him. Alexander trusted people he had known for a very long time, like his boyhood friend Philip of Acarnania; but often he placed trust in people he had just met. One such beneficiary was a Persian shepherd whom his army found after the Macedonians had suffered heavy casualties trying to cross through the Zagros Mountains surrounding the Persian capital city of Persepolis. The key to crossing the Zagros near Persepolis was a narrow, heavily fortified pass called the Persian Gates. Alexander had sent Parmenion with half the troops and all the supplies and siege trains by the longer road around the mountains, and with the other half he resolved to climb up the mountain, go through the pass, and march down to Persepolis, which lay in the plateau below.

Darius' general Ariobarzanes, however, had other ideas. The Persians had by now enough experience fighting Alexander to know that he would attempt the impossible. Climbing the Zagros in good weather was a tough assignment, but doing so with over 20,000 soldiers in the thick of the hard Persian winter was absolutely unthinkable. Ariobarzanes was convinced if it was unthinkable to most mortals, then that is exactly what Alexander would attempt. So with 40,000 well-equipped and-trained Persian troops, Ariobarzanes awaited Alexander's arrival at the Persian Gates. From the safety of the fortress that sat atop the pass, the Persians had a clear view of everything around. Any Macedonian troop movement was immediately noticeable to the Persians because movements stood out against the snow. As soon as the Macedonians neared the pass, the Persians attacked with a volley of stones and arrows. Clinging to their positions on the sides of the mountain, the Macedonians literally were exposed like ducks in thunder. They were so vulnerable that the Persians could have taken them out with slingshots.

Alexander knew he was beaten and asked the bugler to sound the retreat. Their only way over the mountain now was by climbing over the snow-covered peak, rather than through a pass, but there were no trails visible—several feet of snow covered everything. It was then that a shepherd, who had been captured by the Macedonians on suspicion that he was a Persian spy, came up to Alexander and said that he could guide them over. He explained he had been a shepherd in the Zagros Mountains and had been forcibly drafted into the Persian army as a slave before being released a few months back. He didn't like the Persians and would be happy to help. He claimed to know every trail over the Zagros into Persepolis.

Alexander put his complete faith in the shepherd and promised him that if he could lead them over the mountains he would make him wealthy beyond his wildest imagination; on the other hand, if this trail turned out be a trap, he would personally torture him to death.

Historians have long expressed utter shock at Alexander's putting the lives of so many in the hands of someone he had just met—worse, someone who had been captured as a prisoner for fear of being a spy. The shepherd led them over the mountain in that wintry night. The trail he took was the only way they could evade Ariobarzanes' troops. They lit up a few torches from the barks of trees that were above the snow to light their way over and down the mountainside. The Persians slept all through the night, though sentries were a little puzzled by the flicker of what they thought were fireflies along the mountainsides. At dawn they woke up to find the Macedonians over on the other side, preparing for an attack on them. When it came time to belly up the booty, Alexander presented the shepherd today's equivalent of a quarter million dollars—which even today, despite inflation in the price of cattle, buys a lot of goats around the Zagros Mountains. It was a good thing that the Macedonian treasury had collected a few bob in taxes by then to pay the shepherd so handsomely. Once again, just when they had appeared on the brink of victory over Alexander, the Persians were crushingly humiliated.

For modern-day managers, living in a world where trust in their corporations has never been more fragile, trusting others, whether above or below them, isn't easy. Little wonder then that—never more so than today—"whom to trust" remains one of those perennial questions that managers have to grapple with. Lou Gerstner's approach to figuring out whom to trust, when he walked into an ailing IBM on April 1, 1993, was to give *everyone* a chance at earning his trust. Everyone was trusted till proven untrustworthy. This is one approach. For safety Gerstner had also brought along with him—or soon hired—some managers with whom he had a long history of trust.

Most leaders and managers don't enter Gerstner-like situations, nor do they have the clout to bring in with them an army of those with whom they have previously enjoyed a trust-based record. The only way to instill and build trust in a relationship is by a gradual process of positive experiences: "trusting employees with important assignments, publicly defending their positions and supporting their ideas, showing candor and fairness in evaluating their work, and so forth," wrote Fernando Bartolomé, a professor of management in the *Harvard Business Review*.[3]

Whatever approach one takes, however, there is no denying that the way a leader acts and behaves in her professional—and personal—life is the surest way of building trust or the quickest way of destroying it. Trust is always a two-way street. It isn't only a question of whom can a leader trust to get a job done but also one of returning the trust that employees, troops, or political constituencies have placed in her. Political and business leaders caught with their hands in the cookie jar are known to express eye-popping indignation at being abandoned by those they had trusted so completely and for so long, and casting the terms of the abandonment as ingratitude. In the clear light of day, however, it often wasn't trust between the leader and their followers that had been abrogated. It was the leader's exploitative hold over his followers' weaknesses (like the need to hold on to a job) that might have accounted for even Fido-like submission (often mistaken for trust) that snapped, giving way to open—or discreet—nonchalance.

On the other hand many companies and managers are beneficiaries of a deep sense of trust from their employees and even their shareholders. Take Level 3, an Omaha-based fiber-optic telecommunications company that saw its market cap shrink from a high of over $40 billion at the peak in the go-go years of the Internet boom to a mere $1.3 billion in July 2002, by which time the entire telecommunications sector had crashed. Besides the large institutional holders, the owners of Level 3 stock were mainly regular folks from Omaha—most of whom never sold the stock even as it plummeted from its lofty heights. As the institutions unloaded their holdings, residents of the Cornhusker State just couldn't get enough of the stock. The reason: a septuagenarian named Walter Scott, who founded Level 3 and is now its chairman. In Omaha, Scott is highly trusted as a builder—literally, too, since Scott made his money in construction of commercial real estate, dams, and highways. Warren Buffett, the legendary investor, and the other highly trusted citizen of Omaha, says of his friend Walter, "He is also a man who gives you his word, and that's it. He is a person of great integrity. People here have tremendous respect for him."[4] Investors in Omaha keep buying Level 3 for the sheer trust they have in Scott—not unlike the trust that thousands of soldiers and camp followers who followed Alexander over ten thousand miles had in him.

Inspirational Style

As Alexander recovered from his illness near Issus, Darius was getting impatient. His advisers impressed upon him that, not only had Alexander stopped in his tracks, but he had chosen the mountain ranges in southeastern Turkey as a natural defense and eastern outpost for the Macedonian empire. Persian generals convinced Darius that Alexander had stopped his advance. Mountains, as Alexander was to prove, and as Hannibal was to show when he led the Carthaginians over the Alps to take on Rome just over a century after Alexander, provide no defense against armies that are resolute in their pursuit of an objective. Mountains defend nothing but themselves. The French military strategist Jomini wrote, "It has long been debated whether the possession of the mountains makes one the master of the valleys or vice versa."[5]

To meet the Macedonians in the Turkish mountains Darius decided to move farther west toward Issus, near where his scouts had spotted the Macedonian army. Darius sent his baggage train, most of what was in his treasury, as well as many of his family members, to Damascus, Syria, to wait.

As Darius moved west and Alexander recovered, Parmenion and the other generals started the operations to secure an appropriate battleground where the Macedonians, despite their troop size, might have an advantage. The battleground they chose was Issus, a small, sandy enclave surrounded by mountains on three sides and the Gulf of Issus (now Gulf of Iskenderun) on the fourth. The Pinarus River divided the enclave approximately in half. The river flowed from the mountains to the Gulf.

Parmenion instructed the troops to secure all the mountain passes surrounding Issus. These passes were the only way through the craggy mountainsides into Issus. Parmenion was convinced that the best place to take on Darius was Issus. Alexander agreed. He realized that it was going to be difficult for any side to launch any serious flanking or cavalry action due to the confined space at Issus. Moreover, considering the tight spaces through the mountain passes, no matter which pass the Persians used it would provide the Macedonians ample chance to prepare for an attack.

Although Parmenion and then other generals believed that Issus was the place to take on Darius, Alexander wasn't convinced that Darius would come to Issus. In early November, Alexander, now totally recovered, decided to seek Darius out in the plains of Turkey and Syria. He so strongly believed that there would be no attack on Issus till he was to entice Darius into this enclave that he left his sick and wounded behind and marched south in search of Darius. Alexander had planned that once he was spotted by Darius, he would quickly return to the enclave and await the Persian army's arrival.

Leaving the sick and wounded behind proved to be a mistake. While Alexander went in search of Darius in the plains south of Issus, Darius, through sheer serendipity, entered Issus through the northern passess. Alexander had not foreseen this possibility. Even worse, he had not foreseen the senseless mutilation and slaughter of the Macedonian sick and wounded, which is what Darius ordered as soon as he happened upon them. The massacre was "senseless" because if the Macedonians had earlier been less than fully resolute in their desire to defeat the Persians, Darius' actions would soon make them absolutely resolute. When word reached Alexander that Darius was in Issus, he blamed himself for having given up the advantageous position that the Macedonians had enjoyed up until a few days before. His accepting blame for an outcome that he couldn't possibly have foreseen only helped raise the level of confidence the troops placed in him.

The Macedonians immediately turned back and returned to Issus amid a thundershower—they were so inspired by his having taken the blame that they would have walked right through the eye of a hurricane. Entering a southern mountain pass in the middle of the night, they sought refuge in the nooks and crannies along the mountainside, their tents, supplies, and provisions rendered soaking wet. Next morning Alexander's army awoke, drenched and tired, and once again to very grim news and prospects: their path of retreat (even though they weren't planning for a retreat) back to Macedonia had been cut off by Darius, who held the northern pass. But that was not the worst of it. They faced even grimmer news that the sick and wounded they had left behind at Issus had been slaughtered. The expressions of personal grief and sorrow they saw in Alexander's eyes only renewed the vigor with which they now wanted to avenge their comrades' death.

Nothing demoralizes an army more than the knowledge that the communications and supply lines, and most important, the line of retreat have been cut off. But nothing churns an army's stomach more than finding out about the slaughter of their sick and wounded. Undaunted by these setbacks, Alexander ordered a sumptuous, hot meal for his entire army. As they rested on the mountainside and ate (Alexander, like Napoleon many centuries after him, also believed that an army travels on its stomach), Alexander convened a war council in his tent with his commanders to map out their strategy and tactics. The meeting lasted well into the evening.

As night approached, Alexander urged everyone to get a complete night's rest. He had guards posted all over the mountainside to monitor each and every move that Darius made. Several times in the night he woke up to personally reconnoiter the landscape down below, talk to the sentries, and sit watch with them. Nothing moved below except for the flames on the torches kept by the tents in Darius' camp. At the earliest crack of dawn Alexander was up and offered prayers and sacrifices to the gods, from a four-horse-drawn chariot, which he rode into the beach to pay homage to Poseidon, the Greek god of the Sea.[6] Alexander presumably was seeking divine intervention should he be attacked from the sea by Darius' Persian fleet. He was especially worried about the Phoenician fleet from Tyre.

A Rousing Speech

After paying homage to the gods Alexander convened all his troops. He had an enviable ability to motivate and inspire troops by defining battle lines. As Alexander addressed them, their silhouettes came through and disappeared in the rising fog of the valley below:

> *You have already faced and surmounted many dangers, and you ought to take courage from them.*
> *Again we prepare for another battle.*
> *This time our struggle will be between a victorious army and a foe, which has already been beaten.*
> *Moreover, we have already had divine intervention from the gods. Even we couldn't have hoped for a better outcome than if we were generals of our enemy's troops. He has put it into the mind of Darius to leave the spacious plains and shut his army in a narrow cove, where their superior numbers will be useless.*
> *But there is sufficient room for us to march our phalanxes.*
> *Nor are our enemies anywhere near to us in strength or in courage.*
> *We, men of Macedonia, have had long practice in warlike toils and in facing danger. They, on the other hand, are Persians, who have become enervated by a long course of luxurious ease.*
> *We, the most robust and warlike of men from Greece and Macedonia, are arrayed against the most effeminate and sluggish of men.*
> *To crown it all, we are free men.*
> *We are about to engage in battle men who are slaves.*
> *And don't forget that Alexander is commanding you into battle, while they are being led by Darius.[7]*

The entire mountainside echoed to the cry of "Alexander! Alexander!" As it did, the first set of troops started making their way below under the cover of the fog that engulfed the valley. As the sun burned the fog away by noon, Alexander's army of 80,000 troops stood on one bank of the Pinarus facing Darius' much larger army—by a factor of four to eight, depending on which historian one believes—on the opposite bank.

It wasn't clear what Darius was up to on the other side. He had created a screen of light infantry and cavalry all along the riverbank to hide his troop movements and positioning. Alexander was in no hurry either. He slowly brought up his troops to where he wanted them. Parmenion was instructed never to lose contact with the sea on the Macedonian left. Alexander's greatest worry was that Darius would create a flanking operation toward the sea, and the Persians' greater numbers would be sufficient to overcome the superior skills of the Macedonian cavalry positions on the left and thereby enable Darius to stage a flanking move to the left and to the rear of the Macedonian positions.

A modern leader who had the admirable gift of speaking, like Alexander above, in clear, genial, unpretentious, and forceful terms to his constituencies was Ronald Reagan. The terms, some critics argued, were too simple, but they did paint a picture of the opportunity or threat in ways that were comprehensible to one and to all. They were always black or white, never gray. Reagan always invoked the making of choices between these extremes, and there was always optimism in the choices he urged the country to make—or made himself.

While talking about the Strategic Defense Initiative (or "Star Wars" program), for example, he remarked, "What if free people could live secure in the knowledge that their security did not rest upon the threat of instant U.S. retaliation to deter a Soviet attack, but we could intercept and destroy strategic ballistic missiles before they reached our own soil or that of our allies?" Even though the reality on the ground was that SDI was setting off a new and nervous race for offensive nuclear superiority, Reagan's speech gave Americans a vision or perception of being able to take control of their future, which in reality they certainly couldn't. It was not dissimilar from Alexander painting a vision of victory that he couldn't be certain of under any circumstances, simply because he had never encountered Darius before, or an army so superior in sheer numbers.

Take Winston Churchill's inspirational leadership of Britain during the Second World War. Britain knew its weaknesses, including, at the beginning of the war, an unprepared army that would be no match for the German menace. But Churchill knew the power of rousing his nation toward visions of a victory that he himself definitely wasn't certain of, and playing up Britain's strengths. It's strengths lay in its fine navy, its air force, especially its long-range, four-engine bombers that took the battle inside Germany and bombed important assets; an aircraft production capacity that ran continuously, night and day; and the resolve and determination of its populace, which Churchill evocatively captured in his "we shall fight on the beaches" speech. Inspired by Churchill, fight they did, as German flyers could testify. In the Battle of Britain, while Royal Air Force pilots, whose planes were shot, bailed out of their planes and were back at their bases literally for tea and ready for the next flight out, German flyers who bailed were often pitchforked by the farmers on whose farms they fell.

Connective Style

Parmenion's son Nicanor commanded three battalions of hypaspists, the finest infantry troops, on the extreme right of the Macedonian positions toward the mountains. To Nicanor's left stood Parmenion's son-in-law Coenus, with a phalanx battalion, and on Coenus' left stood a phalanx battalion led by Perdiccas, Alexander's close friend and trusted general, who would one day briefly rule Babylon. These three generals led the infantry on the right side of the Macedonian front, under Alexander's personal leadership. Parmenion was the supreme leader on the left side. Under him were four generals, each in command of a phalanx battalion. On the extreme left toward the sea stood Amyntas, then Ptolemy, future ruler of Egypt, then Meleager, followed by Craterus. Amyntas, Ptolemy, and Meleager reported to Craterus, who in turn reported to Parmenion. Every one of these generals knew exactly what he needed to do in battle—plans were drawn up in detail and gone over thoroughly in the strategy session prior to the battle.

Neither Parmenion nor Alexander, who trusted those he empowered to act on their own, ever intervened or second-guessed the generals once battle had commenced. They came to each other's help, but they had gone over the battle plans and strategies so many times that implementing them would come naturally to them—no need, therefore, to course-correct when the battle was in progress. There was also the issue of providing the generals a lot of space. They were all highly accomplished and decorated soldiers. Both Parmenion and Alexander believed that they had picked great people as generals; it was now important to get out of their way.

As soon as all the infantry were in position, Alexander brought up the cavalry: the Companions on the right of Nicanor's infantry, followed by a battalion of lancers, and then Paeonian light and Thessalian heavy cavalries. The Companions obviously were the finest Macedonian troops, highly educated and extremely well trained in all aspects of warfare. Although most of the Companion retinue he had inherited from his father, several of Alexander's friends from Mieza now occupied positions of importance in the Companion ranks at Issus.

To the left, under Parmenion's command, he moved the Allied Greek cavalry, drawn from the various city-states in Greece, just ahead of Amyntas' infantry.

"Getting Himself Over"

Alexander rode up and down the three-mile-long front,[8] stopping before each unit and speaking to the men directly, referring to several individuals by their names and reminding them of the acts of bravery that they had performed in previous battles, while putting themselves at great personal risk. Alexander had that admirable quality to "get himself over" to his troops, was what British field marshal Viscount Montgomery of Alamein referred to as this pivotal skill in military leadership.[9] Alexander's emotionally supportive style here was oriented around motivating people to follow him into battle and to inspire them by building their self-confidence.

Alexander already knew what connecting with his troops could do for morale. He also knew the power of history. As he spoke to his troops about the battle at Issus, and reminded them of their acts of personal bravery in battles past, he also referred to the exploits of great Greek heroes such as Xenophon, who with "the Ten Thousand" had defeated the king of Persia under conditions that were much more difficult than the ones they faced this day. Xenophon's force, Alexander reprised for his troops, did not have the cavalry support they had today, nor any archers or slingers—just a hastily pulled-together band of brave men drawn from Crete and Rhodes who were willing to fight for a cause. If Xenophon could improvise and defeat the king of Persia under such conditions, Alexander reminded them, then they could as well—given their strength and reputation as warriors, as well as their record in battle from the Granicus. Hearing these words of encouragement, his men would walk up to him, clasp his hands in theirs, and beseech him to lead them into battle.

The Companions were always the first to charge into battle, they rode in front of their men, they always fought in the thickest of the battle, and they came to the rescue of a fellow soldier no matter his rank. No soldier ever questioned the moral authority of these men to lead them anywhere. It was an honor to most troops to follow these men, who led by setting a personal example. Playing the dual role of great rulers and great warriors was what ancient Greek heroes were all about. Macedonian rulers and barons exemplified such heroes.

Great generals, Montgomery often said, always connected with their troops, and took every opportunity to get themselves over to talk to them. Reminiscing about his leadership of the British troops in the Second World War, Montgomery wrote in his *Concise History of Warfare* that he sometimes addressed large numbers sitting on the bonnet of a jeep, sometimes a few men standing by the roadside or in a gun pit. "I would also address them less directly by means of written messages at important phases of a campaign or before a battle. These talks and messages fostered the will to win and helped to weld the whole force into a fighting team which was certain of victory."

Compare Monty to Field Marshal Sir Douglas Haig's leadership of the British troops during the First World War. Haig's war of attrition against the Germans, which can be simply summarized as "kill more Germans," is largely considered to have been an abject failure, leading to massive casualties among troops drawn from the British empire. One major British offensive, that of Passchendaele, launched on July 31, 1917, to push north toward the Belgian coast and destroy German U-boat bases, witnessed 10,000 British troops killed or wounded in the first two days of the offensive, and an equal number of casualties on the German side.

Constant rain and bombardment rendered the ground totally useless for tanks and a quagmire for the troops. Almost a hundred days later, when the Great War finally ended, the entire Allied army had barely moved five miles from their positions but both sides had lost 500,000 men between them in that offensive. When Haig's chief of staff (though not Haig himself) visited the troops *after* the battle had ended, he is said to have exclaimed, "My God! Did we really send men to fight in that?"[10] Poets like Wilfred Owen and Siegfried Sassoon wrote some of the finest of all war poems at that battle. Sassoon wrote, "I died in hell—(They called it Passchendaele)."

Part of Haig's failure lay in his inability to instill a fighting spirit in his troops, which, in turn, was a result of his inability and reluctance to "get himself over" to his soldiers. Monty recounted a story where Haig, after much prodding from his staff, finally decided to "get himself over." He asked a soldier at the front, "Where did you start this war?" The soldier, initially perplexed at Haig's question, and then convinced that, given Haig's reputation, this couldn't have been a query about his personal involvement in the war, replied, "I didn't start this war, sir; I think the kaiser did."

Napoleon, too, had an admirable ability to connect with his troops. So much so that his troops gave him the sobriquet "the little corporal." Napoleon earned that on one of the first expeditions he led against the Austrian army. To silence the Austrian guns on a river crossing, the French had to load their cannons faster than the Austrians could fire at them, and Napoleon could be seen carrying the cannon shells and loading them in, just like the corporals whose job it was to load and reload the big guns.

During the Gulf War the general leading the logistics of all the multinational forces, William "Gus" Pagonis, became famous for the management systems he had put in place to stay connected with his troops and officers. Everyone in the 22d SupCom, the 40,000-troop supply command that he was leading, could drop him a three-by-five card on which they wrote in a suggestion, queried a situation, provided an update, or raised an issue. He would go through literally hundreds of these every day and reply to the ones that he had an answer for or forward the query to one of his officers, who had the necessary information or decision rights to answer or do something about the issue. In addition, every morning he held a "stand-up" meeting, which anyone in his command could attend, and, every evening, a "sit-down" meeting, which was open only to his officers and those invited.

Pagonis required his command to use the same overhead or piece of paper that they had used at a prior meeting so precious time wouldn't be wasted in taking in information that they had already seen before. In between his stand-up and sit-down meetings he traveled between his supply depots, met his officers and troops, and constantly barraged everyone with questions.[11] After leaving the army Pagonis joined Sears, Roebuck and Company as its head of logistics, where he has carried on the stand-up and sit-down meeting traditions he created in the army—demonstrating that in matters of leadership, what's good for the gander is fine for the goose.

Aggressive Style

On the other side of the river, in a quick withdrawal of his human screen, Darius revealed his battle position. It was immediately clear to Alexander that his greatest fears had come true: Darius had lined most of his Persian cavalry so as to charge toward Alexander's cavalry positions seaward, where Parmenion was leading and not, as Alexander had been hoping, toward the heavy infantry positions along the hills. He didn't let this realization freeze his moves. Alexander immediately dispatched the experienced Thessalian heavy cavalry that he had stationed on the right behind him to back up Parmenion on the left. He, ordered the Thessalians to ride unobtrusively behind the phalanx ranks so as to be out of Darius' sight. The phalanxes' long spears provided a curtain of steel behind which the Thessalians changed positions.

Aiming for the Macedonian cavalry positions toward the sea was a shrewd calculation on Darius' part, who obviously realized that his infantry would be totally ineffective against the heavily armored, 32-person-deep Macedonian phalanx formations with their fourteen-foot *sarissa* spears or, more appropriately, pikes. Darius had decided to make this a battle of cavalry. The side toward the sea provided greater maneuverability for cavalry action than the side toward the mountains. Darius himself stood bang at the center of the Persian front, which, it had been clear from Xenophon's time was, for all Persian kings, the preferred position for battle. Darius, dressed in Persian regalia, rode high atop an ornate chariot. Surrounding him were the Persian barons, each leading his own regiment. Next to Darius stood an empty, highly adorned and jeweled chariot with a pedestal, which was for the Zoroastrian god Ahura Mazda, who, the Persians believed, accompanied their Great King into battle. Soldiers on both sides often paused by the chariot to admire its rich elegance.

Unlike the generals under Alexander, who trained together, fought together, and lived for months on the road together, the Persian barons only came together on the battlefield at times of national crisis. Therefore, in the early stages of a battle, they spent much of their time adjusting to

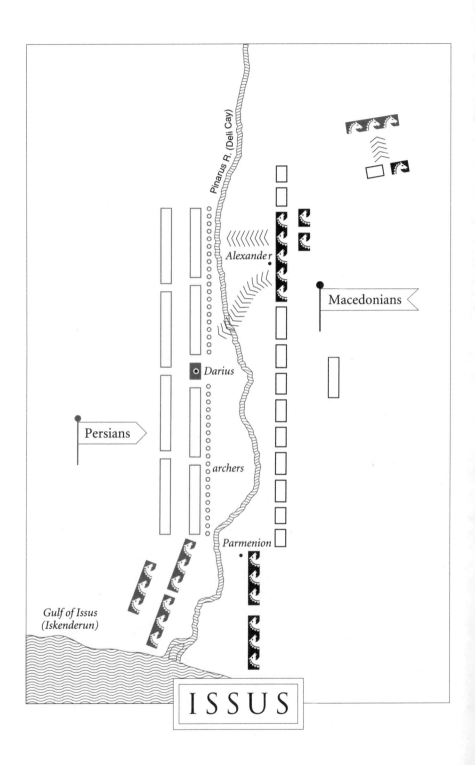

Pinarus R. (Deli Cay)

Alexander

Darius

Persians

archers

Parmenion

Macedonians

Gulf of Issus
(Iskenderun)

ISSUS

the strengths and weaknesses of the other barons leading their charges. Just behind these Persian noblemen were members of Darius' family, which, according to Persian custom, always followed the Great King into battle. As the historian Quintus Curtius Rufus described it, Darius, perched up on his high chariot, as if seated on the proverbial high horse, looked more like a victorious general coming *back from* battle than one *going into* battle.

As a diversionary tactic Darius sent a group of light cavalry up along the side of the mountain to occupy a ridge located just behind the Macedonian right flank, ostensibly to attack the right flank and probably even the rear. The small number in the contingent, as well as the reality learned from the Greek and Macedonian army's previous engagements with the Persian army, revealed that their formation and position meant that this was the contingent of rookies who had just graduated from the Persian military academy. This maneuver suggested to Alexander that Darius had no serious intention of using this force to attack and that the movement could only have been diversionary in nature. Alexander dispatched a band of light cavalry to confront the problem, and most of the Persians made a hasty retreat. The Macedonians dealt with those who didn't.

Although Alexander feared a Persian cavalry charge on his left, none came. Two of the largest armies ever assembled in ancient times just sat staring at each other across a river. It began to dawn on Alexander that despite the great superiority in numbers that Darius commanded, and the attacking position of his cavalry — he might not attack. Some of Alexander's generals started questioning whether Darius possessed the personal resolve and wherewithal for an attack on the Macedonians. They didn't have to wait for an answer.

Alexander had already prepared himself for just this eventuality. Indeed, that the Persians should not attack was an outcome that he much preferred. He was always keen — and had been taught — to be the attacker rather than the defender. It was also in keeping with his personal aggressive style of leadership. He was always the first into battle, he always fought in the very thick of it, and he was always the one pushing deeper and farther into the enemy ranks. He never waited for answers to problems to come to him. He would be the one to seek them out. While other generals might send out lower-level troops to reconnoiter the landscape of a battlefield or seek information or intelligence, Alexander, on the other hand, would aggressively seek out such information himself.

Unbeknown to the Persians, as well as many in the Macedonian ranks, Alexander had kept moving his troops up toward the riverbank of the Pinarus. It was already getting to be late afternoon. Alexander in his short life had seen enough defensive formations to realize that Darius had secured himself in the classic defensive position, and would remain in that position unless attacked. Considering his large army, Darius obviously felt no incentive to change the status quo.

But Alexander had had enough. It was then that he performed what Napoleon would always contend was the most difficult maneuver in battle: moving from a defensive orientation to that of an attacker with sufficient speed and force so as to retain the element of surprise and, simultaneously, be highly effective. Alexander charged—a whiff of sand going up into the air was the sign that his horse was on a gallop. He rode up with a small band of his Companions in close formation, till they were within range of the Persian archers, who immediately sent up a volley of arrows that showered down on the Macedonians. They were harmless against the Macedonian shields. Such was the density of the volley, one historian noted, that they seemed to rise up in the air like a burst of cloud, and many arrows just collided against each other, making them ineffective.

Now that the archers had discharged their arrows, and before they had a chance to reload, to the loud blare of a trumpet Alexander charged toward the archers at the head of his crack Companion cavalry. The Companions had years of training at staging just such an attack. The Companions were, as Admiral Horatio Nelson's captains would be called, "a band of brothers," who knew exactly what to do when they were next to the enemy—like Nelson's captains next to an enemy ship. They were so tightly linked in their sense of purpose and ambition that they were certain every one of them would know exactly what to do.

The effect of Alexander's charge was mesmerizing. Seeing Alexander riding Bucephalus, the shining wings on his helmet gleaming against the late afternoon sun, and his white cape flying in the wind, and the Companions, similarly kitted, riding just behind him, the Persian archers fell back into the Persian light infantry just behind them, their hands frozen midway of a reload.

This was just the kind of confusion Alexander had hoped the charge of his Companions would incite among the archers. He led the Companions up to the Persian left flank, which was protected by the Cardaces. The Cardaces were Persian soldiers who typically joined the army at about twenty years of age, were cross trained in infantry and cavalry, in the use of bows and javelin, and were also used during peace time to plant trees, clean streets, build shields, and care for the cavalry horses. They were indoctrinated in the Persian way of life, and in effect they were almost the ancient precursor to the Hitler Youth Brigade, which meant they were a group of ineffective, inexperienced, and highly immature—even effete—young soldiers.[12] Seeing the Companions charging toward them, they, too, fell in toward the Persian center, which was teeming with troops forcibly drafted into the Persian army from the various parts of Asia that the Persians ruled. They had little interest or incentive to put up a brave fight. The Companions easily drove a wedge into the Persian ranks through the Persian left flank.

By now the hypaspists had arrived on a quick march, and the Macedonian phalanxes had begun to cross the river, marching up at a steady pace, a wall of sharp spears pointing out toward the enemy, with not a visible gap between the spears. The light-armed hypaspists' primary role was to hold the enemy line and possibly push it back. Their purpose was to wait for the phalanxes to arrive and begin the slaughter and mayhem of enemy troops. This is exactly what the hypaspists and the phalanxes did, first pinning Darius' hired mercenaries down, then slaughtering them, as the Companions went around and behind the Persian lines and charged from the rear.

Alexander and the Companions kept pushing inward through the Persian left flank, and directing their energies to come up behind the Greek mercenaries and the Royal Bodyguard units that protected Darius. Alexander's sole objective was to kill or capture Darius. The Persian Royal Household Cavalry tried in vain to protect Darius. Despite their better horses the Persians were no match for Alexander or the Companions, who seemed determined to get their prey. The Companions had been trained to work independently or together in a group. They knew their role here, which was to charge into the Persian center at any cost. In pursuit of that single objective they kept adapting themselves as needed.

The Persian cavalry was trained to maneuver over the vast, wide-open plains of Persia, not within the elbow-room-only confines of a battle in a small cove. The Persian cavalry proved totally ineffective in this tight locale. The Macedonians, on the other hand, found the conditions at Issus to be perfectly suitable, hailing from a country that was largely mountainous and therefore provided small enclaves for cavalry maneuvers. The Macedonians used the advantage that their cavalry had to full effect.

"Hands-Dirty" Engagement

Persian troops and horses fell under the Macedonians' wrath. Alexander located Darius' chariot and headed straight for it—probably the most well-known representation of Alexander is captured in a Roman mosaic from Pompey depicting this precise scene. The horses pulling the chariot went berserk in the fray of battle. Darius' chariot driver fell, and Darius, abandoning protocol, took over the reins. But the horses were terrified and surrounded. Seeing Alexander almost on top of him, Darius leapt from his chariot into a lighter one that had been pulled up for him, and fled the scene of battle. Alexander was about to give chase, but he heard the desperate cry for help from his infantry, locked in hand-to-hand battle with the Greek mercenaries, and he immediately turned his horse and ordered his Companions to follow him in charging up from behind the mercenaries.

This was a very important side to Alexander's leadership: participating in a "hands-dirty" way in the battle itself, leading and inspiring the Companions, and not only keeping an eye on the movements of the hypaspists and the phalanxes but leaving himself flexible enough to come to their rescue when they so needed. Darius, on the other hand, participated in the battle only in those situations where his personal security was threatened but otherwise kept the sort of aloofness that was to characterize the "chateau generalship" of the First World War with, not surprisingly, similar disastrous effects.

Darius had led enough military expeditions in his reign, many against Alexander's father, Philip, to have the benefit of vast experience. But as Darius proved, it was not sufficient to have vast experience. Some people, as Frederick the Great observed, "might have had twenty campaigns under Prince Eugene and may not be a better tactician for all that." Frederick the Great labeled these people "mules." Darius, to be fair, was not a mule, even metaphorically speaking. He was twice Alexander's age at Issus, was a decent man though a weak general who had fought a "soldier's battle," where the general had contributed very little, if anything.

At the sight of their leader, Darius, running away from the scene of battle, Persian morale immediately fell. In the far distance they could see Darius stopping his chariot at the ravines and, jumping onto a waiting steed, abandoning his shield, stripping off his mantle, and even leaving behind his bow as he fled for his life into the early evening darkness that had begun to engulf the cove.

Not surprisingly, soon after Darius' departure the battle ended. The Persian losses were 100,000 infantry and over 10,000 cavalry killed in battle—many Persians had simply been trampled to death in the melee. The Macedonians had massacred the Greek mercenaries and the Persian infantry and heavy cavalry. So huge was the Persian death toll that an observer said that when the pursuit of Darius through the ravines was organized, there were enough Persian dead to form a bridge for the Macedonian riders through the ravines. A total of only 5,000 tallied up the Macedonian dead. Alexander ordered formal burials for the Macedonian and the Persian dead. The only thing he didn't permit were the elaborate, and expensive, Persian burial rituals, which would have seemed an affront to the simple Macedonian funeral rites that were being carried out for his dead soldiers.

Later that evening at Issus, after the sun had set, and darkness had engulfed the enclave, the Macedonian generals divided the spoils of war among themselves and their battalions. Whatever treasures the Persians had brought into battle were divided up.

Defenders Are Toast

Napoleon, too, believed in the principle "When possible, always attack." The function of strategy, according to generals like Napoleon and Alexander, was to make decisive contact with the enemy as soon as possible; everything would fall into place once that was done. This single focus on making contact with the enemy—and attacking and destroying him—was what made generals like Alexander and Napoleon successful. Both in ancient times and modern the function of grand strategy has been to optimize for a vast set of often conflicting objectives, whether military, political, or social. But neither Alexander nor Napoleon would ever allow any other objectives besides attacking and defeating the enemy, confuse their mission in battle. Napoleon said it succinctly: "There are in Europe today many good generals, but they see too many things at once. I see only one thing [in battle], and that is the enemy's body. I try to crush it."

The principles of war taught today in the world's leading military colleges have remained identical to those conceived and practiced by Napoleon and Alexander—especially Alexander, since most of what Napoleon did was inspired by studying him. The principles, as General Wesley K. Clark, defined them in his book *Waging Modern War:* having a clear objective and relying on unity of command to focus all efforts toward this aim. Plans and operations should be simple in conception, massing forces at the most critical points, relying on economy of force in the peripheral areas, and achieving surprise over the enemy. Decisive results are obtained from offensive action and maneuver.

Rudy Giuliani, who until 2002 was the mayor of New York City, packed a brusque and aggressive style in cleaning up the city's crime, filth, and corruption, and, for the first time in many decades, leading a revival that turned the city into one of the safest in the world. One of Giuliani's first acts as mayor in the early 1990s was going after the squeegee men, who, with the pretension of wiping windshields, extorted money from unwilling drivers stopped at traffic lights. They had become a sign of the city's blight and anomie. Getting rid of the squeegees might have been, in the broader scheme of things, a small act—since there were only about two hundred of them. But in terms of perception among New York City's residents and visitors, that effort was a big deal: For the time in New York's recent memory, here was a mayor who was going to go aggressively after the blights of urban life.

Before becoming mayor, in his days as a young U.S. attorney for the southern district of New York, Giuliani had, with similar aggressiveness, gone after white-collar criminals as well as the mob. Up until the early 1980s, when he came on the scene, nobody had really bothered about white-collar crime in New York, since there were so many murders, batteries, and assaults to go after. Giuliani not only went after all types of criminals, he did so with a pizzazz that would send a shiver down the spine of anyone contemplating a similar crime. He didn't just arrest inside traders, he had law-enforcement officials handcuff Kidder Peabody traders in front of their colleagues and march them off to the clink. His reasoning: White-collar crime was more deliberate, planned and committed by people who should have known better. He didn't go after a single mob boss, as previous attorney generals would, he took down entire mob organizations using the RICO (Racketeer Influenced and Corrupt Organizations) Act. Contrary to what Aesop would have us believe, in Giuliani's world, the hare did indeed beat the tortoise.

As mayor he retained his aggressive style, whether going after the little malefactor or the big gun. In the immediate past, New York's political establishment, as in most cities, had had a complicated approach to solving certain issues like homelessness and the racial divide. Unlike other mayors, who would approach these issues with all the resolve of a chocolate éclair, Giuliani urged the homeless to get off their backs and get a job, and on the racial divide took a tough stand. These earned him blistering criticism and venomous invective, but he didn't care. In 1995, when attending a concert at Lincoln Center's Avery Fischer Hall in celebration of the fiftieth anniversary of the United Nations, he asked the Palestinian leader Yasser Arafat, for whom he had no love lost, to leave the auditorium.

On the morning of September 11, 2001, during the attack on the World Trade Center, Giuliani's "hands-dirty" leadership would be visibly witnessed by the world as he coordinated the rescue efforts at Ground Zero, telling television and radio reporters to urge their audiences away from Lower Manhattan, and, while the events of that day unfolded, simultaneously consoling the inconsolable and comforting the grieving with words and behavior reminiscent of Lincoln's sensitive condolences to the mother of several boys lost in the Civil War: "I feel how weak and fruitless must be any words of mine, which should attempt to beguile you from the grief of a loss so overwhelming."

In the weeks after September 11 he urged New Yorkers to pick up the thread that constituted their lives: going out to the ballpark, a night out on the town with friends, or just a weekend of shopping. He himself had recently gone through a lot: A year earlier, diagnosed with cancer, he had dropped out of the Senate race, and a few months before had also admitted that his sixteen-year-old marriage to television personality Donna Hanover was on the rocks. New Yorkers felt that if he had been through such a lot, and seemed to be in control, then they could be as well. His leadership helped bring some semblance of normality to a city that will never be the same.

Humanistic Style

Throughout his career of conquests in lands of differing cultures, Alexander proved over and over again to be a noble conqueror, without the vindictiveness or roguishness that characterizes many of history's winners. There were some notable exceptions to this rule, however; his successes at Gaza, Tyre, and in many battles in India were followed by immense destruction and mayhem. But by and large, humanism prevailed.

When large armies like the Persian or the Macedonian traveled, also traveling with them would be an extended baggage train containing everything they could possibly need for the journey, which could last many years, as well as a train of followers comprising family members, entertainers, prostitutes, doctors, nurses, or just groupies. The followers typically stayed way behind the battle lines as the battle was fought, but, after the battle, as part of the spoils of war, not only was the baggage of the defeated confiscated by the victorious, the followers were also divided up among them. In a major contrast to armies of ancient, medieval, and even modern times, the Macedonians under Philip and Alexander were strictly forbidden from pillaging and plundering anything outside of the battlefields, unless for some reason it was a military decision. Even then it could not be pillage and plunder but a systematic razing of a town or city as the Macedonians did to Thebes, and, as we shall later see, as they would do to the Persian capital, Persepolis, and the Indian city of Multan.

Among Darius' followers were his large harem (exactly 350 concubines, and each musically trained), and their consorts, a large number of entertainers, from wrestlers to belly dancers, to appeal to the varied tastes of the entire Persian army, and chefs and cooks from the various parts of Asia under Persian control. Alexander's followers obviously included some of the above but was well known for also including geologists, cartographers, botanists, and zoologists, whose knowledge he used for intelligence gathering and record keeping. Much of what is known about plants and animals of the ancient world, or for that matter art and architecture, not surprisingly, can be traced back to the writings of people following Alexander on his conquests around the world.

It was close to midnight when Alexander returned to his camp after personally investigating yet another possible sighting of Darius. It had been a long day for him, and his generals awaited his presence at the dinner table in a tent where dinner was beginning to be served. A large hot tub, which once belonged to Darius, had been prepared for him in his personal tent, and as he soaked his tired bones in the warm water, he began to ponder: *So this is what it is to be king.* But the thoughts were interrupted by the distinct wailing of women from one of the Persian tents that had been set aside by the Macedonian generals as part of *his* spoils of the battle. The wailing was loud enough for him to surmise that it must have been coming from a tent very close to his. This ruled out Darius' harem, which was also part of his spoils, but would have been kept away from his personal tent for security reasons. He asked one of his commanders to investigate who was crying and also inquired why their tent should be so close to his. He was told that it was Darius' mother, wife, daughters, and son lamenting over the death of Darius. "They have been informed," one of the commanders said, that "his bow and royal mantle, and his shield have been brought back, and that you have them in your possession."[13]

Hearing this, Alexander jumped out of the hot tub and hastily dressed for dinner. He told one of the Companions to immediately go tell Darius' family that "Darius is still alive; in his flight he left his arms and mantle in the chariot; and these are the only things of his which Alexander has."[14] He then went outside, poked his head into the tent where dinner was being served, and called Hephaistion, a Companion commander and Alexander's closest friend, to come along with him. Accompanied by Hephaistion, Alexander went into the tent to find Darius' mother, wife, teenage daughters, and young son cowering in a corner. Darius' mother, Sisygambis, seeing the two men entering, similarly dressed and of the same age, prostrated herself before Hephaistion, thinking, because he was the taller of the two, that he must be Alexander—a scene poignantly captured by the sixteenth-century Italian master Paolo Veronese in his painting titled "The Family of Darius before Alexander," which hangs at the National Gallery in London. Hephaistion stepped back at about the same time that one of her attendants pointed out her mistake. Visibly embarrassed, Darius' mother bent down to prostate herself before Alexander. But Alexander caught her arms and lifted her up and told her that she had not made a mistake, for Hephaistion, too, was "an Alexander—a protector of men."[15]

He promised her that she would continue to retain all prestige, rank, and position that she had enjoyed in the world under her son's reign. Without looking directly on Darius' wife, Stateira (who was also his sister—marrying close relatives, among followers of Zoroaster was, and is, an accepted practice) he said to the woman with the reputation as the most beautiful in all Persia that she should not be in mourning because Darius was not dead. Alexander kept all the other promises he had made to Darius' family, and then some. It is said that he had a close relationship with Darius' mother, a fearless, regal, and beautiful woman in her own right, who died of grief five days after Alexander's death in Babylon—ten years after Issus. He refused to set eyes on Darius' wife, Stateira, both out of respect for her and because he didn't want to be tempted by the beauty of such a gorgeous woman. All throughout her captivity he made sure that she was well taken care of and her captive condition never taken advantage of. She died two years after Issus, weary and grief stricken, but just before her husband was completely routed by Alexander at Gaugamela.

Learning of her death, Alexander visited with the family immediately. He fasted along with the family, as was the Zoroastrian custom, accompanied her body in the funeral procession, performed every funeral rite that was demanded, and, in so doing, bolstered his richly deserved reputation for mercy and self-control. Some years later he and Hephaistion were to marry Darius' daughters—he to Stateira (named after Darius' wife Stateira) and Hephaistion to her sister, Drypetis.[16] The marriage was a symbolic marriage of the Greeks and the Persians, and Alexander and Hephaistion both entered into these to create the perception of these long-warring nations that they were now one. Following their lead, many Greeks and Persians married each other and settled down in each other's land.

The treatment of Darius' family was of the sort Alexander meted out to those weaker or unarmed or those he came to respect. His humanistic leadership style helped soothe nerves and provide a ray of hope to those caught in stressful circumstances.

Pardoning the Vanquished

At Issus, Alexander had to consider the fate of four ambassadors, sent by three Greek city-states, Athens, Thebes, and Sparta, to Darius to seek assistance in their battle against Alexander. (Once Alexander was away from Greece, Demosthenes was back to concocting nefarious plots.) The ambassadors were captured on the site of battle. The two ambassadors from Thebes he quickly set free, feeling sorry for the destruction and the state of enslavement that the Macedonians had recently unleashed on their city. Any nation, in the state that Thebes was now, would have done the same—sought help from whoever was in a position to offer it. But he never publicly articulated this position.

Alexander's public stance on the release of the representatives from Thebes was different from his private sympathetic stance. He declared that he was releasing the men because of the services that the family of one of them—a nobleman—had performed for Thebes; the other he was releasing in admiration for his success at the Olympic games. The man from Athens he let go because he was the son of a very famous Athenian general who had been helpful to his father. The Spartan he couldn't pardon. He represented a nation that was openly hostile toward him and his people. (In the context of ensuing successes he was to let the Spartan go as well). Alexander made each one of these pardons a personal one, driven by the individual diplomat's lineage, service, or personal accomplishments, assuring, in so doing, that the pardons were not an affront to his current set of men and to the memory of those who had fought pitched battles against these city-states. His troops had no issue with such personal pardons.

Also captured trying to flee with Persian treasures were several members of Darius' close family and staff, including the family of his brother, his generals, and royal courtiers. Parmenion picked them up trying to flee Damascus, Syria, the nearest large city to Issus, with a large chunk of the Persian treasury—the gold itself weighed over two tons. The treasure was important to the Macedonian exchequer, which since the death of Philip (Alexander having abolished all direct taxation in a highly popular move), was raking up huge deficits. The prisoners picked up were all dismissed by Alexander, except for Barsine, the beautiful young widow of Memnon of Rhodes. Barsine was Alexander's Josephine. But unlike Josephine, who was also a widow, Barsine came from nobility and wealth—she was the widow of the greatest Persian general and the daughter of the wealthiest Persian governor, Artabazus, who ruled all of Asia Minor for Darius. Barsine, eight years older than Alexander, never exploited her relationship the way Josephine used hers with Napoleon.

Barsine bore Alexander a son, Hercules. After Alexander's conquest of eastern Asia he appointed her father, Artabazus, as governor of the ancient province of Bactria in northeastern Persia—a region now in Iran, Uzbekistan, Tajikistan, and Afghanistan.

"TREAT ME LIKE A KING"

On his Indian expedition a few years later Alexander was to capture the fearless, learned, much loved, and proud king Porus, who ruled India just north of Taxila—outside Rawalpindi in today's Pakistan. Seeing him injured in battle, yet unshaken in his will to fight on, Alexander sent several emissaries to Porus to ask him to give up, since he was completely surrounded. Porus initially turned these emissaries back and even charged on some of them. Not until Alexander sent an emissary who was Porus' friend did Porus surrender.

Alexander had come to admire Porus' fighting spirit and resolve. Unlike Darius, here was a king who refused to leave the theater of war and save his own life. Alexander inquired of the six-and-a-half-foot-tall Indian king what he should do with him.

"Treat me like a king" is what every Indian high school student learns when he or she reviews one of the most famous—and the earliest recorded—encounters between India and the West.

"Indeed, that will be done," Alexander is reported to have said. But there must be something that the Indian king he had so come to respect must want for himself?

"Everything is contained in this one request," Porus replied.[17]

Alexander had never heard such an answer. He had heard pleas for mercy, clemency, and surrender. But he had never witnessed such pride and self-esteem even in defeat. Trained by Aristotle to comprehend the subtleties of human behavior, Alexander realized that even in defeat the grandeur, posture, and self-image of this king hadn't been destroyed. Alexander reinstated him to his throne, enlarged his kingdom, and promised him the security of the Macedonians, now the most valiant army in the world.

It's not common to find the sense of humanism in modern leaders—indeed it is a rare quality that stands out only among a handful. No leader has expressed such a sense of reconciliation and humanism as has South Africa's Nelson Mandela toward his former adversaries and captors—even after undergoing harsh treatment as a prisoner, stitching gunny-bags and breaking quarry stones at the hands of the white Afrikaners, who had him imprisoned for twenty-seven years.

Mandela has been quoted as admonishing his followers not to humiliate the opposition. "No one is more dangerous than one who has been humiliated."[18] As he negotiated with his former foes, he expressed, and encouraged his followers to express, a belief in the principles of democracy as well as a moral integrity that forbade revenge for all the decades of apartheid. Indeed, the Truth and Reconciliation Commission, headed by Mandela's friend, the Anglican archbishop Desmond Tutu, was charged with investigating and bringing closure, without revenge, not only to the atrocities committed by the white Afrikaners against South Africa's majority blacks and mixed races but also to the acts of violence committed by members of the African National Congress, which Mandela headed, against black collaborators with the apartheid regime.

In his fascinating biography of Mandela the British journalist Anthony Sampson writes of Mandela's proclivity to quote Shakespeare's lines from *Julius Caesar*: "Cowards die many times before their deaths; the valiant never taste of death but once." Mandela's life is one of valiant triumph over the most excruciating adversity. No wonder that, like the two men whose work he followed the most, Mahatma Gandhi and the Reverend

Martin Luther King Jr., his courage and his moral purpose have made him a towering hero of our times. As Nadine Gordimer, the South African Nobel Prize–winning novelist—with whom Mandela visited soon after being released from prison—wrote in her brilliant and moving political novel *Burger's Daughter,* to many South Africans it must be "strange to live in a country where there are still heroes."[19]

Commanding Style

Aristotle had taught Alexander some of the principles of effective leadership. The commanding style, according to Aristotle, required a leader to be "angry with the right person, in the right way, at the right time, and for the right reason." Over time Alexander became more and more suffused with his own sense of power and turned somewhat ruthless later in life, but after Issus he was in peak form as a strong commander. Take his treatment of the offer by Darius to legitimize Alexander's conquest at Issus for return of his family. Darius not only offered land in the western parts of Persia to Alexander but also the hand of his daughter Stateira to Alexander in marriage.

"For the future," Alexander is reported to have written Darius, "whenever you send to me, send to me as the King of All Asia, and do not address to me your wishes as to an equal. But if you are in need of anything, speak to me as the man who is lord of all your territories."[20] If he didn't, Alexander threatened to pursue him like a common criminal. Similar in style was Civil War general Ulysses S. Grant's reply to General Simon B. Buckner's proposal to negotiate the surrender of Fort Donelson. Known for his action-orientation in his written and spoken language, Grant wrote to Buckner: "No terms except an unconditional and immediate surrender can be accepted. I propose to move immediately on your works."[21] Like Alexander's letter, to the point.

Alexander reminded Darius that he seemed to have forgotten who the victor was and who the defeated, and if Darius had any misconceptions in his mind about who was who, he shouldn't hesitate to reengage in battle; that Darius had no business offering him what wasn't his anymore: the land he offered was already Alexander's; and the daughter he offered in marriage was in his captivity. To Darius' remark that his empire was very large and that Alexander would need to cross many rivers such as the

Tigris, Euphrates, and the Hydaspes, before he could even begin to think of himself as a conqueror of the Persian empire, and along which rivers, Darius promised, his troops would fight Alexander tooth and nail, Alexander is said to have inquired: What threat did rivers pose to those accustomed to crossing oceans?[22] Alexander made sure that everyone knew the contents of his reply to Darius in his commanding style.

The Killing of Philotas and Parmenion

Alexander the commander became more ruthless as he moved to finish his conquest of the world, in part because he began to trust fewer and fewer people in his entourage. A few years after Issus, campaigning in Bactria, Alexander again heard of a conspiracy against him, which he had initially heard on his Egyptian campaign, distantly involving Philotas, son of Parmenion.

According to Ptolemy, Alexander's friend, general, and ruler of Egypt after his death, Alexander sent for Philotas, who had been up until then one of his most trusted lieutenants. It was Philotas whom he had relied upon as the commander of his crack Companion unit at the Battle of Issus. It was Philotas who again commanded the Companions at Gaugamela (a battle we shall read about in more detail in the next chapter), which some historians have described as the greatest battle fought in the ancient world. It was at Gaugamela where Darius was once again routed, and all of the Persian empire fell into Alexander's hands. Professor B. I. Wheeler, writing in his book *Alexander the Great* (1925), said about the battle: "The issues of centuries had struck their balance in a day. The channel of history for a thousand years had been opened with a flying wedge." The wedge was the wedge formation into which Alexander and Philotas organized the Companion unit before plowing through the Persian ranks with devastating effect.

Because of the high military position Philotas' father, Parmenion, held in King Philip's kingdom, Alexander had seen Philotas literally from the day he was born. But even that level of closeness did not prevent him from doing what he needed to do when someone so near to him threatened his personal security.

Philotas was brought before a military court to stand trial, where Alexander made his charge and brought forth witnesses who knew that Philotas was aware of a conspiracy to kill him. Alexander's most convincing charge was not that Philotas himself would participate in the assassination, but that knowing of the plot, he had not warned him of its existence even though he conferred with Alexander at least twice a day. Indeed, the charge was even weaker as regards Philotas' personal participation in the plot itself. It turned out that he had no knowledge of how the assassination would be carried out or even who the plotters were; his crime was not to have offered a Macedonian who knew of the plot an audience with Alexander. From Alexander's point of view Philotas, given the position and personal trust he enjoyed, was as guilty as the conspirators, if not more so. Philotas was stoned to death.

The Roman historian Quintus Curtius Rufus provides a vivid picture of what transpired immediately after Philotas' death. Alexander sent one of Parmenion's closest friends (whose brothers he held as hostages) to Media (in today's northwest Iran near the Caspian Sea), where Parmenion was stationed. This friend of Parmenion carried with him four letters personally written by Alexander: three addressed to Parmenion's three deputy commanders, instructing them to kill Parmenion, and a fourth to Parmenion himself, which was to be given to him only moments before his death.

Alexander reminded Parmenion's friend that they had all been victims of Parmenion's crime. But none was a greater victim than he, the friend, who had been so completely deceived by Parmenion. "To hunt him down and punish him I have decided to use your services—observe the confidence I have in your loyalty."[23] Having said that, Alexander also told Parmenion's friend that till the job of killing Parmenion was accomplished, he would hold his brothers as hostages. Moreover, he must go to Media at once, outrunning the speed with which rumors have a tendency to travel.

Ten days later Parmenion's friend strolled into the fruit orchard surrounding Parmenion's house in Media. And as the seventy-year-old general, who had achieved a lot before Alexander and without whom neither Alexander nor his father would have achieved anything, came rushing to greet his friend, who handed him Alexander's note. As Parmenion read the note, his deputies slit his throat. Even though there was no suspicion of Parmenion's involvement in the assassination plot against him, Alexander decided he could not risk such an influential person as Parmenion living when he had killed his son Philotas in such a brutal manner. Parmenion's influence was not only in the Macedonian troops he had led so many times to battle but also among the Greek contingent, who had come to respect and admire him as the greatest general they had had a chance to serve under. Parmenion alive, according to Alexander's calculations, was not a risk worth taking.

THE KILLING OF CLEITUS

As his command became more and more autocratic and less and less tolerant of criticism, several close associates died or were silently spirited away and killed. His teacher Aristotle's own nephew, Callisthenes, was killed when the historian refused to prostate himself before Alexander—as was the Persian custom.

Of these, the killing of Cleitus was the one for which Alexander expressed deep remorse and self-flagellation, as England's King Henry II did after having had the archbishop of Canterbury, Thomas à Becket, murdered in 1170. Cleitus was a pugnaciously mercurial man, which meant that having him on your side today was no guarantee he would be on your side tomorrow. But at the end of the day Cleitus served as Alexander's commander. He was a great commander. Cleitus had saved Alexander's life at Granicus. Alexander would have died at that battle, and disappeared as a footnote in the mists of history, if it were not for Cleitus.

Cleitus, some twenty years older than Alexander, was also the brother of the nurse who had looked after him from the day he was born. Cleitus unfortunately was also outspoken. The one downside to Cleitus' nonconformity was that every now and then it drove him over the deep end. Cleitus, in many ways, was like Civil War general George B. McClellan, who expressed open disdain for those around him—especially his superiors. McClellan fought with the senior cadets and teachers while at West Point. He privately disparaged civilian superiors when he worked in the private sector, and he publicly disdained politicians—including his boss, President Abraham Lincoln, against whom he would go to extreme lengths to keep information away; not surprisingly, with disastrous results—in a few months he was dismissed from his command.[24] Similarly, in one of the greatest-ever public fallings-out, President Truman, in April 1951, fired General Douglas MacArthur from his position of supreme commander, when the highly decorated general tried to bypass the President and sent a letter to the Speaker of the House advocating an attack on China in the Korean War. Of course, Cleitus never withheld information from or bypassed Alexander, but he often expressed open disdain—even disgust—at what Alexander had become.

The night Cleitus died in late summer of 328 B.C. in today's Samarkand,

Uzbekistan, both he and Alexander were roaring drunk. Other commander colleagues tried to stop Cleitus' harangue about Alexander's embracing of Persian clothes and customs, and temporarily even escorted him out of the tent where they had all sat drinking. But Cleitus returned and, quoting from Euripides' play *Andromache*, remarked about the evil customs that today pervaded Greece.[25]

Alexander ran him through with a spear, instantly killing him. As he stood horrified over his friend's dead body, he pulled the spear out and would have run it through his own throat had it not been for the other commanders who stopped him. Alexander retired to his tent in grief and lay there for three days. He grieved for his friend; but mostly he grieved for himself—that he was now suffering from the powerful man's conceit that he had seen engulf his father, according to which anyone who disagreed with him must be morally flawed.

History is strewn with the remains of organizations, and fallen leaders, who made criticism unacceptable. Even in organizations with large groups of leaders, the quickest way of losing direction is when challenging the status quo, or questioning and criticizing accepted practices, becomes a career-limiting, even career-destroying, move. Great military, and business, leadership is about risk taking, and Alexander worried that his killing of Cleitus would send the message that he did not wish to be questioned or have his decisions challenged. After three days, when he came out of the tent, he went straight into a meeting with his commanders and ate crow. This was not the way he wished to lead.

The right to disagree with him was a fundamental freedom that Alexander believed he ought to protect—including the expression of criticisms that might be ludicrously puerile or intimately vile. That was what Aristotle had taught him. Disagreements or criticism had nothing to do with lack of loyalty. Rulers and leaders who confused those two, Alexander was aware, were certain to create around them an environment rife with cronyism or cliquery. As many business and political institutions have seen, nothing erodes an institution's moral fabric as quickly and easily as cronyism. An environment of cronyism breeds distaste for disagreement. There will, of course, be the brave few who will yet disagree, and often loudly, despite the consequences. It is the meek, however, who can render greater damage. The ones to fear, Napoleon said, "are not those who disagree with you, but those who disagree with you and are too cowardly to let you know." They will pull the rug out from beneath you at the first opportunity.

Marauding Style

It was 326 B.C.—seven years after the Battle of Issus—when the Macedonians invaded India. They were tired after trekking over some of the tallest mountains and the most inhospitable deserts in the world. Much to their surprise they also faced stiff resistance from the armies of the local kings—the kind of which they had never experienced before. As the Macedonians invaded each town and city, often after fighting a blistering battle, they looked for complete surrender of its populace. Fleeing was considered tantamount to waging battle, and many of those who fled were followed and struck down by Macedonian cavalry. It was even believed that the Macedonians scoured the forests for refugees who might have fled their land, and killed them.

Although such cruelty was the hallmark of many armies at that time, the Macedonians had not, according to most historians, engaged in, by and large, the systematic annihilation of escaping civilian populations—though some eminent historians, like California State University's Victor Davis Hanson, have forcibly, and thoughtfully, challenged that view.[26] Whatever might have been the case before India, and there were examples of plunder and annihilation by the Macedonians in Thebes, Gaza, Tyre, and Persepolis, among others, it was certain that by the time they reached India their priorities had changed.

Some have reasoned that the choices for control of regions in the outer reaches of their empire were total subjugation or extermination on a massive scale to serve as a lesson for those who were spared. With their far-flung empires they could not risk the rise of a rebellion as soon as they had turned their backs or left the region. They needed to quash the possibility of any such rebellion in the future. These are the fundamental tenets of deterrence. Thomas Schelling wrote in his influential book *Arms and Influence* that the power to hurt is what provides armies, nations, or, for that matter, businesses, bargaining power over their adversaries.[27] By hurting, or using the threat of hurting, a nation can make its opponent afraid—very afraid—of suffering unacceptable consequences.

Multan in the Punjab province of India was one Indian city that witnessed retribution of gargantuan proportions after Alexander had exhibited the inspirational, aggressive leadership style that had brought him this far. The city of Multan, which still stands on the banks of the Ravi River, had a large population and was well defended by a wall surrounding the city, in the midst of which stood a massive citadel. The riverbank on which the city stood rose high above the water level, providing the city with a natural defense against invaders.

Some 50,000 Indian troops stood along the riverbank to thwart any Macedonian excursion. Alexander, with an army of 5,000, rode up to the opposite bank and, instead of stopping for reinforcements to arrive to counter the much bigger Indian presence, forded the river. While the Indians attacked in a closely aligned, linear formation, Alexander ordered the Greek phalanxes into position and attacked in column formation at the flanks or the rear. The Macedonians quickly regrouped after each attack, and before the Indians could regroup their large formation, the Macedonians charged. Soon morale gave way, and the Indians retreated into their formidably secure citadel, where children, women, and the elderly had already sought refuge.

Alexander commanded his troops to break through the walls of the citadel. Battering rams went into action, but the well-reinforced walls wouldn't give way. Alexander beseeched his troops to act more forcefully. He ordered them to concentrate their efforts on a single point in the wall, believing rightly that if one point in the wall was breached, the siege was over. He ordered scaling ladders to be lined against the citadel walls, and leapt up the second one arrived. With his shield held above his head to protect him from the arrows raining down from the citadel towers, Alexander clambered atop the citadel walls. There, waving his sword and his white cloak fluttering in the air, his helmet "so polished that it shone like the brightest silver," as the historian Quintus Curtius Rufus wrote, he spoke to his disillusioned men to accompany him into yet another victory—a speech that in motivational spirit was not to be matched till Shakespeare's Henry V cajoled his troops to attack Harfleur with the words "Once more into the breach, dear friends, once more. . . ."

Inspired thus, several Macedonians clambered up the scaling ladders. Under their weight the ladders broke. Despite frantic pleas from his troops below to fall back, Alexander jumped into the citadel, swinging his sword wildly to stave off enemy attacks. Three of his trusted lieutenants, including Peucestas, who carried the shield of Achilles borrowed from the Temple of Athena in Troy, also jumped into the fray. An arrow struck Alexander, piercing his chest. If Peucestas hadn't hovered over him, using the fabled shield to stave off further arrows, both of them would have been dead; the other two Macedonian soldiers who had jumped in were dead.

As Alexander fell to the ground, struck by the arrow in his chest,

Macedonian troops arriving on the parapet above announced to those below that their king was dead. The rumor of his death spread like wild-fire, and the Macedonians struck their battering rams into the city walls much harder, and one of the walls gave way—just in time for Alexander. Indian troops were poised to finish him off, when they heard the shouts of the Macedonians through the breaches in the citadel walls. As they turned to fight the Macedonians streaming in through the breach, Alexander was spirited away out of the citadel, where the arrow was surgi-cally removed. The Macedonian army was so torn up by the news of their king's death (and without the knowledge of his survival) that they slaugh-tered the entire population of Multan. Though they hadn't acted upon orders from Alexander, they had clearly adopted a new vengeful, vindic-tive mindset, one very different from the earlier days of conquest in Egypt and Persia.

The unwarranted killing of civilians and destruction of property re-mains in the annals of warfare one of those intractable questions for which there are no clear answers. The notion of "strategic warfare," which implies not only the slaughter of combatants and military posts and forts but the killing of noncombatants as well as the systematic destruction of civilian property and pillage of towns and cities, came to the fore during the U.S. Civil War, when Union generals like William Sherman, out of necessity, changed the nature of battles. As entire towns and cities— including their civilian populations—became voluntary or involuntary participants in the war effort, the targeting of farms and food stocks, rail depots and rail lines, workshops and factories, communications and postal facilities, became legitimate. Although Union soldiers believed that only civilians who had furthered the war effort should be persecuted, many Southern historians have claimed that retribution befell many innocents, especially toward the end of the war when the Union army cut a wide swathe of destruction in its "March to the Sea" in November 1864—out of Atlanta toward the Atlantic, which would witness, among other devasta-tions, the razing of two thirds of Columbia, South Carolina, on February 17, 1865.

Several massacres of civilians have consequently followed the pursuit of deterrence: the Allied bombing of Dresden in the Second World War to instill fear in Nazi German about the sort of retribution that would be-fall them; Winston Churchill allowing the bombing of the British city of Coventry in November 1940 rather than compromise a highly placed in-telligence source;[28] the bombing of the Basque culture's most historic town of Guernica by Hitler's aircraft friendly to General Franco in the Spanish Civil War; the massacre of over three hundred children, women, and elderly by American troops in the village of My Lai in Vietnam; the killing of several hundred Indian civilians attending a peaceful rally at Jallianwallah Bagh (Garden) by British general R.E.H. Dyer in April 1919; and obviously Hiroshima and Nagasaki.

In business, too, the marauding style is often witnessed in the aggressive way CEOs manage their business to win at any cost, in a supercompetitive, take-no-prisoners style. While some companies have been reported to go to any lengths to win a competitive edge, including carrying out an espionage campaign against a rival or threatening to put a rival out of business, they haven't fundamentally crossed the line of legally doing business nor are they, on the other hand, held up as paragons of moral virtue.

Some CEOs can also appear hypercompetitive to change an otherwise stolid organizational culture. Take Jamie Dimon, the CEO of the Chicago-headquartered Bank One—a company that was formed through the 1998, $29-billion merger between Bank One of Columbus, Ohio, and First Chicago NBD. Dimon, who is successfully turning around what was till recently a troubled merger, inspires his troops by his rousing invective against the bank's much larger competitors. "What do I think of our competitors?" Dimon asked a gathering of Bank Oners at Chicago's McCormick Plaza. "I hate them! I want them to bleed!"[29] These words are spoken to inspire the company's troops and to lend a sense of competitive spirit to the culture. There is nothing wrong with this.

Often, though, the hypercompetitive style, especially if it leads to atrociously high levels of profits, can boost one's ego and vanity, so that what was formerly a competitively inspirational style transforms itself into a marauding one—often pushing the organizations so led over the edge. When the bond-trading scandal hit Salomon Brothers in 1991, many were not surprised that the firm was tied up in such unethical dealings, considering the overly aggressive "ready to bite the ass of a bear" culture fomented by its leaders.[30] Traders were encouraged to focus on the short term and generate profits at any cost. There was very little transparency in the management of the organization, but it was well known that departments producing excess profits were highly rewarded, and secret deals often got made to award individual departments much higher bonuses than others. It was reported that in 1990 senior leadership had struck a deal with the risk-arbitrage department such that they could keep as much as 15 percent of all profits and distribute it among the traders. If such an incentive would get the department to generate higher profits, then that was what was done at Salomon. Not surprisingly, the department generated extraordinary profits and awarded its traders magnificent bonuses.

Not that anyone at Salomon was lowly paid to begin with. But where the typical trader would have walked away with $1- or $2 million in annual bonus, that year of the incentive one trader in risk arbitrage got in excess of $20 million.[31] One could say that the institutional mechanisms for a massive scandal were in place at Salomon months before it actually happened. When it happened it shook the very foundations of the U.S. financial system, because it was in the highly sensitive and sacrosanct treasury-bill auctions where the scandal occurred.

Treasury-bill auctions determine the underlying T-bill interest rate, which affects everything in the U.S. economy from mortgage rates to car loans and interest on savings accounts. To ensure no single institution can overly influence this important leg of the U.S. economy, securities law prohibits any institution to bid more than 35 percent of a T-bill auction. When the canaries began to sing, it turned out that Salomon had tried to clean up the auction by bidding over 90 percent in one auction alone. In addition, rather than investigate and punish the rogue traders, senior leadership's initial impulse was to cover it up, and they undertook one cover-up after another till Salomon fell on its face like a house of cards—not unlike the disastrous results that Alexander's army was scoring in India. Although victorious, their victory was costly, and even the troops who had followed Alexander for so many years were surprised at the grotesque, egotistical human beings they and their leader had become.

Without a shadow of doubt Alexander was a master strategist and tactician. He was a great general. He was smart, refined, cultured, and intelligent. And, he had very human flaws. And`he demonstrated all these qualities starting from the age of twenty. But his strength was an ability to choose from a quiverful of leadership styles depending on the situation. At least that was what made him a remarkable leader during the early part of his campaign. Unfortunately, toward the end of his reign, he began to suffer from a type of megalomania that afflicts the style of many successful leaders. The reasons for delineating these different styles are not so we can follow them all (the last two leadership styles are worthy of nothing but derision), but because these represent the diverse styles that we might observe in leaders we interact with. We may choose to develop some of these leadership styles ourselves, emulate some, and actively avoid others.

SUMMARY OF THEMES

1. TRUSTING LEADERSHIP STYLE.

Despite being warned by Parmenion that the medicinal potion he was given by his doctor, Philip, was poison, Alexander put complete faith in his childhood friend and drank the potion—and only after that revealed to Philip the concern that Parmenion had raised. He would place his complete trust in people he had just met—such as the Persian shepherd in whose hands he trusted the safety of half the Macedonian army.

2. INSPIRATIONAL STYLE.

Alexander had an uncanny ability to inspire his troops. He reminded them of past battles and victories, talked to them about the higher purpose that they were following beyond winning the battle at hand, and inspired them with stories of past heroes who had succeeded in much rougher conditions.

3. CONNECTIVE STYLE.

Before any battle he would ride up and down the front, speak to his men directly, call out to familiar faces by name, and remind them of previous acts of bravery. Not only would that boost morale, but his men also knew that their contributions were being recognized.

4. AGGRESSIVE STYLE

Alexander always tried to position himself as the attacker—never the defender—because he knew the advantage most attackers enjoy. Surprise was among the most important, followed by an ability to shape the direction of the battle the way he wanted. He also enjoyed the goodwill of people as a "liberator" rather than an "aggressor."

5. HUMANISTIC STYLE.

Despite the cruelty demonstrated in battle, Alexander always made sure that even the enemy's troops got a decent burial. Alexander could be valorous and magnanimous off the battlefield. He made sure that Darius' wife, mother, and children were well taken care of and their captive condition never taken advantage of. When Darius' wife died two years after Issus, weary and grief stricken, just before Alexander routed her husband at Gaugamela, Alexander visited with the family immediately. He fasted along with them and accompanied her body in the funeral procession.

6. COMMANDING STYLE.

Alexander knew his place in the world. If someone stepped outside of the boundaries, he was quick to act. Even with Darius he was prompt to point out who the victor was and who the vanquished was, and if the vanquished wanted any forgiveness, he must ask for it in the appropriate fashion. Eventually, he became more paranoid, which led to the sudden killing of several of his close friends and confidants. The deplorable killing of Parmenion as well as his son on rumors of plots, or the killing of Cleitus in a drunken stupor, point out that Alexander was a highly insecure, judgmental human being who could often behave like a despot.

7. MARAUDING STYLE.

The killings of thousands of innocent civilians at Thebes, Gaza, Tyre, Multan, and elsewhere have always raised the question about Alexander: Was he a great leader or just another barbaric killer? Many historians have chosen to take extreme positions on one end of the question or the other. Unfortunately, we will never know the truth. What is important, however, is to take the position of either end of the spectrum with a pinch of salt— or a large dose of it, depending on how vociferous the position is. Reality probably is, as with most things, somewhere in between.

CHAPTER 7

A GLOBAL STRATEGY TO
UNIFY THE WORLD

Now that, after Issus, he had money from the Persian treasury to pay his troops, Alexander decided to consolidate his conquests in the eastern and southern Mediterranean before pursuing his foe—who was quickly moving inland toward the safety of the Persian summer and winter capitals of Susa and Persepolis. Although there were several sightings of Darius, Alexander's focus was on consolidation of his empire, not chasing down his enemy. His greatest fear was that the Persian satrapies along the eastern and southern Mediterranean—Syria, Palestine, Lebanon, and Egypt, in particular—could launch an assault on Greece or Macedonia while he was deep inside Persia. The Phoenicians, who operated out of Tyre and Sidon (modern Saida) in today's Lebanon, were to be particularly feared because of their naval prowess.

Each of these satrapies also possessed key capabilities the Macedonians could exploit for their campaigns ahead. The Phoenicians, for example, were among the greatest seamen of their time, and Phoenician naval architects, shipbuilders, and sailors would equip Alexander with a much-needed capability. Egypt represented a very different win. According to the Egyptians, whosoever conquered Egypt was designated pharaoh, and importantly, "Son of God," and was therefore viewed as possessing divine powers—a useful designation for any conqueror because it was sure to encourage his troops and instill fear in his enemies.

Planned Globalization

Alexander's geographic expansion policy followed a precise, systematic pattern, even though it often appears to many historians as nonlinear, convoluted, and overly complex. Wherever Alexander went, he did so with extensive preparation. It was therefore not surprising that he often got drawn into long entanglements, even though he hated them—like the seven-month siege of Tyre to dismantle the Phoenician fleet.

In a speech he gave before leading his army down the Mediterranean coast, he laid out the choices his forces faced: They could chase Darius now (last seen galloping toward Babylon) and end the Persian threat once and for all; or, they could invade Phoenicia and Egypt and thereby ensure that those two powerful nations, under Persian control, would not make a run on Greece, while they were deep within Asia chasing Darius later. The Spartans had already been preparing for a war with Macedonia and all of Greece under Macedonian control, and it would be easy for the Persians to cobble together a force from the navies of these two powerful nations and launch an attack on Greece in alliance with the Spartans. Moreover, Athens' loyalty to Macedonia, which was derived from fear rather than goodwill, couldn't be counted on to thwart a joint Persian-Spartan war.

As long as Egypt and Phoenicia were under Macedonian rule, Alexander realized, there would be no threat of an attack from the sea on Greece. Moreover, the Macedonians' reputations as warriors would be greatly bolstered if they subdued the Egyptians and Phoenicians; both had a reputation for military prowess, which could make the invasion of inner Persia easier.

The Macedonians needed a beachhead to expand into Phoenicia and Egypt. Although there were smaller towns like Sidon, which surrendered to the Macedonians as soon as they had arrived at the town gates, Tyre was the prize of Phoenicia. Tyre was a perfect beachhead because it was the center of Phoenician naval architecture and warfare, and the gateway to the dense forests of Phoenicia and Assyria. The Macedonians needed to augment their capabilities in naval architecture and warfare, and they needed timber to build a formidable Macedonian fleet. Moreover, Tyre had well-developed ports, which could facilitate the transport of the timber into Egypt, where the Macedonians planned a naval base from which to control the southern Mediterranean; Egypt had no forests.

East India Company:
Traders, Drug Runners, and Empire Builders

Alexander planned to use Tyre as a base for further expansion into Phoenicia (today's Lebanon and Syria) and Egypt, and consequently Libya and other parts of Africa. Similarly, in business, companies are encouraged to identify a compelling beachhead — "a customer segment that has the most compelling need for the firm's offering and can serve as a base for expansion into related segments and application markets," according to Northwestern University Kellogg Graduate School of Management professor Mohanbir Sawhney. Sawhney believes that "a good beachhead should offer connectivity and access to rich territory beyond," and not be an island like Hawaii, which offers little potential for further expansion.[1]

No company had thought about and exploited a beachhead as much as the English East India Company did in the seventeenth, eighteenth, and nineteenth centuries. No other company, either, had the longevity or the all-encompassing hold over its market that the East India Company did. Finally, no other company has had as much influence on modern-day corporate management as this company: it was the first entity to organize its corporate governance system in the form of directors, with fiduciary responsibility, who were elected by and reported to the shareholders of the company. It has, not surprisingly, been the model on which even today's U.S. and British corporate governance systems — of professional managers overseen by a board of directors elected by the shareholders — are based.

The company's beginnings go back to December 31, 1599, when Queen Elizabeth I granted a newly formed company, representing a group of London merchants and shippers, exclusive rights to all trade with India and Southeast Asia. Elizabeth believed that the new century would bring vast riches from the East to the island nation. England had pretty much been locked out of the East but now, only a decade since the defeat of the Spanish Armada, had asserted itself as possessing the mightiest naval force in the world. Trade with the East was a natural consequence of England's exploiting that strength for commercial purpose.

Early on, the focus of the company was on the spice trade with the East, which was largely dominated by the Portuguese. Vasco da Gama had discovered the sea route to India from Europe (around the Cape of Good Hope), and the Portuguese had exploited that discovery by being the first to establish trade links with India and the Far East. The Dutch had followed the Portuguese, and the two European colonists had a virtual lock on the trade.

The East India Company's early forays into the spice trade were met with intense competition, price rigging, and even violence—Dutch traders once set fire to an English ship in Indonesia with its human and commercial cargo all on board, forcing the British to bow out of the Far East spice trade altogether and focus on India.

The traders arrived in India with the desire to sell British broadcloth, the main British export item in those days, but found few takers for the inferior cotton from its mills in Manchester. The Indian cotton industry was already well developed, and, although homespun, Indians had become used to wearing much higher grades of cotton than was being offered by the British traders. On the other hand, the traders found that there was huge demand for Indian cotton and silk fabrics back home in England. So although they had approached India as a consumer base for British products, it didn't take long for the East India Company to realize that India was a much more profitable supplier of goods like paisley shawls, floral chintzes, and cotton shirts and dresses that commanded a premium in Britain.

By 1612 the East India Company had set up a textile factory in the western port city of Surat (in today's Gujarat state), situated near the Arabian Sea. Surat, derived from the Urdu Bunder-e-Khubsoorat ("The Beautiful Port"), was a major trading post of the Mughals who then ruled India. Using Surat as the beachhead, representatives of the East India Company ventured inland into India. They made frequent, gift-laden appearances at the Mughal court in Delhi of Emperor Jehangir, and endeared themselves to him. One company functionary, Captain William Hawkins, even succeeded in impressing Jehangir with his hard-drinking habit. Jehangir, an alcoholic, gave Hawkins temporary command of one of his cavalry units.

While Surat was exceptionally well placed for commerce with Indian traders and merchants on the West Coast of India, as well as with the Arabian and Persian merchants who came across the Arabian Sea to trade here, the city didn't quite deliver access to the vast untapped vistas of India.

So the East India Company focused on securing more trading posts. Their next three were built in the large port cities of Madras (today's

Chennai) in the south, in 1641; Bombay (today's Mumbai), which they leased from British monarch Charles II in 1688 for ten pounds sterling a year; and Calcutta (today's Kolkata) in eastern India, in 1699. Like Alexander the Great the East India Company had all shipping routes covered. Of these Calcutta, the capital city of the richest Indian province of Bengal, was the most important. Moreover, now almost a hundred years after its founding, the East India Company wanted political control over its market. Trade alone wasn't enough to assure the profit growth its English shareholders were expecting.

The East India Company had started to raise an army, which it financed from the outlandish profits it made buying low and selling high. The army it raised, ostensibly to protect its factories, ships, and warehouses, became so big that by the time the company built its trading post in Calcutta, it rivaled the British army in terms of size and manpower.[2] It was a vicious army too: When weavers working for Indian traders refused to weave cotton for the company, the army chopped off the thumbs of the factory workers. To ensure they fully controlled the entire market for raw materials, the army destroyed warehouses and factories of Indian traders and ran them out of business.

About the time the company was establishing itself in Calcutta, Britons were expressing an almost insatiable desire for tea. In Calcutta the company had vastly enlarged its presence in tea, since Calcutta was only a few hundred miles from two of the world's greatest sources of the crop—Assam and Darjeeling. But Indian tea wasn't enough to satisfy thirst in Britain. So using Calcutta as a base, the company used its muscle to pry open some of the old trade routes that it had been locked out of earlier—especially China, which was the other major producer of tea. Demand for tea was so high that almost 5 million tons of it were imported into England every year from India and China. Tea was used to conquer and control Britain's newer colonies, stretching from the Americas to Asia, and was viewed by the colonists as a tool of oppression. "That obnoxious commodity" was how Thomas Jefferson described tea, when shiploads of it arrived in Boston harbor. "The worst of plagues, the detested tea," was how patriots in Massachusetts labeled tea from the East India Company before a group of them, led by Samuel Adams, with active participation from Paul Revere, their faces blackened, dunked ninety thousand pounds of it into Boston harbor—a crucial event in the history of American independence, aptly named "the Boston Tea Party."

The East India Company paid for everything it bought in silver, because that was the only currency Indian and Chinese merchants were willing to accept. When there wasn't enough silver to buy all the tea needed back in Britain, the company pushed ahead with its plans for territorial domination in India and entry into the opium trade in China. In 1757 a midlevel officer of the company, Robert Clive, defeated the army of a Mughal prince, Siraj-ud-Daula, at the Battle of Plassey (1757), only one hundred miles outside of Calcutta. Other small princely states fell under the company's military onslaughts.

Now that it was in political control of parts of India, the East India Company would no more need to ship silver from its vaults in London to buy cotton in Surat or tea in Calcutta—tax revenues from its Indian domination sufficed. Over half of the British government's total expenditure of £7 million sterling was paid for by taxes collected in India. To finance the China trade it entered opium cultivation. Opium was raised in India and shipped to China in exchange for tea. By the nineteenth century the opium trade had become so big that the British navy escorted merchant ships of the East India Company carrying opium to China. Because the Chinese emperor had banned the use of opium, the ships dropped anchor in the South China Sea, from where drug runners carried the contraband inland—the largest government-sponsored drug ring ever.

With the company's success came arrogance in its managers. The company's approach had been to expand at any cost, including bribery, torture, and murder, and some of its ways began to rub off in its inner workings as well. Its top managers were frequently charged with corruption, and leaders like Clive were brought back to England to stand trial. In 1857 after a massive rebellion among the Indians in the army (called the Sepoy Mutiny), the British crown was forced to step in and take possession of the territories under the company's control. That was the beginning of the Raj and, with it, a new history of colonial plunder. In 1873 the company shuttered its doors forever.

Just as Alexander had used ports of Phoenicia from which to launch his naval operations and the people and the forests of Phoenicia to design and build his ever-enlarging fleet, the East India Company, too, had used India to stage its global commercial operations, and through it brought about, as Edmund Burke wrote in 1769, the notion of a political system largely dominated by the "principle of commerce." But the corruption it unleashed and "the disdain for the individuals who were affected by their policies,"[3] brought about its fall.

The Siege of Tyre

The siege of the Phoenician city of Tyre began in midwinter, 333 B.C. and lasted seven months. Alexander's siege of Tyre is considered the greatest siege in history; only Napoleon's command of the artillery guns in the siege of Toulon against the British navy and that of Russian defenders of the city of Stalingrad against the invading Germans in the Second World War come close. At Toulon and at Stalingrad the defenders successfully pushed back the attackers; Tyre remains the greatest offensive siege. Every generation of military generals studies the siege because it shows conclusively that no amount of physical fortifications can ever defend against a determined enemy.

Tyre was the finest and strongest naval base of the invincible (till they encountered Alexander) Phoenician navy, situated on an island two miles long and a little less wide, defended all around by the sea and a towering wall. The Phoenicians had built the new city of Tyre as an impregnable fortress. The Tyrians were famous mariners of the ancient world and, besides their bravery and success at sea, were known for their prowess at resisting sieges. The old city, on the mainland, had withstood a siege from a Persian general for thirteen years. The new city was built even more strongly than the old, and was equipped to withstand almost every kind or duration of siege possible in those days.

When the Macedonians neared Tyre, the Tyrians offered to surrender to them as long as they promised not to set foot inside their island fortress. The condition was unacceptable to Alexander, even though that was precisely the accommodation the Persians had reached with the Tyrians. Alexander wanted to pray and offer a sacrifice at the temple of the Tyrian Heracles. Because Tyrian custom held that only their king could offer a sacrifice, permitting Alexander to pray would have been tantamount to capitulation.

With virtually no ships, having destroyed all those he had sailed on to cross the Hellespont, Alexander launched the siege. He set out to build a causeway from the mainland (old Tyre), situated half a mile from the island. This would be his primary means of access to the fortified city. The Tyrians thought that he was out of his mind. Tyrian sailors aboard their ships would sail by the workers building the causeway and berate them for foolishly thinking that they could ever get the better of Poseidon— the Greek god of the sea. The Macedonian soldiers, together with every available worker they could find, kept building their two-hundred-foot-wide causeway. Waves from the Mediterranean, reinforced by southwestern winds, lashed and destroyed the work on most days. But the men persevered and threw entire trees around the causeway to still the sea. The more the attrition of their causeway, the deeper the Macedonians pushed piles into the bottom of the sea, reinforced with stones and wood from the old city.

After several months, as the causeway approached the island, the work became more precarious and difficult, partly because the water near the island was very deep, but mostly because the Tyrians used every possible method to literally sink the Macedonians' efforts: They sent divers to undermine the causeway at night; they sent ships armed with catapults, slingshots, and archers to harass the workmen; and they attacked from atop the ramparts of their walled city with boulders, firebombs, even boiling oil. In some ways they were practicing the ancient equivalent of Napoleon's artillery shelling at Toulon. To defend the French city against the British siege, Napoleon had all the artillery guns moved to the top of a cliff overlooking the harbor, from where artillery barrages rained down on the British ships. The Tyrians were also brutal to any prisoners they took. One captured shipload of Greek and Macedonian seamen were slaughtered on the ramparts of their fortress, and their bodies tossed into the raging sea.[4]

Alexander built two towers at the end of the causeway to keep the Tyrians at bay. But one day, with a wind behind their back, the Tyrians loaded a ship with twigs, sulphur, naphtha, and other combustibles and sailed it out toward the causeway. Sailors aboard the ship set it on fire and swam back to the safety of their walled city. The fire destroyed the towers, siege engines that had been built, and finally the causeway cracked below the smoldering top and was washed away. It took less than an hour to destroy the work of months.

Alexander immediately ordered the construction of a bigger causeway—twice the size of the one that had been destroyed, so he could put up many more towers to defend his workers. He also realized that he needed to wrest control of the seas from the Tyrians. Like business organizations that either build up their local organizations or ally with established local companies to realize their global aspirations, Alexander, with the objective of building up his fleet in Tyre, took a small contingent of his army and rode to the Phoenician port of Sidon. The city had previously surrendered to him, and he took command of eighty triremes that were berthed there.

The king of Cyprus, watching which way power in the Mediterranean was shifting, also sent in his fleet of 120 ships. Rhodes followed suit as well. Soon Alexander returned to Tyre with a fleet three times the size of Tyre's. He equipped these ships with missile launchers, rams, ballistas, and bridges for landing. Although most of these engines were ineffective against the 150-foot walls of the fortifications, they gave the Tyrian ships a run for their money. Even though he was a relative neophyte at warfare at sea, Alexander's audacity helped him win. In naval warfare he practiced what would be known, almost 2,100 years later, as the Nelsonian doctrine: "that no sea captain could go very far wrong by landing his ship alongside his enemy's." The triremes created the expected havoc. Tyrian ships either sank or quickly retreated toward their harbor.

The Tyrians, from atop the relative safety of the vertiginously high ramparts, witnessed their ships sinking or surrendering to the Macedonians. It was only a matter of time before Tyre fell. The 30,000-man Tyrian garrison surrendered to the Macedonians, but not before waging an intense battle in which 8,000 Tyrians were killed, 15,000 were spirited away to safety by the Sidonians (Tyre's neighbors, who had thrown in their lot with the Macedonians), and the rest were sold into slavery. Alexander's causeway between old and new Tyre turned the land into a peninsula, as which modern-day Tyre exists today and prospers.

Siege Mentality

The long history of physical fortifications—from Tyre, the Great Wall of China, and the Roman Hadrian's Wall that cuts across the northern parts of the British Isles, to relatively modern fortifications like the Berlin Wall—suggests that walls do nothing but temporarily—and only temporarily—keep outsiders out, but more insidiously, insiders locked in. Often, these fortifications can also reside in people's minds; as fundamentalist Islamic movements have tried to create mental walls to prevent any western cultural influence on their followers' minds or as even forward-thinking, developed nations like France have done the same, trying to block the influence of Hollywood and American fast foods on that nation's citizens.

An interesting example of the futility of fortifications, physical and mental, is witnessed in the way Quebec, the largest province in Canada—the world's second largest nation—has tried to prevent physical and intellectual encroachments through fortifications. Quebec was the first part of

North America to be settled by Europeans. In the early seventeenth century French explorers like Jacques Cartier and Samuel de Champlain systematically mapped the region, and many settlers from northern France moved to the vast vistas of the province to settle down—those who could brave the province's freezing cold winters. In 1763 the French lost the Seven Years' War to the British for domination of the region, and most French settlers who could packed up their bags and moved back to Normandy, from where they or their forefathers had come; the less economically fortunate remained and, as the British conquered the territories, came under the subjugation of mostly Scots who settled here.

The Battle of Quebec was the pivotal battle of that war, wherein, after a long siege of Quebec City, the only walled—and like Tyre, considered invincible—city in North America, a 4,500-strong British contingent under the leadership of Major General James Wolfe climbed the 350-foot-high, almost vertical cliff that separated the fortified city from the waters of the St. Charles and the St. Lawrence rivers below. Early morning, when they were spotted on the Plains of Abraham, the French, under the leadership of the marquis de Montcalm, instead of staying in their citadel, at one end of the walled city, and awaiting the arrival of reinforcements, which were less than ten miles away, decided to engage immediately. In less than thirty minutes Quebec City fell to the British and one of the two greatest sieges in North America—the other being Union general Ulysses S. Grant's successful siege of Vicksburg in the U.S. Civil War—ended.

The domination of English language and culture over their French has continued, since their defeat at the Battle of Quebec 250 years ago, to be a deep problem for Canada's 7 million French-speaking population—most of whom live in Quebec. For generations the French-speaking Quebecois felt, and indeed were, oppressed—surveys have revealed that in the early 1960s a French-speaking worker in Montreal earned a third less than an English-speaking one. But between 1960 and 1975 Quebec witnessed what is termed the "Quiet Revolution," which not only brought about economic parity but also in its wake created a breed of French-speaking professionals, artists, and businessmen, who brought a sense of joy and pride to the region.

Along with the new sense of identity, however, came an unmitigated sense of political and linguistic righteousness. The secessionist Bloc Quebecois came to power in 1976, and, with it, the imposition of French as the official language of Quebec, and the policing of all labels, signs, and instructions in French against any foreign-language incursions. Even recent immigrants into the region are forced to quickly study the language, because in Quebec it's either the Quebecois way or the highway.

Today Quebec's Office de la Langue Française polices the usage of the French language throughout the province. No exceptions are allowed. In 1996 the Jewish residents of the province were especially infuriated over what is now described as the "Matzogate" affair, when an overzealous language inspector disallowed the entry of kosher matzos—for the Jewish Passover—into Montreal because the labels on the boxes were in English.

Quebecois French, its usage and its imposition, has become the tall, Tyrian fortress wall behind which stands a people resistant to change. Unlike French in the mother country, which continues to grow by leaps and bounds—though appropriately moderated by the French Academie de la Langue Française—Quebecois French has been stuck at the same place where it stood when the first French settlers arrived. The language has unfortunately become not one for communicating or interacting with the outside world, but a means of sealing out the world's winds of change, and its cultural and linguistic influences.

Quebecois French's protectionist practices might well lead it to the same moribund state in which Walloon, a French dialect spoken in southern Belgium, has found itself. The fall of the fortress isn't far. As Alexander believed, all that is needed to bring a fortress down is to concentrate one's forces at one point—as soon as the wall is breached there, the rest crumbles like a sand castle. Quebec grapples with several religious and social forces: climbing divorce rates and abortions, rapidly declining church attendance, and a withering away of its people's attachment to age-old traditions. All these will certainly contrive to stall Quebec's quest for independence. One among these forces could bring the fortress down.

Encouraging Multiculturalism

Alexander allowed the cultures and social mores in the nations he conquered to flourish alongside the Macedonian or Greek cultures and mores. A few months after Tyre, and about a year after his victory at Issus, Alexander arrived by road in Egypt; all his baggage, siege engines, and several thousand of his troops were sent by sea in the recently acquired naval fleet. The Persians had only recently conquered Egypt. Alexander felt that he wouldn't face much resistance there, much of the Persian garrison having surrendered or been killed at Issus. Indeed, Egypt, the richest nation on the southern Mediterranean, surrendered to his forces without loss of a single person.

As he went through Egypt, he was careful not to offend the spiritual sensibilities of the Egyptians. At Memphis, the religious center of Egypt, he made a sacrifice to the most venerated of Egyptian gods, Apis, who takes the form of a bull sacred to the Egyptians, as well as other gods like Isis and Ra. Alexander took pains to ensure that his sacrifice was in keeping with the rites sacred to the Egyptians. After the religious sacrifices he staged equestrian, gymnastics, and musical contests in which Greeks and Egyptians both participated. Alexander's approach was distinctly different from that of the conquering Persians. The Persians had desecrated Egyptian temples and found every way to insult them—for example, knowing full well that the bull was a religious symbol for the Egyptians, they sacrificed bulls to intentionally humiliate them.

In response to Alexander's respect and honor, priests at the most important Egyptian temples addressed him as pharaoh (although whosoever conquered Egypt automatically received that title, to be addressed and respected as such by the influential Egyptian high priests was quite another matter). Hieroglyphic inscriptions also reveal they attached a further explanation to the pharaoh title: "He who hath laid hands on the lands of the foreigners."[5] This suggests they even accepted him as one of their own deities and an incarnation of their greatest gods.

Sailing down the Nile, toward the delta, Alexander saw a large stretch of land rising above the delta and the Mediterranean beyond. This is where he decided to build a vast city that would be the center of naval operations—defense and merchant—and be the center of art, culture, and education. He called the city Alexandria, the first of about eighty cities that he would either build or inspire the building of during his reign (twenty of them would be called Alexandria)—though some historians contend that *he* genuinely didn't build more than about a dozen.[6] Borrowing barley from the supplies of his troops, he rode around this stretch of land marking the city's outer limits.

He designed the city with wide-open avenues, canals, and waterways. He had a deep interest in reading, and always carried Aristotle's personal copy of *The Iliad,* from which he read a few pages every night. At Alexandria he decided that he would share his love for reading with others and conceived of creating—as Benjamin Franklin would do in eighteenth-century America—the first public library. He even conceived of the first museum that humankind had ever known. Although both the library and the museum msteriously disappeared many centuries ago, their collections helped maintain literary and artistic connections with the ancient world. By the time Alexander's successor in Egypt, Ptolemy, actually built the library, it was found that many distinguished works of prose had already permanently disappeared from human memory (reading aloud and committing to memory was the customary way that such works got passed around and were transmitted from generation to generation). At least a dozen of Euripides' plays, for example, had already gone missing, less than two hundred years after his death.

The Ptolemaic emperors were determined to make Alexander's dreams for a great library come true. The collection in Alexandria's library, in a few generations, had surpassed five hundred thousand books. Any visitor to Alexandria was required by the Ptolemies to deposit his books at the library, in return for which he received a certificate for their deposit with the royal seal on it. The book was copied, then visitors were given their books back before they departed Alexandria. Ptolemy III (grandson of the first Ptolemy) was also reputed to have run a vast borrowing scheme with the main library in Athens, which had recently been set up, modeled after the one in Alexandria. He paid a handsome sum of money for the privilege of borrowing a book for the purposes of making an exact copy. The originals of the books he borrowed were never returned to Athens—the copies were. Athens was in such disarray that no one bothered to check whether they were receiving back their originals or facsimiles.

The library had real impact. For example, Euclid, who lived during the era of the first Ptolemy, used the books on geometry collected at the library to synthesize the first treatise on the subject called *Elements*. Modern geometry traces its roots to Euclidean geometry. Because of their interest in reading and collecting, the Ptolemies also had the Torah translated into Greek. This translation is believed to have been much closer to the original than surviving Hebrew texts, because the version it was translated from not only predated the oldest Hebrew text that survives today but also was synthesized from the various versions of the holy book in existence then. No one knows when the library was destroyed—some archeologists claim that it happened when Julius Caesar invaded Egypt and accidentally set fire to the library; others contend it happened during the reign of one of the caliphs who ruled over Alexandria in the fifteenth century. Suffice it to say, the search for the ruins of the library continues.

Macedonians and Greeks were invited to come settle in Alexandria, but the interests of the local Egyptian population were protected as well. Alexander decreed the Egyptians free to practice their religious and social customs and adhere to their established forms of political governance. Finally, laws continued to be written and administered through the long-standing Egyptian judicial system. Alongside that, Alexander conceived of—and Ptolemy created—a Greek assembly, appointed Greek magistrates, and established a democratic system through which the foreign and military affairs of the state—closely coordinated with the Egyptian judicial system—were conducted.

Alexander understood the unprecedented nature of the political system he was trying to build. Eschewing the highly regimented pyramid structure of governance in place in Egypt, with serried ranks of Persian civil servants, he developed an innovative structure that protected the interests of the Egyptian inhabitants and the foreigners who arrived there, as well as the empire's security requirements. He asked the two Egyptian governors who ran Upper and Lower Egypt before the Persians had invaded Egypt to come back to their jobs. He appointed two Greek governors to the outlying and sparsely populated areas of Egypt, in what would be today's Libya and the western end of Saudi Arabia (along the Gulf of Suez). Two Macedonian generals, commanding 4,000 troops, and an admiral with 30 triremes protecting the approach to the Nile, were all the defense force he left behind. All seven reported directly to him.[7]

Alexandria today is a large city of close to four million people, and a center of trade and maritime commerce (out of the same harbors that Alexander built). Over the centuries the cosmopolitan and pluralistic nature of Alexandria has attracted traders, scholars, and artists from all over the world, and there still exist the Egyptian, Greek, Italian, and Jewish enclaves. Although Egypt's nationalist fervors in the sixties, led by its charismatic President Gamal Abdul Nasser, witnessed the exodus of many of Alexandria's nonnative Egyptian residents, the city even today continues to be a thriving international center with a healthy cosmopolitan mix—though physically exhibits all the characteristics of a "dump."

Global Approach, Local Opportunities

Globalization as a trend isn't new: In 200 A.D. northern Britons were walking around in shoes cobbled in Rome; in the 1340s the entire Florentine banking infrastructure was almost ruined by defaults on loans made to the

British monarchs; and in the early nineteenth century ice makers in Cambridge, Massachusetts, shipped ice from frozen ponds and lakes in New England to Europe, Africa, and Asia as far as Calcutta. Almost 150 years ago American companies such as gunmaker Colt and sewing-machine maker Singer opened factories in England to supply their local customers. And yet, after such a long record and experience with globalization, why do some of the world's leading global companies still have difficulty succeeding, while relative neophytes at globalization like Alexander the Great created dominions that lasted for several hundred years? The answer may be in many business organizations' lack of understanding of their local markets.

Unlike Alexander's organizational structure, whereby local Egyptians governed their local populations, global companies are often saddled with large Soviet-style bureaucracies, which can be woefully out of touch with local demands and tastes. Country managers of soft-drink makers complain of wanting to introduce a new product in, say, Brazil, and waiting for a decision back home in New York or Chicago from someone who has never been to Brazil. In the early 1980s Nestlé's glass-and-chrome headquarters overlooking Lake Geneva in Vevey, Switzerland, was mockingly described as "the Vatican." Country managers complained of three levels of managerial clearance from headquarters before even a press release could be issued. Thankfully that has all changed and Nestlé occupies its rightful place as a preeminent global company. "There is a popular misconception among managers," wrote Gurcharan Das, the former CEO of Proctor & Gamble India, "that you merely need to start with a brand name, create a standardized product, packaging, and advertising, push a button, and bingo—you are on the way to capturing global markets."[8] Even today few global companies really seek to understand their local customers, build and market products that cater to local tastes, and learn from their local successes to, in turn, build global brands.

In recent years some companies seem to be scoring a few successes, but only when they take special effort. A senior manager at Kraft said that it was imperative for everyone in her group to get out into the real world and find out about consumer tastes. Describing how she once took all the people in her business into the Spanish and Asian enclaves of Los Angeles, she explained. "We took the most Connecticut-type people and dumped them in the middle of a Spanish bodega and said, 'See what you can find.' They came up with great ideas—ideas that will be part of our business plan next year."[9] It is this type of local experience that leads McDonald's to introduce gazpacho in Spain and lamb burgers in India.

Similarly, when the Honda Accord went through a massive redesign in the mid and late eighties, Honda engineers were sent out to U.S. shopping malls to scour the parking lots and watch how Americans placed shopping in their trunks. Out of that came Honda's innovative redesign of its trunk whereby shoppers didn't have to bend over the trunk to place their shopping in—but could slide it in. Not surprisingly, the Accord emerged as the one of the most—in some years, the most—popular car in the United States.

Companies often fail to understand local sensibilities and possible reactions before entering a new geographic market. Even giant retailer Wal-Mart, which is legendary for its business successes, was misinformed about the backlash it would receive when it moved into Germany, a nation renowned for protecting its small shopkeepers. When Wal-Mart started offering its low prices to consumers, and was matched in its pricing by German retailing giants Aldi Nord and Lidl Markets, the German cartel office stepped in and forced all three to raise prices for fear they might run the small shopkeepers in Germany's towns and villages—the backbone of Germany's domestic economic muscle—out of business.

Companies lack an understanding of their markets partly from not having a sizable number of local managers or decision makers to influence the steps that a multinational company needs to take in a specific local situation, and partly from not knowing how even to begin to recruit such managers. In that regard it isn't surprising that Unilever is among the world's most successful globalizers. As far back as in the 1940s the British-Dutch consumer-goods giant started attracting local talent to replace British and Dutch managers. And train them together. So successful has Unilever been with global expansion that some of its country subsidiaries, like Hindustan Lever in India, are identified as local companies rather than local subsidiaries of a global company.

Achieving local status didn't come easy. Unilever took a long-term view to its commitment to India by building brands targeted at Indian consumers. It invested in understanding its consumers in a fashion that even the Indian government doesn't understand its citizens. Many observers of the Indian consumer market believe that Hindustan Lever has a deeper understanding of the economic makeup of consumers even in the remotest villages of India than what the Indian census provides. It knows the buying power, the buying habits, the tastes, and, most important, ways to reach these consumers much better than any private or public entity in India. Its distribution system in India through trucks, rails, planes, automobiles, boats, rickshaws, cycles, and even plain human feet is the most sophisticated of any company—and it can deliver anything it wants to the remotest part of India with absolute confidence that it will have reached the consumers it was designed to reach.

The company, which is one of the leading companies in market capitalization in the Indian stock market, not only understands, for example, that a certain type of shampoo is in demand but packages that shampoo in various sizes of bottles as well as one-time-use plastic satchels because the buying power of some Indian consumers prevents buying the shampoo in sizes larger than for a one-time use. Being local has another major advantage: In the mid 1970s, when a nationalist fervor saw the ejection from India of such large U.S. multinationals as IBM and Coca-Cola, Hindustan Lever, because of its local orientation, wasn't even considered for ejection. Hindustan Lever is no stepchild within the Unilever constellation either; for decades the head of Hindustan Lever has occupied a board position in Unilever's global board, and managers from the Indian subsidiary are constantly provided global opportunities to grow and develop, just as managers from Unilever's non-India country organizations are often sent to India on short-and long-term assignments. Like Alexander's global expansion strategy, which was to bring the best of what Greece and Macedonia had to offer but protect the best of the nation he was in, Unilever has managed to strike the right balance between being global, while simultaneously being local.

Decentralization Wins

A decentralized form of organizational structure didn't find its way into U.S. business until the 1920s, led by Alfred P. Sloan's efforts at General Motors, and it wasn't until the 1950s that it became the prevalent way that companies such as General Motors, Dupont, and General Electric managed themselves. But decentralization thrived under Alexander the Great and would reach its paragon in the administration of the Roman empire, especially under Julius Caesar. Decentralized decision-making was the only way Alexander could control and manage his vast empire.

On the other hand, the end of the more than two-century-old Persian Achaemenid empire can be traced directly to the lack of decentralized decision-making. In the two years since his defeat at Issus, Darius had recruited the largest army that the Persians ever had. He cast a wide net for recruits, going as far as today's Pakistan, Afghanistan, Turkmenistan, Kazakhstan, Syria, Iraq, and Iran. As at Issus, his most experienced fighters were the well-trained and experienced Greek mercenaries. Conservative estimates put the number of the infantry in the new army at 200,000 (though some estimates have ranged up to a million) and 40,000 cavalry.

Darius introduced many innovations into the Persian army after Issus. He armed his cavalry with lances instead of javelins; and he replaced the Persian scimitar, which was designed for close, hand-to-hand combat, with a long sword. He equipped chariots with sharp blades or scythes on their sides and yoke. Launched at high speed, the chariots, pulled by two or four horses, were capable of slicing through infantry or cavalry ranks like a hot knife through butter. Each one of the national contingents was titularly headed — not led — by the Persian satrap (the governor) of the region.

Unfortunately, Darius made all decisions about *where* to engage the enemy and *how* to fight them. He alone considered the various options: Should he, for example, draw Alexander and his troops farther east into Persia and engage them on familiar terrain; should he follow a scorched-earth policy, and starve the enemy; should he engage the Macedonians across one of the two fast-flowing rivers that ran through the region where they were playing cat and mouse—the Tigris and the Euphrates; or should he just await Alexander's arrival in Babylon? These were issues that Darius wrestled with alone. Darius alone decided even issues of tactical minutiae such as how many horses should pull a chariot or when a division should engage the enemy.

Darius's centralized decision-making system would be the cause of the rout of the Persian army at Gaugamela, and of the end of the 227-year reign of the Persian Achaemenid empire founded by Cyrus the Great in 558 B.C. The unfortunate outcome of Darius making all strategic and tactical decisions by himself was that, while he was determined *not* to make any of the mistakes of the Battle of Issus, there was no one around to challenge him or persuade him to look for disconfirming evidence.

With his work done in Egypt, Alexander set off in spring 331 B.C. toward the ancient city of Babylon, situated about fifty-five miles south of today's Baghdad, Iraq. Babylon was the largest and, according to historians such as Herodotus, the most splendid city in the world. Its hanging gardens were considered by the ancients to be one of the Seven Wonders. It was a trading city, cut by the River Euphrates, which flowed right through it (the river has since changed course).

Lined along the river were quays for merchant ships to anchor and warehouses to store their inventory. The great temple of Marduk was the centerpiece of the city, laid out on a vast circular base with towers built in stages each stepped back from the one beneath it. According to myth the gods stopped this complex and ambitious construction by confusing the language of the workers so much that they couldn't comprehend one another.[10] This was the inspiration behind the Tower of Babel of Genesis 11:1–9, "with its top in the heavens."

Alexander continued his march toward Babylon with the fast-flowing Tigris on his right. (The Tigris and the Euphrates are almost similar in length and importance in West Asia as the Mississippi and the Missouri Rivers are in the U.S.) He learned from captured Persian scouts that the Persians were massing on the right bank. Crossing the Tigris, four feet deep and with severe currents, posed a challenge. He stationed a line of horses up the river to break the strong current, and another line down the river to catch any soldier who might be swept away. He constructed a makeshift bridge with wooden piles to ferry across supplies and siege engines.

Mazaeus, a very senior general in Darius' army, was given 3,000 cavalry (2,000 Greek mercenaries and 1,000 Persian infantry) and specifically instructed to attack the Macedonians if they tried a crossing of either the Tigris or the Euphrates. Those were the specific instructions given to him—attack if they tried a river crossing. Twice Mazaeus found wooden piles driven into the rivers to hold makeshift bridges to facilitate a crossing, but because he didn't see any Macedonian trying to cross the river, he had to await instructions from Darius as to what to do next. Even though he was a general, he had no authority to destroy the pilings to thwart a possible crossing. In business this is called the "principal-agent problem," which Michael Jensen and others have long identified as a core problem afflicting organizations: How does an owner make an employee operate in the owner's interest?

Darius' solution to the "principal-agent problem" was to hoard all decision-making himself. He wouldn't trust anyone, including his generals, to act in ways that would further the objectives of the Persian empire. It is amazing how even almost 2,500 years after these events the issue of whether a local manager or general has power to exercise authority and act upon an opportunity that has presented itself in the interests of the owner of the business continues to be a deeply intractable one in the annals of management. When Arthur Sulzberger Jr. became the publisher of *The New York Times* in 1992, he held a series of retreats to suggest to his managers what he expected of them. "Any executive or manager has only two drawers in his desk," Sulzberger was quoted as saying, "One says 'centralize' and the other says 'decentralize.'"[11] There are no other drawers, Sulzberger is said to have elaborated. It was up to the managers to choose which was the style most appropriate to them in which situations, but once chosen they needed to stick by their choice or run the risk of hindering their direct-reports' ability to make critical decisions. Some historians still maintain that the reason why Vietnam turned into such a quagmire for the U.S. was that President Lyndon Johnson had chosen the "centralize" drawer to the extent of choosing specific sites for aerial bombing and fretting all night whether the operation had been executed well—rather than relying on his ground commanders to select and execute such specifics. Johnson, like Darius, wouldn't trust his generals to make the most effective decision.

Alexander, aware that the drawer the Persians always opened was the one marked "centralize," exploited the Persians' decision-making approach to cross the river. Macedonians engineers would therefore exploit Mazaeus' inability to do anything about the pilings in the water to full extent. They would hammer in piles at various points in the river to confuse the enemy as to exactly where they intended to make the crossing. Then they would suddenly appear at a point on the river, lay down wooden planks over the piles to serve as a bridge, and before the Persian command structure was able to send a message to its commander at the site, the entire Macedonian army—men, machines, and horses—would cross over.

A great example of the tyranny of centralized decision-making can be witnessed in the exploits of the great Carthaginian general Hannibal. Approximately a century after these events in Persia, Hannibal was defeated in a famous naval battle—Rome's first naval victory, the Battle of Mylae. Hannibal had entered the battle because he thought he had a chance to sink the Roman navy, which he had spotted. If he had to await a decision from the senate back in Carthage about whether and how he ought to exploit the opportunity that had presented itself, it would be lost. Carthage, like Persia, subscribed to centralized decision-making, whereby all major decisions lay in the hands of its democratically elected senate, who were convinced that they, rather than the field commanders, were the only people who could make decisions in the best interest of Carthage. Unfortunately for Hannibal the gamble he took to engage cost him his entire fleet.

Hannibal, fearing reprisal from his fellow Carthaginian citizens, therefore, sent a deputy back to Carthage to tell the senate that he had been dispatched by Hannibal who inquired whether he, with two hundred Carthaginian ships under his command, should engage a Roman fleet of one hundred and twenty ships? The senators rubbed their hands in glee and urged Hannibal to immediately engage the Romans.

Hannibal's deputy went on to inform the senate, "Very well. That is just why Hannibal fought. Unfortunately, we have been beaten. But since you commanded it, he is relieved of the blame."[12] The victory of the Battle of Mylae was especially rejoiced over in Rome because the Carthaginians, who so far had commanded the seas, had suggested to the Romans that given their primitive knowledge of seafaring they should not dare to even wash their hands in the sea. The Romans, for their part, had warned the Carthaginians that they had a record as pupils of always getting the better of their teachers.[13] At Mylae they certainly proved that they were better learners of seafaring than the Carthaginians were teachers.

The Battle of Gaugamela

To stop Alexander's advance into Babylon, Darius' army of 200,000 infantry-men and 40,000 cavalry awaited Alexander's arrival on the plains of Gaugamela on the night of September 30, 331 B.C. Far into the Kurdish countryside smoke billowed from villages and fields, which Darius' army had set afire to deny Alexander supplies. The Macedonians were well rested, having relaxed for four days before arriving on these sweltering plains.

Alexander's scouts had apprised him of the three fairways that Darius had built on the plains to afford his cavalry and chariots even ground to maneuver. Darius had been told that the only reason he lost at Issus was because the Persians had had no space to maneuver, and he was therefore going to make sure that there was now plenty of space. The fairways had also been spiked facing the enemy, much like spikes built in the entry ramps at car rental drop-offs. As many generals do, Darius had prepared to fight the last war. He did not realize that if at Issus he had played poker, the Battle of Gaugamela would resemble a game of chess. Darius wasn't prepared for that.

Alexander, on spotting the enemy some four miles away, asked camps to be set up for the night. He then took a posse of his commanders and galloped into the night to reconnoiter the terrain and study the Persian positions. Like the great generals such as Napoleon and Wellington who followed him, Alexander insisted on seeing everything himself. It was as if Alexander already understood what Napoleon was to say 2,000 years later: "A general who has to see things through other people's eyes will never be able to command an army as it should be commanded." Alexander, although known for his audacity in battle, never led his army into any action whose probabilities of success he had not previously calculated. Part of his drive to see everything for himself stemmed from his desire to see the possibilities, but part of it was to prepare for every conceivable eventuality. In no sphere of human endeavor does Murphy's Law—Everything that can go wrong, will—hold truer than in war. The Prussian military strategist Carl von Clausewitz called this reality "friction"—the conspiring of unforeseen circumstances to wreck one's carefully prepared battle plans. Only those who could adapt to these would win.

Alexander saw that the entire Persian army had been drawn up in battle order, with their positions stretching four miles wide. He called a meeting of his officers. Parmenion advocated a night attack. To which proposal Arrian quotes Alexander as saying, "I will not demean myself by stealing victory like a thief."[14] We aren't sure whether Alexander actually said that or whether this quote was assigned to him for its propaganda value, but it remains an oft-quoted maxim.

Then, turning to his officers, he said that there was no need for him to encourage them to do their duty; he had seen enough courage in the last few battles to know that if they all gave their best, they would win; anything short, and they would lose. They were fighting, not as they had fought before, for the future of Syria, or Egypt, or Phoenicia; this was a battle for the soul of all Asia. Every officer was told to remind his troops of the discipline expected of them—to march in silence; and at the opportune moment "to roar out their battle cry and put the fear of God into their enemy's hearts."[15] He then ordered everyone to get a night's sleep.

Darius, on the other hand, with his troops lined up in battle formation, awaited an attack from Alexander all night. None came. The next morning, after a hearty breakfast, the Macedonians got ready for battle. Darius had a traditional battle line with infantry at the center and cavalry on the flanks of his four-mile-wide formation; chariots were peppered all across the line, and elephants stood front and center. It was clear to Alexander from the four miles that separated him from his enemy that Darius hoped to break up the Macedonian order by using his elephants and the scythed chariots, and then envelop the ranks with his cavalry.

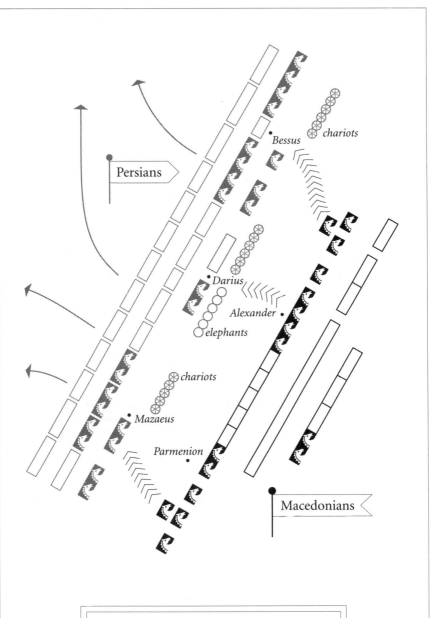

Persians

Bessus

chariots

Darius

Alexander

elephants

chariots

Mazaeus

Parmenion

Macedonians

GAUGAMELA

Indeed, considering that Alexander's entire formation was only as wide as Darius' center, in the hands of a good strategist and tactician, Darius' gambit was highly plausible.

Fortunately for Alexander, Darius was neither a strategist nor a tactician. Alexander marched the first three miles of the gap separating him from Darius, giving his enemy the impression that he was entering the "fairway" trap that had been laid for the Macedonians. But when the Macedonians were within a mile of Darius' formation, he suddenly gave the order to his troops to orient them in Epaminondas' "oblique order," with the right flank leading in the front and the left "refused." This formation implied that the Macedonians were going to focus on a specific point of the enemy's front, drive a wedge through it, cut through the Persian army, and kill it.

Darius tried to extend his left flank to be prepared for the Macedonian right, which was about to attack, but his five-times-larger army couldn't adapt at such short notice. He gave the orders for his chariots to roll, but by then the Macedonians had cleared themselves of the fairways, and managed first to scare the Persian horses pulling the chariots by banging their swords and lances on their shields, and then to ride and drive their swords into them. The horses that turned back in fear were spiked in their hoofs.

Seeing the chariots rendered ineffective, Darius ordered the infantry and cavalry units in the center to charge; some of them already had moved leftward to meet Alexander's right wing, and a gap had opened up in the Persian center. Alexander, who always observed every movement on the battlefield, seeing the Persian gap opening up, wheeled his Companions around from the right, and charged into the Persian center in a "wedgelike" cavalry formation, with serried banks of Macedonian cavalry converging on the very spot where Darius stood atop his ornate chariot.

Alexander himself led the charge, but the Macedonians had practiced these maneuvers so many times that that they could form and re-form their maneuvers in their sleep. Their performance resembled that of the Vienna Philharmonic, which has never had a permanent conductor—the musicians playing nightly at the Vienna State Opera practice and play so often that their music onstage flows together as effortlessly as the somnolent breathing of an old married couple. Persian defenses began to melt away as the Macedonian cavalry battered in, and very soon, with his charioteer speared by a Macedonian lance, Darius turned around and fled the scene of battle.

As he prepared to chase Darius, Alexander received an urgent message from Parmenion that the Macedonian left, which he was leading, was under heavy attack. With dust clouds swirling behind the hoofs of their horses, the Companions wheeled around to help Parmenion. Seeing Alexander returning to engage them from their rear, the Persian right flank began to slither away. The Macedonians won the battle, but Alexander's objective to kill or capture Darius had again slipped away. Ordering Parmenion to once again capture the Persian baggage train, he rode off in search of Darius. Although estimates of losses vary wildly, conservative estimates put the Persian losses that day at over thirty percent; the Macedonian losses were a mere 1 percent.

In the next few months Alexander invaded the principal Persian city of Babylon, and then the Persian capitals of Susa and Persepolis. Though he captured the towns and the wealth of the Persian empire almost intact, Darius was nowhere to be found.

For almost a year after Gaugamela, and five years after Issus, Alexander relentlessly pursued Darius, as he expanded and consolidated his empire. By now it stretched from Greece in the north to Egypt on the southern side of the Mediterranean Sea, through Syria, Mesopotamia, and Persia in western Asia.

Alexander found Darius alive—but only moments away from his death. Darius was stabbed by his own generals and left to die in a wagon on a dusty road between Iran and Afghanistan. Alexander found the dying king with a small band of loyal Persian soldiers protecting him. The meeting between the two great emperors has since been captured in various versions of romantic poems and miniature paintings. According to the tenth-century Persian poet Firdausi, who wrote the *Shahnama (Romance of the King)*, Darius thanked Alexander for the treatment of his mother, wife, and children. Greek myth has it that the Persian king officially handed Alexander his kingdom. It is generally believed that all that Alexander did was wrap Darius' body in his cloak, pay his respects to a worthy enemy, and have his body shipped to the Persian capital Persepolis for burial next to the other great Persian emperors.

SUMMARY OF KEY THEMES

1. MAP A STRATEGY FOR GLOBALIZATION.

Alexander's expansion style was systematic. The pursuit of Darius was held up during the siege of Tyre or the invasion of Egypt, though Alexander was aware the diversions would provide Darius the time to bolster the wrecked Persian army after the Battle of Issus. But because he was more interested in his broader objective of ruling the world, conquering Tyre and Egypt would provide him a naval base, enhanced capabilities in naval warfare, and ready access to the timber of Phoenicia and Assyria to build his navy, and prevent those two nations from attacking Greece or Macedonia.

2. PRESERVE VALUE.

Alexander always sought to avoid a war of attrition, aware that the longer a war, the less value the geography to him. He positioned himself as a liberator of the people from the harsh rule of the Persians, and citizens of many nations found his appeal persuasive enough to willingly switch to his side.

3. PENALIZE THOSE WHO REFUSE TO ACCEPT HIS RULE.

When Tyre finally fell, eight thousand Tyrians lost their lives and the rest were sold into slavery. Like the destruction of Thebes, his treatment of people after the siege of Tyre, and thereafter Gaza, were signals to the people not to resist him.

4. ENCOURAGE PLURALISM TO STRENGTHEN SOCIETY.

Alexander allowed—indeed, encouraged—the cultures and social mores of the nations he conquered to flourish alongside the Greek ones. In Egypt, for example, he built Alexandria with wide-open avenues, canals, and waterways. Most important, though, he ordered the writing of laws compatible with the existing Egyptian judicial system.

5. HARNESS LOCAL TALENT.

In Egypt he asked the two Egyptian governors who ran Upper and Lower Egypt to stay on in their jobs. He signed up all the naval architects, designers, and builders in Tyre for his army.

CHAPTER 8

"TEETH VERSUS TAIL"— LOGISTICS STRATEGY

THE MACEDONIANS WERE KNOWN FOR THEIR LIGHTNING SPEED AND surprise tactics. They managed both while moving unprecedented numbers of people and goods across extensive deserts such as the Libyan, Nubian, Syrian, Arabian, Thar, and Makran, some of the world's tallest mountain ranges like the Caucasus and the Hindu Kush, and among some of the most warlike tribes and populations anywhere. The Macedonian army was the most efficient logistics operation that man has ever known, and became the model for Napoleon's as well as relatively modern armies of the two world wars. Alexander would supply forward bases by ship, then dismantle and carry the ships over land to another river en route to the next forward base. Similarly, Alexander initiated the notion of a single point of contact on logistical issues, ensuring simplicity of military objectives, which every logistician clearly understood and targeted his performance against. Not surprisingly, many successful business and military institutions and operations still study Alexander's logistics as a way of thinking how they ought to tackle their own.

A popular military maxim says that amateurs talk about strategy and professionals discuss logistics. Cardinal de Richelieu of France, who in the seventeenth century helped end the overpowering influence that the Spanish and the Habsburg dynasties had over Europe, wrote in his political manifesto that history had witnessed more armies succumb to want and disorder brought about by ineffective logistics than faced defeat at the hands of the enemy.[1] Take the experience of German Field Marshal Erwin Rommel in the Second World War. Rommel became a highly decorated general when in 1940 he led Germany's invasion of France. In 1941, appointed as head of the Afrika Korps, the "Desert Fox" and his combined German-Italian army in northern Africa were finally defeated by British Field Marshal Bernard Montgomery about sixty miles from Alexandria at El Alamein. The German tanks were better equipped than the British ones, and the German troops fought well. But each night, while the Germans went *back* to their base to restock, the British moved forward—they had planted several forward supply bases from where they restocked. The Germans lost because they were tethered to what some military historians have called "the umbilical cord of supply." Imagine a stretched rubber band. The British stayed put at the farthest stretch of the band, while the Germans would go back each night to where the band returned to its normal state. The British finally won because Montgomery appreciated the role of logistics to his strategic success. He even acknowledged that as much as eighty percent of the problems that the Allied forces had in the Second World War were of a logistical nature.

Burning the Wagons Before Entering Afghanistan

Darius was dead, the Achaemenid throne was in Alexander's hands, and Darius' heirs were his prisoners. Every Persian capital was in Alexander's hands. With the Mediterranean, northern Africa, and much of the Caucasus and Persia under his control, Alexander paid off Greek troops with the treasures captured from Persia and made arrangements to send them home. Those who voluntarily remained were given a bonus.

Alexander did not let the Macedonians go, even though his refusal risked a revolt from men who had been on the road for several years. There already were mild signs of a mutiny brewing among some sections of his troops, and Alexander decided to address the issue head on. In a powerful speech he persuaded them that as long as the entire Persian army had not succumbed to the might of the Macedonians, Persia wasn't under their control. As long as Persian generals and governors like Bessus, who was the architect of Darius' murder, roamed Persia, victory wasn't complete. He asked them to take up their arms and follow on ahead.

News soon arrived through Persians coming over to the Macedonian side that Bessus had proclaimed himself heir to the Achaemenid throne and had taken to wearing the Persian crown with the upright tiara, parading in the royal robes, and had even given himself the title Artaxerxes V.[2] Bessus, the Persians added, had proclaimed himself the "King of Asia" and was moving around attended by Bactrians (from today's northern Afghanistan and Turkmenistan). The news, from Alexander's perspective, couldn't have been better. It gave him just the ammunition to rally his troops into battle.

As the columns of troops lined up to march toward western Afghanistan, Alexander realized that his army was staggering under the weight of their accumulated spoils. There was no way that this army could march forward at anywhere near its customary thirty-five miles a day. If Bessus was north with the remnants of the Persian army and organizing a force through alliances, the Macedonians needed to move up quickly and thwart its formation.

Two other critical logistical issues loomed. First, although Philip, Alexander's father, had banned the accompaniment of women and forbade relationships developing between his troops and local women in lands they were conquering, Alexander had, since turning away from the Mediterranean inland toward modern Iraq and Iran, allowed his men to marry local women. Marriage stemmed the yearning for home and women (and consequent children) and helped maintain a sense of order and decorum in the army.

Second, although Turkmenistan itself was well settled and bountiful in food, the path through today's eastern Iran and northern Afghanistan would take Alexander through the sparsely vegetated and human-swallowing Kara Kum Desert. Moreover, while he had positioned himself as the liberator of people, and they had voluntarily surrendered supplies that he needed when he was the "liberator," he realized that people would be less forthcoming with supplies for the new ruler of Persia, "since the local populations are antagonistic toward their new rulers."[3]

Alexander ordered the wagons filled with luggage, excluding necessities. Once filled and gathered together, he ordered the mules and horses to be freed. Alexander then lit a torch and set fire to the wagons carrying *his* luggage. Then he ordered the rest of the wagons set afire. The Macedonians watched all their excess luggage and the loot that they had collected on their campaign go up in smoke. Just like that. No one objected. No one rushed to save their luggage. They just watched the embers and flames. Although disappointed, they had not lost their renowned self-control and discipline[4] after so many years on the road. They were delighted that their load had lightened and would be particularly thankful for it in the weeks ahead. Many generals would follow the example set by Alexander, including Napoleon, who did exactly the same on his ill-fated retreat from Moscow.

Don't Carry What You Don't Need

Just as Alexander burned his cargo to a bare minimum and carried only those pieces of supply that were the most essential, the U.S. military in "Enduring Freedom" (the U.S. and British military's code name for ridding Afghanistan of its Taliban regime and of the operational base of Osama bin Laden's international terrorist network) asked its troops to carry only the essentials. Computers track what they need and when they need it, refill and replenish depleting stores and supplies, and automatically generate requisition orders to buy fresh stocks from suppliers.

Transportation of high-priority items, which used to be performed exclusively by the military's own aircraft and ships, is now done through FedEx and DHL. From the Second World War up until "Enduring Freedom," combat units, however large, were invariably supported by an equally large, if not larger, support system. In most wars, therefore, the "teeth-to-tail" ratio—the standard comparison of the size of the fighting unit (teeth) to the support infrastructure (tail)—was about 1:1. In "Enduring Freedom" the "teeth" were much larger than the "tail."

One can understand the use of overnight freight in times of national crisis, though not everyone can use FedEx, UPS, or DHL for their supply transportation needs or the costs would be prohibitively expensive. Retailers who sell sporting equipment like treadmills, for example, have to rely on the sophisticated use of logistics networks—or the logistics costs associated with its delivery could wipe out the entire profit margin.

Just as Alexander made trade-offs between what to carry and what not to carry, most retailers are also forced to make trade-offs between what to stock at a store and what not to, and what to have supplied overnight and what not to. Most consumers do not realize that stores—especially at shopping malls and city centers—are high-priced locations where holding stock of fast-moving items like fans and air-conditioners in the summer or snowplows in the winter makes sense in season but not out of season, where these items are better stocked at regional warehouses from where they can be delivered, as needed, directly to customers. On the other hand furniture retailers like IKEA and general retailers like Wal-Mart can carry their entire stock, or at least much of it, at a store because of their off-city-center locations, where they build massive, warehouse-style stores. The reason why IKEA can stock a dining table, for example, while a typical furniture retailer might take eight weeks to deliver one, is that IKEA appeals to a certain segment of the consumer base that is willing to take on the most difficult part of the furniture business' value chain: assembly.

Underlying the speed of "Enduring Freedom" was an operational technique first mastered by Japanese automobile manufacturers and suppliers in the late 1970s and 1980s, called "just-in-time" delivery, whereby all the parts and supplies needed to make an automobile were delivered daily or hourly—"when they were needed." A five-year study conducted by the Massachusetts Institute of Technology on the future of the automobile reported that by 1982, over fifty percent of all Japanese suppliers were delivering parts to the major automotive assemblers like Honda, Toyota, and Nissan daily, and thirty-one percent were making hourly deliveries.[5] In the United States, on the other hand, as late as 1988 a paltry ten percent of suppliers were delivering either daily or hourly.[6]

The Japanese further revolutionized the mass-production mindset of the automobile industry, first developed in the U.S. by Henry Ford and Alfred Sloan, through the creation and adoption in the 1990s of "lean production." Today this technique is revolutionizing the ordering, manufacturing, and delivery of everything from Dell computers to Boeing aircraft. "Lean production," which cuts excess, shrinks inventory, and has been shown to halve the time it takes to build an aircraft, requires tight information and materials flow between the customer, supplier, and the manufacturer or assembler.

It has been working for the military as well. In 1997, when a Marine stationed at his base in Camp Pendleton, near San Diego, placed an order for a spare part, it typically took a week to get that part from the stock rooms of the same base.[7] In Operation Enduring Freedom, because of a redesigned and revitalized logistics chain, the same spare can reach that Marine in a matter of hours at his position in a foxhole on a battlefield anywhere in the world. The difference in time it took to have the part delivered is like the difference in ordering furniture from a typical furniture maker, and waiting six weeks for it to arrive, and ordering a similar item from L. L. Bean, and having it arrive the next day.

To be fair, however, the U.S. could achieve what it did logistically in Afghanistan because it didn't have a large ground force to equip and feed. In the Gulf War, for example, it took the U.S. four months to build up enough supplies to prepare for the arrival of all of the half-million ground forces that were deployed in Saudi Arabia. In Afghanistan the troops deployed were a few thousand, and because they were mainly Special Forces, they were trained and equipped to be self-sufficient for as many as thirty days of combat right from the word go.[8]

The army could therefore keep its supply lines to a minimum and, in doing so, also avoid any chance of the supply lines being cut off. As historians have been quick to remind us, Afghanistan had been the "graveyard of numerous armies in history,"[9] from the two British expeditions—in 1839 and 1878—to the decade-long Soviet occupation beginning 1979. In a country that is eighty percent mountainous, guerillas would cut off supply lines, ambush convoys, and eventually sap the resolve of those who survived.

Forward Supply Bases

A key element of Alexander's logistics operations was highly sophisticated intelligence gathering. Alexander had eschewed the practice of running a spy network, as the Persians did, by feeding false stories, bribing officials, and instigating rebellions. Instead, his intelligence came from two main sources: professionals such as botanists, zoologists, meteorologists, surveyors, cartographers, and historians; and local knowledge, from people he met or conquered. From the latter group he sought disconfirming evidence for a strategy that he and his advisors might have agreed upon. This way he avoided unexpected situations arising from issues he might not have adequately addressed. Obviously, Alexander had a remarkable ability to synthesize these disparate sources of information and arrive at an estimate for how many troops the land ahead could support. This information determined his next steps. For example, when he invaded the Persian capital of Persepolis, he did so with only 17,000 troops, principally because the terrain could only support that many—not the 87,000 troops and close to 9,000 pack animals that were in his entourage.[10]

Whenever a military campaign loomed, Napoleon would send for all the relevant books on a region—historical, topographical, botanical, zoological, geographical, and others—to apprise himself as closely as possible from as many different angles as possible. In the Gulf War, military satellites had closely mapped every rail line, oil depot and refinery, and oasis in the Iraqi desert, and these were all rolled into the U.S. Army's logistics plans, so that if needed, the U.S. tanks, trucks, and troops could capture these supply resources in a prolonged offensive — to break the Iraqis' logistical chain or commandeer it for their own use.

Alexander's superior information and intelligence gathering was an important reason why the Macedonians crossed difficult terrain where other armies suffered casualties from starvation and dehydration.[11] Alexander could have boasted, as did the duke of Wellington, that there were many who could command an army, but only he could feed it.

It is generally believed that Alexander was the last person to successfully conquer Afghanistan (after he died, the nation first became part of the empire of Seleucus Nikator, and then, through an arrangement, for three hundred years part of India's Mauryan empire, which was established by a twenty-four-year-old Indian named Chandra Gupta Maurya, who also became Seleucus' son-in-law). The reason why Alexander conquered Afghanistan and that nation remained for just above three hundred years as part of the empire he bequeathed to his successors was because Alexander invested in building cities and towns, and connecting Afghanistan to other parts of the world.

As he built his first city in Afghanistan — Alexandria-in-Areia (modern Herat) in western Afghanistan — Alexander mapped his pursuit of Bessus. His intelligence-gathering efforts suggested to him that even though parts of northern Afghanistan were densely populated and arable, he would have to cross through large tracts of highly inhospitable deserts.

In search of a cultivated region, where food would be plentiful, Alexander led the Macedonian army south of Areia toward the Helmand Valley to ride out the winter. This took him hundreds of miles away from his destination in ancient Bactria (northern Afghanistan and Turkmenistan), where Bessus had stood with his army.

The thousand-mile trek from Areia to another city that he would build, Alexandria-in-Arachosia (modern Kandahar), was not an easy one, because it took the Macedonians through the 150-mile-long Desert of Death, where no one lives and nothing grows, and where "the Wind of One Hundred and Twenty Days" sandblasts everything in sight — buildings, hills, and people.[12] Many previous would-be conquerors, like the legendary eighth-century-B.C. Babylonian queen Semiramis, had been stopped in their tracks, because their horses foundered in the hot desert sand, and were forced to return. Alexander accomplished it by breaking his army into small units, which would each forage for its food requirements itself and, if a large amount of food was found, would hold it in store for the other units.

The army rested out the winter in Kandahar, anxiously awaiting the late-winter harvest of wheat and barley, which was plentiful in the region. Kandahar, since its founding by Alexander, has been a strategic post in the many conquests of history, and each conquest has left its mark on the city in some shape or form. Some doctors in Kandahar, for example, still practice ancient Greek herbal medicine ("Yunnani"), which was brought to the region by Alexander's physician, Philip of Acarnania.[13]

During the harvest Alexander sent grain ahead to forward supply bases. The three-hundred-plus-mile trek from Kandahar to Kabul was through the arid vistas of Arachosia, where food and water were not available. The journey through several mountain passes of the Hindu Kush was also going to be extremely cold, and arduous enough to not leave any scope for hunting parties to span out in the search for food—even were there any to be found. The choices, therefore, were simple: either carry all required food and water on the march or store stocks in supply bases as forward as possible. This was a revolutionary concept then and is a revolutionary concept now. Forward supply bases implemented by the British army in North Africa during the Second Word War and by the U.S. Army in the more recent Gulf War are notable exceptions in military history.

With the highly slimmed-down baggage train, Macedonian troops had to carry all their clothes and equipment; horses and mules carried pieces of the siege engines, catapults, ballistas, rams, scaling ladders, and other armaments. Food consumption was in excess of 200,000 pounds of grains, 200,000 gallons of water, and over 100,000 pounds of fodder for animals— per day! Add to that whatever fruits, vegetables, and meats they could muster up. Since there was no option of foraging any food from the desert, and troops couldn't carry it, forward supply bases were therefore stocked with grains, fodder, and water. Troops would need to carry rations sufficient for at most three days of travel, which, simple and insightful calculations by Donald Engels reveal, is about the optimum amount of food individuals could carry themselves; add another day of travel without a refueling stop, and the Macedonians would have needed over 10,000 pack animals.[14]

"Good Logistics Is Combat Power"

It was on August 4, 1990, "a particularly hot, humid, and gritty day in Georgia,"[15] that two-star general William "Gus" Pagonis got the call to start the logistical planning for the multinational forces' logistical buildup in Saudi Arabia. On August 2 Iraqi president Saddam Hussein's troops had swept into and occupied Kuwait, and the objective of the U.S.-led military operations was to oust the Iraqis from Kuwait. When Pagonis, along with a couple of officers, landed at the King Abdul Aziz Airbase in Dhahran, Saudi Arabia, on August 8, units of the 82d Airborne had already started arriving in what would be an eventual buildup of 550,000 multinational troops, all arriving by air, and over 7 million tons of supplies, equipment, and arms, arriving mainly by sea.

By the time the ground offensive began on February 24, 1991, the biggest mobilization in history had moved four times the number of people and supplies in one third the time it took to launch the highly time-sensitive Berlin Airlift of 1948.[16] There was enough food and water stocked up to feed the troops for a month, enough ammunition for forty-five days, and fuel to keep everyone moving for five days continuously.[17] At the heart of the logistics operations were eight forward logistics bases, less than ninety miles apart from one another and permitting trucks to make a round trip in twenty-four hours or less. This way, like Alexander's troops, when the multinational forces were on the offensive, they could be supplied all along their path and wouldn't be tethered to a single supply base behind them.

Two of the forward logistics bases had been set up almost inside enemy territory, suitably camouflaged from enemy eyes behind dozens of sand bunkers that blended in with the desert around. Trucks were loaded up with all the supplies necessary to create further forward bases, so when the offensive started troops wouldn't have to worry about where their meals, fuel, and ammunition were coming from. "My basic rule of thumb," wrote Pagonis, "was that the depots from which the corps took their supplies had to be located close enough to the front so that once the troops advanced, they could still resupply from these depots."[18] According to Pagonis, this logistical design was based on his studies of the strategies and tactics of both Alexander the Great and the British army that fought Rommel in North Africa.

The entire logistics system was designed to support a flanking maneuver derived from the flanking operation that Alexander the Great first implemented at the Battle of the Hydaspes (see next chapter). In this end run in the Gulf War, popularly titled "Hail Mary" (after the last-minute throw-the-ball-toward-the-end-zone-and-hope-for-a-catch prayer), the heavy-armor VII Corps moved on the offensive almost 250 miles north toward the Euphrates River, and cut off the communication and supply lines of the Iraqi army, and emerged behind the rear of the divisions facing Kuwait and Saudi Arabia. The large, gas-guzzling tanks of the VII Corps refueled from bladders of fuel carried by trucks. Borrowing an idea from the British in North Africa, the U.S. Army had its tanks carried on trucks to the front, so they would not require any maintenance or repairs in traveling there—breakdowns of even the most sophisticated tanks in the desert is a common problem.

The lighter XVIII Airborne Corps started its movement from behind the VII and, because of its speed, crossed the VII just before it entered Iraq. The XVIII headed west and confronted the Iraqi army from the front. The XVIII also had to accomplish what Alexander had first demonstrated in warfare: moving from a defensive position (protecting Saudi Arabia) to an offensive position against the Iraqis, while it was on the move. The pincer movement by the VII Corps and the XVIII Airborne Corps forced the surrender of the Iraqi army within four days. It was in keeping with the simple objective of the Gulf War, which in General Colin Powell's words was "First we cut off the Iraqi army, then we kill it."

The forces' supreme commander, General H. Norman Schwarzkopf, had decreed that logistics was to occupy a central role in the campaign, and in pursuit of that goal, just before the ground offensive, had General Pagonis promoted to a three-star general, which gave him equal say and profile as the most senior tactical commanders in the campaign. It was something that Alexander had first instituted, when he not only made logistics central to his campaigns but also made sure that it was led by one of his top generals. Parmenion headed logistics operations frequently, and each time the Macedonians won, he was made responsible for capturing the enemy's baggage train and bringing it home. Other generals who played the top logistics role were Coenus and Craterus, both senior commanders in the army. Like Pagonis these generals of Alexander were, during their individual commands, the one person with whom the buck stopped on logistical issues.

Successful business organizations, too, invest in developing top-notch logistical processes and designating a top manager as the person with whom the buck stops. Nowhere is the importance of logistics more evident than in personal computer assembly and distribution. For years everyone looked at Dell's direct-to-customer model of doing business, whereby a computer would only be assembled once a customer order had been received, and then shipped within a day or two through a well-oiled transportation system. To competitors like Compaq the Dell model represented a niche market, which, they believed, would only appeal to buyers of relatively simple computers, while unsophisticated buyers would require a dealer's help in selecting even basic systems; complex systems would need the services of VARs (value-added resellers) for installation. Dell's "niche," unfortunately for Compaq and others, turned out to be pretty large. Compaq, like many other assemblers, chose a build-to-forecast model whereby each month or quarter a forecast of sales would be made, and computers built to that forecast. Compaq had a fledgling direct-order business, and most of its computers were sold through retailers or VARs who would also add on customized software or hardware for the needs of their commercial customers. Compaq would receive forecast numbers from its sales force and build sufficient units and ship them out to retailers and VARs—except over time a large inventory of computers began to build up in its warehouses, and with its retailers and VARs, because forecasts, as they always are, were out of sync with demand. Often rapid technological shifts would make certain pieces of hardware or software obsolete even in the one- to six-month duration that a computer might wait till it was sold. Compaq's "forward bases" therefore frequently stocked up inventory that customers did not want. They were also more expensive. (Dell, by buying components just before customers needed them also managed to benefit from the average one percent decline per week in electronic component prices.)

Unlike smart clothing retailers like Zara (the Spanish retailing sensation that's conquering the world) and the Limited, who, understanding how fickle customer tastes can be, move even hot new items by running continuous sales, Compaq never did that or did it too late; sales on Compaq computers would be on items that were, as teenagers would say, "so last year." Little wonder, then, that Compaq's build-to-forecast model failed. Dell, meanwhile, continues on its merry way enlarging its market share of the personal computer market.

Compaq learned the hard way, as have many other venerable firms, that logistics can either make or break a company—especially one that thrives in making and selling short-life-cycle items like computers or fashion goods. British retailer Marks & Spencer for years was held up as a paragon of logistics—notably for its highly successful, direct replenishment of inventory right at its stores on British high streets, which eliminated even intermediate warehousing of products. The company faltered precipitously, however, when it moved into fashion merchandising in the late eighties and early nineties, where logistics was a matter not just of physical distribution of goods but was tied closely to predicting, testing, and stocking next season's fashion wear. Previously, its direct-replenishment logistics system had catered to filling its food aisles with fresh produce and its clothing aisles with inexpensive, high-quality, and reliable products that could be worn both by one's dowdy aunt and by the daughter devoted to perfect seams. When it moved into "fashion" merchandising, it needed to make the leap to a much higher level of logistical sophistication, but like many companies—and unlike Alexander—it took time to realize that logistics was much more than physical distribution. "To today's managers, preoccupied as they are with more immediate challenges," wrote Graham Sharman, a leading authority on the role of strategy and logistics, almost twenty years ago, "logistics may seem an unlikely battleground in the contest for future competitive advantage. But it is, indeed, where much of the battle will be fought"[19]—a reality that many companies find out the hard way. It is amazing that Alexander understood the role logistics would play in his success.

Crossing the Hindu Kush to Control Afghanistan

The tall mountains of the Hindu Kush ("Killer of Hindus") rise majestically behind Kabul and disappear into the landscape before merging with the highest mountain range of the world, the Himalayas. Successive conquistadors from Heracles and Dionysus to relatively modern ones like Tamerlane and Genghis Khan have used the passes through these mountains to sweep into the valleys beyond. The mountains paths are littered with the bones of soldiers accompanying these campaigns, most of which ended in defeat. The Pashtuns who live in the surrounding valleys are among the most warlike people in the world; it is said that they are most at peace when they are at war. Moreover, as the British learned in their two ill-fated missions, it isn't just the men they needed to worry about; the women, too, were dangerous. Rudyard Kipling, who knew a few things about Afghanistan, warned in his poem "The Young British Soldier" that if injured on the plains of Afghanistan, it was better to blow your brains out with your own rifle than fall into the hands of the Afghan women, who would certainly cut you into pieces.

After waiting for the stragglers to catch up with the army, Alexander decided to take his entire army, baggage train, and even the followers, over the Hindu Kush into Bactria in pursuit of Bessus. Of the three major passes through the mountains, the Salang Pass was the most traversable: It was the lowest of the three and had some vegetation, which could have ameliorated to some extent the Macedonians' supply problems. (The Soviets used this pass for their invasion of Afghanistan.)

Unfortunately, to deny Alexander any supplies, Bessus had scorched the soil around the pass, so nothing was in bloom when Alexander reached the mountains. The second pass led to Bamian, a center of Buddhist study, where the giant statues of the Buddha had been carved into rocks almost two centuries before Alexander (only to be destroyed by the fundamentalist Taliban regime in the 1990s). This pass was the main route of the Buddhist monks who traveled between India, China, and Afghanistan. Unfortunately, it was narrow and would lead the Macedonians away from where Bessus had sought refuge in Bactria. The only pass, therefore, available to him, which was capable of allowing the over 100,000 people traveling with him—two-thirds troops and one-third families and followers—was the Khawak Pass, situated almost twelve thousand feet above sea level.

At forty-seven miles Khawak was also the longest. Bessus had gambled that with the Hindu Kush separating him from Alexander, and the only possible pass for the crossing being the snowcapped Khawak, where the cold Siberian wind comes howling down the plains of Central Asia before ripping into the Hindu Kush, Alexander wouldn't pursue him into Bactria. Bessus was wrong.

In early spring 329 B.C., over five years of travel from Macedonia, Alexander strapped his pack animals with as much luggage as they could hold and, with three days of food, started the arduous journey to cross the Hindu Kush. No one had ever dared such a feat before with so many, and no one ever would again. Every subsequent military expedition would be smaller, and either conducted on horseback or mules or on helicopter gunships and transporters.

It was not an easy journey, even for the hardened Macedonians. The crossing over the mountain took sixteen days. Food, which was being doled out at half rations, completely ran out on the sixth day. At eight thousand feet the mountain was completely covered with snow, which meant there was no food to forage, so they subsisted on wild berries and leaves. Tired, cold, and hungry, the Macedonians staggered on. The air got thinner as they climbed, and some began to hallucinate; many just keeled over and died. Stones marking where the bodies were buried stand even today, spread out in the circular shape common to ancient Greek burials.[20]

The several-mile-long procession was also exposed to the threat of the sword-wielding mountain horsemen, who would silently ambush the procession and hack as many as they could to pieces before vanishing as silently and surreptitiously as they had arrived. Anyone who has witnessed the Afghan national game of *buzkashi* already knows how skilled Afghans are at horsemanship. To say *buzkashi*, which literally means "goat grabbing," is a dangerous sport is to put it mildly. It is the equivalent of playing rugby—on horseback. The game involves highly skilled riders on well-trained horses fighting over the carcass of a headless goat. The Macedonians, who had several times defeated armies four—even ten—times their size on the plains, were taken aback at the surprise, speed, and viciousness with which the Afghans harassed them on the mountain. In a few weeks after the crossing, in one ambush, they lost 2,000 infantrymen and 300 cavalry—the highest toll suffered by the Macedonians in over twenty years.

As the procession came close to the summit, there was the real threat of mass death through starvation. Alexander gave orders to kill some of the pack animals for meat. With no wood for fires Alexander gave orders to eat the meat raw. It was then that the physicians and the botanists in the entourage came to the rescue. Identifying for its medicinal value a small plant type growing in the snow—the plant, which we know as asafetida,[21] still grows in the region, producing a resin which is used by the Yunnani doctors for treating wounds and curing stomach ailments—they encouraged troops to eat meat with droplets of the resin. The botanists and the physicians saved the troops from starvation. (Several ancient descriptions of Europe, Africa, and Asia's plants and animals owe their origins to the scientists accompanying the Macedonian army—who studied those that they had never seen before, wrote extensive descriptions of them, and analyzed the ones suitable for eating; just as many detailed descriptions and facts about Egypt in modern times owe their genesis to the scientists and surveyors accompanying Napoleon's army.)

All through the crossing Alexander encouraged and cajoled his troops and spun stories about how the cave of Prometheus could be found on the other side of the mountain. Finally the troops and their followers arrived in the Kunduz Valley, where they reassembled in the Bactrian capital of Bactra (modern Balkh) for a race in pursuit of Bessus.

Bessus, the self-proclaimed emperor of Persia, was so surprised and horrified at the Macedonians' resolve that he sped farther north, crossing the Oxus River (modern Amu Darya) for the safety of the interiors of today's Central Asian "stans": Turkmenistan and Tajikistan first and Uzbekistan, Kyrgyzstan, and Kazakhstan beyond.

The eighty-mile stretch from Bactra to the Oxus River is hot, baking, sand-duned desert, where temperatures of 110°F are considered positively balmy. Sand grits strike the face like embers from a fire. Cold mountain temperatures in the night, and the hot, dry heat during the day, caused heat strokes and convulsions. Alexander ordered the troops to rest by day and travel by night. Bereft of water to quench their thirst, some took to drinking the high-alcohol wine in their supplies—and fell sick. Four days later, when they neared the Oxus, several jumped into the warm, disease-infested waters and drank out of the river. Fever and dysentery raged through the Macedonian army.

Leaving the sick on the banks, Alexander organized rafts made of animal skins and tents, and whatever wood and dry grass the troops could muster up. The infantry took five days to cross the Oxus, but the cavalry and their horses had crossed over on the first day and gone after Bessus. Messengers working for Bessus' commanders met the rapidly advancing cavalry and offered to surrender Bessus if Alexander would stop the chase. Alexander was in no mood to negotiate.

Learning from the messengers that Bessus was headed toward Maracanda (today's Samarkand), Alexander asked Ptolemy to lead the Companions in a chase.

Despite the heat and the unknown country, Ptolemy rode so fast that he covered the ten-day ride that separated Bessus from them in only four days. So astonished were the commanders accompanying Bessus that they placed him in a wooden collar, stripped him naked, and left him lying on the side of the main road to Samarkand. Bessus was brought back to stand trial in a small Persian court set up by Alexander.

Every society has its own form of justice. Eskimos sit around their confessors and remind them that despite their crime, they are still loved. In many Islamic cultures criminals are stoned to death. In ancient Persia the court of justice included family members of the victim. Presided over by Darius' brother, the court tried Bessus, where he was found guilty of high treason. His earlobes cut off, as was the Persian custom, and flogged before all assembled, Bessus was finally sent back by Alexander to Ecbatana to be judged by the highest court of the Persians. The court in Ecbatana again found Bessus guilty, and he was impaled to death.

Alexander thought that he now had complete control over Afghanistan, but he was to be totally surprised in a few months by a ferocious rebellion fanned by a commander in Bessus' army. Alexander realized that Bessus hadn't been the true leader of this band after all—nothing is as it seems in Afghanistan. Not surprisingly, after Afghanistan had been completely conquered, five divisions of 10,000 Macedonian troops each rode up and down the entire countryside for five months, making sure that there were no pockets of possible resistance. Alexander and his troops scoured the land with a fine-tooth comb, determined that the Afghans should never re-form as a threat.

Alexander's legacy in Afghanistan continued for over three hundred years—first under the Seleucid empire, named after his top general, Seleucus Nikator; then under the Indian Mauryan empire, named after his contemporary and friend Chandra Gupta Maurya, who struck a peaceful arrangement to bring Afghanistan under his rule in return for a gift of five hundred war elephants to Seleucus; and then under the Kushan Dynasty. The cities he built—Alexandria-in-Areia (Herat), Alexandria-in-Arachosia (Kandahar), and Alexandria-under-the-Caucasus (Begram), just north of Kabul—all survive today. So do several cities in Tajikistan, Kyrgyzstan, and Uzbekistan, including Samarkand, which became the central city of the Silk Route.

None of this would have happened had Alexander not mastered the art and science of military logistics, a legacy that remarkably continues into contemporary warfare and business.

SUMMARY OF THEMES

1. KEEP IT SIMPLE.

The underlying principle of Alexander the Great's logistics system was simplicity. Where other armies of the ancient world typically carried as many followers as troops on an expedition, with the followers carrying the rations and other supplies of the troops, both Philip and Alexander trained their troops to carry everything they needed themselves. This reduced the logistical train that went ahead or followed and also allowed the Macedonians to achieve lightning speed.

2. SET UP FORWARD SUPPLY BASES.

Most ancient armies, and indeed most modern ones as well, are tethered to their supply bases. Tactical operations are often lost because the supply chains of the advancing armies don't arrive in time or are cut off by the enemy. The key success factor of the multinational force's quick win over Iraq in the 1991 Gulf War was based on a principle first seen in Alexander the Great's army: forward supply bases, which would be set up in anticipation of the arrival of the troops.

3. PLAN FAR IN ADVANCE.

Because of the subsistence level of agricultural production in ancient times, and lack of roads and communication facilities, Alexander's army could not entirely depend on foraging from the land as Napoleon's well could. So before he set out on the next stage of a campaign, Alexander always made sure that an advance team had been sent out to capture supplies from a local magistrate or ruler. Most towns and villages willingly surrendered to the advance team, but in those instances where they didn't he arm-twisted them into surrender. In those areas where there were no towns and villages, Alexander made sure he consulted with the botanists, zoologists, meteorologists, and logisticians in his entourage about climate conditions, and the availability of animals, fruits, and vegetables that could be garnered for the large army.

4. BREAK INTO SMALL UNITS.

If there was no certainty of advance supply bases, Alexander split the army up into smaller units, which set out on different courses to reach the same destination. Each unit was responsible for taking care of its own forage and if any came across a large enough supply, they requisitioned it for other units. Very often, his advance intelligence team would provide him accurate estimates of how many people a town or city ahead could sustain due to the subsistence level of agricultural production, and Alexander would always take only that many troops, leaving behind the rest at a point where supplies were more plentiful.

5. ESTABLISH A SINGLE POINT OF CONTACT.

Alexander the Great made many decisions on logistical issues. But by and large he delegated logistics-related decisions to one of his senior commanders, such as Parmenion, who was responsible for planning and executing them. Everyone knew with whom the buck stopped when it came to logistics.

CHAPTER 9

THE ART OF
DECEPTIVE STRATEGY

IT WAS 328 B.C. WHEN ALEXANDER PREPARED TO INVADE INDIA. THIS NA-
tion was the last frontier before the world ended in a vast ocean—that is
what Aristotle had told him. Now that he had every nation from Greece to
the farthest eastern outposts of Persia under his rule, Alexander resolved to
stand on the sands of the ocean and proclaim himself "Ruler of the
World"—a world unifier. That was the first reason behind his desire to
conquer India. Nothing would cause him greater grief and disappoint-
ment than the realization in a few months, after entering India, that the
ocean he had been told was the end of the world was none other than the
River Ganges—on the opposite bank of which began the Nanda empire,
with a large and fiercely valiant army.

Alexander had one other reason for wanting to invade India: It was a
challenge he couldn't pass up. No foreign invader had conquered India,
and the experience of some of the greatest rulers who ever lived but failed
to conquer India was the stuff of legends. Heading the list was the legendary eighth-century-B.C. Assyrian queen Semiramis. In her long reign
she had accomplished such remarkable feats as rebuilding the city of
Babylon, destroyed by the Hittites almost a thousand years before. In her
attempt to conquer India, however, her troops foundered in the desert
crossing through Afghanistan. Nebuchadnezzar, who never gave up on
anything—he was the one who laid the thirteen-year siege of Tyre—tried
in the sixth century B.C. and failed. Cyrus the Great, the founder of the
Achaemenid Empire, who had conquered all of Asia and even Greece,
could only reach the outskirts of India—no more. Even the divine Hera-

cles, who came through India in his quest to complete his "Twelve Labors," failed to conquer the nation. That's how stacked the decks were against Alexander.

There was hope, however. The mythic Dionysus (or Bacchus), the god of wine and ecstasy, had succeeded (albeit because he was brought into India as a baby). If this son of Zeus could succeed, Alexander, who by now was convinced of his divinity, believed so could he. In the spring of 327 B.C. Alexander's army crossed over the Hindu Kush from northern Afghanistan into the Kabul Valley. There, after resting awhile, he persuaded his troops to undertake the arduous journey into India.

The invasion of India had been meticulously planned—and spun. The army was split into two, the main body led by Hephaistion through the Khyber Pass into the sweltering plains of India—the main route through which succeeding waves of conquering armies would, over the next two millennia, sweep into India. Alexander led a smaller contingent over the mountain north into the Himalayas—into the Vale of Kashmir, to be precise. His mission: to secure the absolute north of India, where the nation ended in the Himalayas, and, from atop the mountain ranges, keep an eye on Central Asia beyond. So high are the Himalayas and so flat Central Asia that one can almost see the curvature of the earth from up there—not that Alexander knew the earth was round.

The Macedonians could feel the snow shifting under their feet and hear the heartbeat-skipping sounds of ice cracking, as they made their way through mountains and valleys where no human had traveled before. Alexander had told his troops that this was the road that Dionysus had taken many centuries before. This was therefore not a conquest, but a pilgrimage. A Macedonian advance team ascertained that there were plenty of ivy vines growing alongside the route, so there would be no uncertainty about Dionysus' travels through here. The Macedonians on their long journey had not seen ivy, a key ingredient of bacchanalian orgiastic rituals. So they accepted the notion of a pilgrimage hook, line, and sinker.

Alexander's objective in northern India was the capture of the citadel atop Mount Aornos (modern Pir-Sar) in the Himalayas. Mount Aornos towered over forests of fir and pine and fields of saffron crocuses for as far as the eye could see. The citadel sat next to a volcanic lake.

Alexander had heard that a tribe of invincible Indian warriors lived in the citadel, adequately supplied from the steep rice terraces and the fruit orchards up on the flat mountaintop—about the size of Cape Town's Table

Mountain. The warriors were let down and hauled up with ropes and chains from the top, but once these necessities of mountain climbing were gone there was just no way for any human to climb the steep slopes surrounding three fourths of the seven-thousand-foot-high mountain. The one side the slopes weren't so steep was a deep ravine that separated the mountain from the forests beyond. Legend had it that even Heracles had been thwarted in his ambition to conquer the citadel. Of course, wherever legends existed, Alexander went, but the military purpose served by Mount Aornos was that it could serve as a natural observation post.

As Alexander rode toward Mount Aornos, word reached an Indian town on the way that the Macedonians were coming. To escape Alexander's wrath the townsmen came out and surrendered to the Macedonians and claimed that their town was Nysa (near modern Jalalabad, Pakistan), after the imaginary hamlet in Greek mythology where the Greek god Hermes is said to have brought Dionysus for his upbringing. We don't know how far Alexander was taken in by their deception, but his troops certainly were, and danced all night by torchlights to the strains of "Euoi, Euoi."

Some historians have compared the similarity between Alexander's march toward Mount Aornos and the Spanish conquistador Hernán Cortés' toward the Aztec capital of Tenochtitlán in August 1519, also situated next to a lake about seven thousand feet high, where stood the holiest of Aztec shrines. The town was connected to the land around by three causeways. When threatened the Aztecs had only to pull up the bridges connecting their town to the causeways, and they would be sealed off.[1]

Similarly to Alexander, to spur his troops on, Cortés talked about the divine nature of their expedition, whereby the Christian God would be served, he claimed, if the conquistadors could turn the devotion that the Aztec people had for their own gods towards their "superior" God[2] except, Alexander wasn't on a religious mission. His mission was to unify the world as "One World"—culturally, politically, and economically.

Phantom Threat

Alexander, on reaching Mount Aornos, decided that he needed to create a phantom threat to bring the Indians down from the safety of their mountain abode. With that in mind he dispatched a large contingent of troops led by Ptolemy to advance and secure a forward base on the mountain.

Ptolemy and his troops were constantly harassed by the Indians and pummeled by showers of stones, rocks, and boulders that came plummeting down from the top of the mountain. Despite heavy losses, after a long struggle Ptolemy was able to secure a position on a promontory of the mountain. The Indians kept their eyes glued to Ptolemy's movements, ready to drop more boulders if they caught the sight of any Macedonian troops.

What the Indians did not realize was that Alexander had created a feint. While they were preoccupied defending themselves against an attack from Ptolemy, Alexander led the rest of the troops around the other side of the mountain, where the slopes weren't as steep. He decided to accomplish what everyone, most especially the Indians, would have thought was impossible: bridge the ravine. To build the bridge he divided his troops into three groups: One felled timber, which was plentiful in the forests, another moved the timber and boulders toward and into the ravine, and a third hammered them into the ravine to construct the bridge. The troops worked in shifts all day and all night—an effort similar to the Allied prisoners of war building the railway bridge connecting Thailand with Myanmar across the Khwae Noi River (or popularly, the River Kwai) in the Second World War.

By the third day the bridge was strong enough to move siege engines and ballistas, which once in place would make short shrift of Indian resistance. As Alexander moved forward over the bridge to attack from the base of the side that was relatively not so steep, the defenders realized their mistake. They now moved around to attack Alexander's troops. But they had to come down from their mountaintop position to attack the bridge, which they did. It was exactly what Alexander had wanted.

Now that they were within the range of his siege engines and balistas, the Macedonians heaped rocks and arrows upon them. So engaged were the Indians in the fight with Alexander that they forgot about Ptolemy, who inched his way along the several-mile-long mountainside with the garrisons and surprised the Indians from the rear of the Indian defense. Mount Aornos was conquered and a garrison established at the citadel to watch over the land all around. The capture of Mount Aornos again revealed how physical advantages like a mountain could not stand against the will and guile of a determined leader like Alexander.

Alexander's determination, and ability to stage feints, is also witnessed in one of the most astonishing military victories of his career, which was scored only a month before his Indian expedition. This was at the Sogdian

Rock, a steep mountain—though not nearly as high as Mount Aornos—on top of which was a fortress. Snow covered everything in sight. When Alexander ordered the surrender of the Sogdians (Uzbeks) holed up in the fortress, they laughed. Some mocked his troops to spring wings to fly up and get them. Undaunted, he ordered three hundred mountain climbers to scale the snow-covered mountain in the night using ropes and pegs, and carrying Macedonian flags.[3]

These troops worked all night, and when dawn arose, several flags could be seen fluttering on the mountain's sentry posts from heights well above the fortress—the Sogdians, in keeping with the mountaineer's maxim "Climb high, sleep low," would abandon their posts at night to sleep in the fortress. Although over thirty Macedonian climbers had fallen to their death, their bodies had been quickly removed, and the rest of the troops below hidden from the enemy's sight, so when the Sogdians looked out of their fortress in the morning to mock the Macedonians, they didn't find any more than a few standing below. Those below now mocked at them and asked the Sogdians to look behind and above them. There, clinging to the mountainside above them, were Macedonians waving their national flag—ready to jump into the fortress. The Sogdians couldn't look at the side of the mountain below them, where most of the Macedonians stood hidden from their sight. Thinking that *all* the Macedonians had climbed or were climbing up the mountain, the Sogdians surrendered.

Among the Sogdians Alexander met was Roxanne, the daughter of the tribe's chief. So infatuated was Alexander with Roxanne that he married her. She was his true and only wife—Barsine was his mistress and Stateira (Darius' daughter) would be a symbolic wife to suggest the marriage of Macedonian or Greek culture and society with Persia's. After Alexander's death Roxanne and her son by Alexander—Alexander IV—would return to Macedonia. Both would meet unfortunate deaths.

Feints in the Business World

The creation of a phantom threat to battle an enemy, while a matter of course in military warfare, is less prevalent in business—though not non-existent. The reason it is much less prevalent than in military warfare is because regulatory and corporate reporting requirements inhibit cloak-and-dagger moves among competitors. In the pharmaceutical and many high-tech industries, for example, it is not entirely uncommon for drug makers to seek patents in therapeutic areas where they have no intention whatsoever of competing—the only value of the patent being to throw off or block off competitors from coming near their core technology.

One of the best examples of a competitor creating a phantom threat happened in the pet food industry. In the late 1980s and early 1990s the health and fitness craze hit the pet food industry. Iams, a pet food company established in the mid-forties by a former Procter & Gamble salesman named Paul Iams, as well as Colgate-Palmolive's Hill's Pet Nutrition Unit, rushed into the health-conscious segment by offering pet owners lean diets for their pets. These companies sold their products through specialized pet food retailers, breeders, and veterinarians—partly because they were locked out of the supermarkets and partly because they wanted to create the veneer of their products as premium brands, which could only be found at the specialty retailers; similar to high-end shampoos, which are only sold through exclusive hair salons.

St. Louis–based Ralston Purina Company, the dominant oligopolist (in plain English, the eight-hundred-pound gorilla) in the pet food business then with over thirty percent of the market share in pet foods, largely ignored these emergent market segments and consumers. Ralston sold its dog and cat foods through supermarkets, and as long as Iams or Hills kept its high-priced, premium products off the supermarket shelves it believed it didn't need to bat an eyelash. Unfortunately for Ralston a new form of distribution channel for pet foods was creeping up in the form of large, specialized pet-food retailers like Petco and PetSmart, which stocked a broad variety of pet foods, including the gourmet meals. While these retailers attracted massive numbers of pet food buyers through their aggressive pricing and promotions, it was still the case that the supermarkets were where most pet owners shopped more frequently than any other outlet. So Ralston stocked its products at the Petco's and PetSmart's of the world, but protected the supermarket channel with all its effort and energy.

To further force Iams and Hills into concentrating their resources *away* from the supermarkets, and into these specialized channels, Ralston developed its own range of gourmet products, which it priced below its competitors' offerings and stocked at the specialty pet-food stores. Ralston, in effect, was practicing one of Sun Tzu's precepts about deception: Create an opportunity that seems so attractive that your enemy is enticed into it with lures of high profits.[4] Some companies create "phantom" products to steer competitors away, but Ralston created a real product that caused a "phantom" threat.

Seeing Ralston come into what they had considered was their exclusive territory, Iams and Hills expended even greater resources in developing and bringing to market more and better gourmet products. To stave off Ralston's forays and price positions they positioned themselves as premium brands. Indeed, so enamored were they of their premium-brand positioning that they even went to the extent of suggesting that their products *could not* be purchased at the local supermarket.[5]

That is exactly the kind of positioning Ralston wished to force its competitors into articulating. Once Iams and Hills locked themselves out of the supermarket channel, Ralston then introduced a line of gourmet products for its supermarket channel—so shoppers would have little incentive to go anywhere else for their pet food needs. Ralston had a foothold in all the channels that Iams and Hills competed in, but a lock on the supermarket channel. By forcing its competitors to divert all their resources into defending their turf in the specialty pet store market, Ralston, bought by the Swiss consumer goods giant Nestlé in 2001, had locked them—at least temporarily—out of an important channel.

In 1997 warehouse club giant Costco forced Colgate to sell its Hills brand of gourmet pet food through its stores, or face delisting of its other products, including its eponymous toothpaste. While Colgate initially resisted, and Costco did carry out its threat, eventually the company relented and today the Hills brand is carried on its shelves. In 2000 P & G bought the Iams brand, and this gourmet pet food is today sold everywhere that other P & G products like Crest toothpaste, Tide detergents, and Pringles potato chips are sold. The new competitive dynamics in pet foods, as they say, is an entirely different story.

Into the Heartland of India

Alexander, now that the north of India was secure and in his control, galloped back at a blistering pace to rejoin the larger contingent of his army, which was moving under Hephaistion's command toward Taxila—about twenty miles outside of modern Rawalpindi, Pakistan. Taxila was the great university town that he had heard about from many, especially his teacher Aristotle. Taxila was where, several centuries before Alexander's arrival, the Buddha would come for medical treatment whenever he was ill. The Buddha, who died at the age of eighty-six, often visited the medical faculty here or was visited by members of the faculty for treatment. The city-state was ruled by the Indian king Ambi, who, hearing of the Macedonians' arrival through the Khyber Pass, had sent ambassadors to notify them that they would be welcome guests.

As Alexander arrived at the university town with 80,000 troops, the gates of the city opened and inside stood King Ambi with 30,000 troops astride horses and elephants. Not sure whether the colors painted on the flags, shields, saddles, and howdah were meant as a welcoming gesture or a call to battle, Alexander ordered his phalanxes to form and his cavalry to position themselves in the center and the outer flanks. Ambi realized that there must have been some misunderstanding.

He therefore rode out of the city walls to greet the Macedonian king. Seeing the Indian king come toward him alone, Alexander also did the same. Ambi, in his broken and sparse Greek, hastily picked up from the Greek faculty at Taxila, surrendered his throne and invited Alexander in.

Alexander stayed in Taxila for a few weeks, setting his sights to conquering the interior of India. He and Ambi got into a contest of generosity, which displeased some of the Macedonian commanders. Ambi's personal philosophy was that the only things worth fighting for were water, the basic necessities in life like food, and knowledge. If these were plentiful, who cared about the rest? He was willing to give Alexander everything he had, and Alexander, taken in by such display of generosity, in turn offered him everything *he* had.

But in the brief respite at Taxila, Alexander planned. Although the Western world from which Alexander came believed that the world they lived in ended in the ocean (or the River Ganges), getting to the ocean required crossing five major tributaries of the River Indus. Along each one of these tributaries lay many cities and towns, each ruled by its own king or prince. Unlike the Persians the Indians had a strong reputation as warriors, their military craft and technology were well developed, and their armies were very large and well trained. While he rested in Taxila, Alexander received reports of troops massing on the banks of the Hydaspes (the modern Jhelum River), one of the tributaries of the Indus.

Despite the reports he wasn't going to spoil his stay in Taxila. It had been several years since Mieza, and he had yearned these years on the campaign for rigor and the challenge of the intellectual pursuits he had enjoyed so much at Mieza. Alexander walked around the town every day and met many intellectuals and teachers. He frequently dropped in on debates, discussions, and classes. He had a stream of visitors from the university, with whom he engaged in serious, substantive discussions. What free time he had left, he generously showered on letters to Aristotle and his mother about the place. (Writing home from his campaigns, as well as reading *The Iliad* every night—Aristotle's personal copy, which the teacher had presented to him at Mieza—are two common themes that have consistently recurred in many historians' writings about his personal interests.)

Weaving a Tangled Web

"Oh, what a tangled web we weave when first we practice to deceive," wrote Sir Walter Scott in 1808.[6] One of the first widespread applications of elaborate and extensive deception in war was at the Battle of the Hydaspes (Jhelum) against the Indian king Porus, who was everything that the king of Taxila, Ambi, was not. Valorous, fearless, and proud, Porus massed his troops alongside the Hydaspes, across from the banks where Alexander would arrive. The Battle of the Hydaspes certainly provides the most insightful lessons about Alexander's subtle, indirect approach to warfare through outmaneuvering, outflanking, and outthinking the enemy.

Many military historians contend that not till the Second World War, well over 2,000 years after the Battle of the Hydaspes, would the world witness anything close. Only Napoleon, for whom the Battle of Hydaspes was the most intriguing ever fought, was to undertake tactics that came close. There were a few other generals, Julius Caesar, Hannibal, Scipio, Marlborough, Frederick the Great, Wellington, among them, who would exhibit, in parts, the penetrating insight and control of Alexander—but only in parts.

By and large, however, the world would eschew Alexander's subtlety, intrigue, and sense of timing as to when to move and when not to in favor of massive mobilization of large forces in battles, whose outcomes would be decided by sheer numbers or willpower. This Clausewitzian approach would be challenged by military strategists and historians like Liddell Hart, who, after the needless loss of millions in the First World War, were to call successfully for a reexamination of military strategy and pave the way for one that, like Alexander's and Napoleon's, depended not so much on numbers as on guile, surprise, speed, and skill.

It would have been easy for Alexander to overwhelm Porus at the Hydaspes on the strength of sheer numbers: He had more than twice as large an army as Porus' 35,000—unlike most battles against the Persians, where he was vastly outnumbered. The lore of the Macedonians' successes was now the stuff of legends. And if the Persians, the world's largest army, could not put up a fight against Alexander, surely the army of a small provincial kingdom, whose greatest exploits involved rubbing out minor border incursions from the neighboring kingdom of Taxila or apprehending cattle stealers, would prove no match against the Macedonians.

Despite the Macedonians' superior reputation and formidable track record, King Porus and his troops bravely geared up for a fight. Porus' army, comprising 30,000 infantry, 5,000 cavalry, 300 chariots, and 100 elephants, lined up along the banks of the swelling waters of the River Hydaspes. The troops polished their iron swords, sharpened their spears, and tightened the scythe blades that lined the wheels of the chariots. The archers chiseled the tips of their three-foot-long arrows and felt the tautness of their five-foot-long bows.

The monsoon's rains had broken and the river's normal half-mile width had doubled, ravaging the banks of either side, flooding portions of the countryside. This was the first time, after Egypt, that the Macedonians had experienced such torrential rains, and their meteorologists confidently proclaimed that these rains were caused by the climatic shifts over the Ethiopian plains—as they had previously proclaimed caused the rains in Egypt. When lotus was found growing in ponds and crocodiles found basking in the sun, scientists accompanying Alexander, for a brief moment, jumped to the Aristotelian hypothesis that the Indus and the Nile must be connected—only to have their hypothesis later demolished.[7]

Porus had hoped that the May monsoons and the rising tide of the Hydaspes would either halt Alexander's progress or, at the very least, give them a brief respite from the stress and tension of standing across from the greatest army in the world. They had not realized that the monsoon rains were exactly what Alexander had been waiting for. While most armies battling in Asia called it quits during the monsoons, Alexander wanted to attack under the pervasive sense of lull that engulfed armies during them.

Although Alexander had previously charged across rivers to engage the enemy—at the Granicus and Issus, for example—he had never confronted any river like the Hydaspes. Moreover, even though he had a larger and more experienced army than Porus', he was unwilling to shed lives needlessly. Instead, he rested his army on the riverbank, laid down massive stores of wheat and corn, and instead of massing his army along any specific section of the bank, and building temporary quarters, he changed their positions every day along several miles of shore. This way the enemy on the other side could never guess from where to expect an attack.

Every day the Macedonian army staged cavalry marches and noisy infantry exercises. Although Alexander's troops numbered 80,000, he had in addition about 40,000 civilian followers—wives, children, entertainers, philosophers, prostitutes, physicians, poets, soothsayers of various nationalities, surveyors, geologists, tutors, and so on—tagging along. Every evening there was loud singing, boisterous dancing, and drinking of massive quantities of cheap jug wine. But there would be no attack. There would be lots of movements of supplies and troops, and Porus on the other bank would move his horses, chariots, elephants, and troops to keep up with the Macedonian movements—but there would be no attack.

Every day the ruse was played out. Troops would be moved, placed in position, taken off position, reassembled, reconstituted, and repositioned for an imminent attack, and then nothing would happen. Lunch would arrive, followed by equestrian games, and then an entire evening of partying. All this as they were drenched by incessant monsoon rains. This went on for weeks. Porus' army, waiting for the inevitable attack, first grew restless and then was lulled into a sleepy boredom. Opposing armies facing each other over long periods develop a bond with the other side—the Germans stopped shelling of British positions during the Great War in the late afternoon when they knew the Brits would retire for tea. Porus' army rather enjoyed the mirth and merriment on the opposite side.

SHROUDING TRUTH IN A BODYGUARD OF LIES

Like Alexander's moves to throw the Indians off on the other side about the exact location or timing of an attack on them, in the late summer of 1943 the Allied armies' military planners wrestled with a similar issue: How do they dissuade the Germans from believing that an invasion is imminent? They knew that it would be difficult to persuade the Germans that an invasion was not being planned—especially since they had spent the previous two years trying to impress upon them that an invasion was coming. But as they applied the finishing touches to Operation Overlord—the invasion of France, which would be launched in Normandy on June 6, 1944—they reluctantly concluded that, while it might be tough to persuade the Germans that an invasion was not imminent, it would be highly beneficial at least to keep them guessing as to when and where the attack would come.

The Germans had spent several years shoring up their defenses along the coast of northwest France: The Atlantic Wall is considered to be the most fortified defense ever built in history. All along the beaches and towns bordering the sea were concrete bunkers with heavy guns and machine-gun nests and pillboxes. Beachfront properties—inns and vacation homes—had been seized by the Germans, and behind sandbagged windows sat German machine gunners constantly scanning the blue sea. The waters and beaches had been mined to rip apart any landing craft or ship that might arrive in their proximity.

To deflect the German army's attention from the planned invasion site, the Allies concocted and undertook a massive scheme of deception—not unlike Alexander's equestrian games and social binges. The Germans had always believed that when, not if, an invasion of northwest France took place, it would be at the Pas-de-Calais—just as Porus believed that whenever the Macedonians would cross the Hydaspes, they would do it right across or from somewhere very near—after all, the armies stood facing each other at the point where the river was the narrowest.

From most people's perspectives the Pas-de-Calais made a lot of sense. It was right across from the English seaside town of Dover, with large harbors to support an invasion. The Strait of Dover, which separated France from England, was the narrowest part of the English Channel. On a clear day one could stand on the shores of France and watch the seagulls waft past the white cliffs of Dover—the subject of many romantic poems. For the Allied aircraft stationed in the numerous airfields in Kent, Pas-de-Calais would literally be a puddle jump. So convinced were the Germans about Pas-de-Calais as the landing site for an invasion force that they had extended and deepened the Atlantic Wall near the French seaside town.

The Allied military planners had no intention of disabusing the Germans of their conviction. Indeed they did everything to strengthen it. This is how Operation Fortitude got launched. Fortitude had two parts to it: Fortitude (North) concentrated on creating a screen of deception to lead the Germans to believe that the Allies planned an invasion of Norway; Fortitude (South) focused on creating the illusion of an attack on the Pas-de-Calais. As part of Fortitude (North) an entire fictitious army group was created to train and launch an attack on Norway from Scotland. Cardboard soldiers as well as dummy boats and military vehicles were created to look like a large invasion force, and the operation even created fictional radio traffic in easily decipherable code to suggest an imminent invasion. Even the Soviets cooperated by spreading a story about senior officers being sent to England to complete the arrangements for an invasion.[8]

So completely deceived were the Germans about Fortitude (North) that even several days after the real invasion began at Normandy, Adolf Hitler was still awaiting news of the invasion of Norway. It was in the context of briefing each other about these deceptive actions that Winston Churchill famously remarked to Stalin in Teheran, "In wartime, truth is so precious that she should always be attended by a bodyguard of lies."[9]

Fortitude (South) was even more ambitious. For months before the actual landings Allied aircraft had bombarded towns, railway lines, supply depots, roads, convoys, radar installations, ammunition dumps, and airports. But of the 200,000 tons of bombs dropped in northwest France, only a third were dropped in the area of the actual planned invasion, which was Normandy, and most around the Pas-de-Calais—thus furthering the deception that Pas-de-Calais was where the invasion was planned. For example, of the airports bombed, eleven were in the Pas-de-Calais and only four in the vicinity of Normandy.[10]

Even the preparations back in England were designed to throw the enemy off. Although elaborate preparations were already under way to mobilize, train, equip, and transport thousands of troops to their real destination in Normandy, parallel efforts were also under way in southeast England (across from the Pas-de-Calais) to prepare for the noninvasion of the Pas-de-Calais. German spies at work in England had been converted into double agents, who, just prior to the invasion of Normandy, passed on information to their German bosses that the Allies would launch an invasion against Normandy as a feint to draw the Germans away from the Pas-de-Calais; the real invasion would begin when the German forces had been drawn toward Normandy.

Hitler and his generals bought the deception completely. As little as a week before the landings at Normandy the Führer arrived at the conclusion that an invasion was coming (the Allied preparations were too large to have gone unnoticed); that there would be an initial landing at Normandy or Brittany, but the real invasion would begin with the opening of a second front across the English Channel near the Pas-de-Calais. Germany would like nothing better, he is said to have claimed, than to be given the opportunity of engaging the enemy as soon as possible.[11] The rest, as they say, is history.

The Battle of the Hydaspes

For over two months the Macedonians rode, drank, sang, and danced. Then one night it happened. Like George Washington's crossing of the Delaware near Trenton, New Jersey, two thousand years later, Alexander commandeered a highly select group of his cavalry, 5,000 in all, and 10,000 infantrymen, and rode under the concealment of the dark monsoon clouds, a misty rain, and the hills along the river. He had left most of his troops behind to continue to distract Porus' attention as he rode up the hilly riverbank, toward the chosen spot for the crossing—some fifteen miles from his original position. Porus could never have guessed that the very point that Alexander had chosen to make the crossing was where the river was at its widest.

Unlike George Washington's revolutionary army, which corralled all the fishing boats on the Delaware River that night for the crossing, Alexander's had first to wade into the snake- and crocodile-infested waters of the Hydaspes and then swim across. Unknown to Porus the reason why Alexander had selected the widest part of the river was that this is where the currents would be the weakest. Yet the current and undertow were strong enough to carry away and drown some of the troops and horses. By the time Alexander began the crossing, the drizzle had given way to a heavy downpour, and the thunder and lightning that accompanied it would have persuaded any reasonable man to turn back.

Alexander, however, was no reasonable man. Riding his horse, Bucephalus, he led his men into the raging waters. The horses wobbled about in the water, till they found their bare footing on the river bottom—it was about a century before the invention of the horseshoe.[12] Their riders held on to them, by their knees—neither stirrups nor saddles had found their way out of India—and some riders and horses clambered on to boats, which had been cut in half to bring them up the land route and quickly reassembled to facilitate the river crossing. Makeshift rafts from reeds and animal skins were jumped on by the infantrymen, and like surfers getting out into the ocean to catch the perfect curl on their surfboards, the infantrymen used these rafts as floatation devices to paddle across.

Anyone who has witnessed the migration of the wildebeests through the Serengeti Plains of Africa knows that more lives are lost in the river crossings than to thirst in the scorching heat of the African plains or even to the surprise attacks from animals such as lions and tigers who feed on them. We also know that getting into the water, once the initial fear is overcome, is the easy part. Clambering up the muddy, slippery riverbank on the other side, while fighting others for a footing, is the tough part. The others here included 5,000 horses and their riders, and 10,000 very wet and tired infantrymen with their heavy breastplates and other pieces of armor and their long spears. Thousands of wildebeests die each year as they compete for a footing on the banks of rivers. It was a miracle that Alexander's troops, horses, and armor made the crossing.

It was as the first light of dawn broke over the lush green Indian landscape that Porus' reconnaissance men spotted a few hundred very wet and tired Macedonians on their bank. The king immediately dispatched his son and 2,000 of his troops to investigate. By the time they arrived at the Macedonian crossing point, enough had made it across to gather their armor—and their wits and courage—to successfully repel an attack. Porus' son was killed in the skirmish.

Porus realized he had been deceived. Across from him on the other bank stood a large contingent of the Macedonian army getting ready to cross. Someone was impersonating Alexander, even to the extent of wearing a plumed helmet and barking orders. He knew in his heart, though, that the crossing had already happened. Porus now ordered his troops to turn toward the Macedonians up the riverbank.

The Macedonians on the other bank directly across from him were beginning a crossing, but he knew that this was a feint designed to focus his attention on them—and away from those who had already crossed up the river. He positioned his elephants at the front and center of his formation. The position of the elephants was designed to scare off the horses of the Macedonian cavalry and to trample through the phalanxes. His infantry was behind the elephants, holding the center. On the flanks were the chariots and the cavalry.

Once every Macedonian soldier had crossed over, Alexander rode along the river downstream with his cavalry and surveyed the enemy's positions. He didn't want a full-frontal assault, especially against war elephants—whose capabilities in battle to him were still unknown. He positioned his infantry at the center. Always a believer in attack, Alexander didn't wait for the Indians to come get him. He led the Macedonian cavalry in a charge against the Indian cavalry and chariots on the left flank. As they were riding toward the Indians, he ordered Coenus to lead two corps of the Macedonian cavalry in a break away from the charge, to ride behind the hills and surprise the Indian cavalry on the right flank from their rear.[13]

Seeing the Macedonians charge toward their positions, Porus ordered the Indian chariots and cavalry to meet them. They seemed to be going for his left flank, so he ordered the cavalry on the right to move to support the left. Alexander had timed his arrival to meet the Indian cavalry in such a way as to allow for Coenus to arrive just after the engagement had begun and surprise the Indian cavalry from its side or rear. That is precisely what happened.

Just as the opposing cavalry units neared each other, Alexander ordered his horseborne archers to unleash their arrows. In the ensuing melee in the Indian cavalry ranks, as the arrows struck home, the Macedonians found gaps in which to charge. By now the Macedonian cavalry that had broken away to ride behind the hills also entered the fight. Squeezed by the Macedonians all around them, the Indian cavalry began to fall. The Indian chariots had been pushed so far toward the river that many bogged down in its muddy banks. Stranded thus, the troops astride the chariots became sitting targets for the Macedonian cavalry, which slaughtered many.

Alexander had instructed his infantry that when they arrived upon the Indian center, they should spear the elephants' feet. He had no better idea for dealing with the elephants. That is exactly what the infantry did. Seeing the Macedonian infantry on the horizon, Porus unleashed his war elephants, behind which charged the Indian infantry. As soon as the pounding elephants came within striking distance, the Macedonian infantrymen in the front of the phalanxes speared their feet; the infantry behind clanked their shields to create an ear-piercing sound so loud that fear overcame the elephants. It had the desired effect, and more. The hurt and frightened elephants reversed the direction of their charge, trampling through Indian infantry positions. Finally, after eight hours of battle, in the early afternoon, the Indian defenses broke down and Porus surrendered. So impressed was Alexander at Porus' bravery and actions that he made him the ruler of all the land along the Hydaspes, and they remained close friends till Alexander died.

Nothing like the Battle of the Hydaspes had ever been witnessed in the ancient world: neither the double-envelopment cavalry action nor the conduct of the battle shrouded under deception and guile. The Chinese military strategist, Sun Tzu, wrote in *The Art of War*, about 150 years before Alexander that "all warfare was based on deception. Hence, when

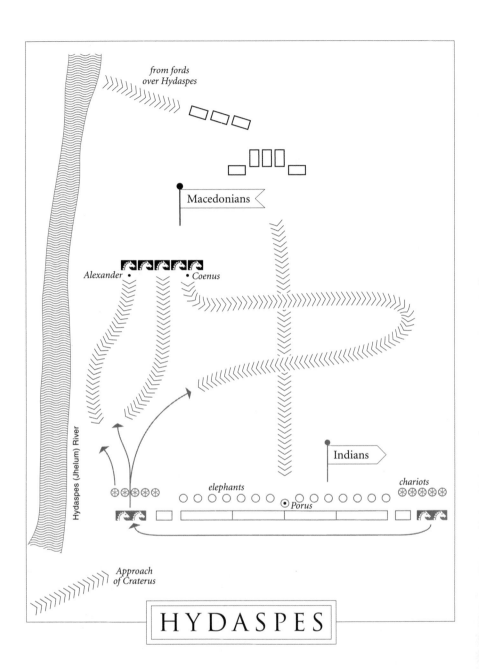

from fords
over Hydaspes

Macedonians

Alexander • • Coenus

Hydaspes (Jhelum) River

Indians

elephants

⊙ Porus

chariots

Approach
of Craterus

HYDASPES

able to attack, we must seem unable; when using our forces we must seem inactive; when we are near, we must make the enemy believe that we are away; when far away, we must make him believe we are near. Hold out baits to entice the enemy. Feign disorder, and crush him."[14]

Does Size Matter or Speed?

Alexander had forced Porus to line up his entire army on the opposite bank of the Hydaspes facing the Macedonian army, while he had no intention of attacking the Indians there. In business, too, companies frequently resort to such "strategic resource diversion"—forcing a competitor to focus their resources on a product or geography where the company has no plans ever to enter. Take Boeing's recent tactics against the European Airbus Industrie. For the past decade or so there has been a race between these two leading builders of commercial aircraft to come up with an efficient long-range superjumbo to meet the estimated tripling of demand in air travel over the next twenty years.[15] Boeing has held the lead in the commercial aircraft market, but in the high-density, long-haul market it has enjoyed almost a thirty-year monopoly with its 747s.

Despite this monopoly, and despite many highly publicized efforts to develop the superjumbo, Boeing did not immediately follow up with its announcement to actually build one when, in December 2000, Airbus Industrie announced that it would proceed with the development of the 555-seat A380. Indeed, three months later, in March 2001, Boeing announced that it would withdraw from the development of a superjumbo and concentrate on building the 250-seat Sonic Cruiser, which would fly almost at the speed of sound.

Obviously, it is too early to predict whether Boeing's Sonic Cruiser would be more successful than Airbus' A380. Boeing is ostensibly gambling on the superfast plane based on the hypothesis that greater deregulation of airline markets will facilitate greater and more frequent point-to-point, rather than hub-to-hub, travel.[16] If Boeing's hypothesis is correct, the world will need smaller, and preferably faster, planes like the Sonic Cruiser. If, on the other hand, hub-to-hub wins out, there will be need for larger aircraft like the one Airbus has staked its future against.

There are several different interpretations as to why Boeing, the leader in the long-haul, bulk-capacity market with its 747s, would not preempt competitive encroachments on what has traditionally been its turf. One interpretation holds that Airbus benefited from a launch subsidy from its

European owners—the British and French governments, primarily—to get its efforts for the superjumbo off the ground, while Boeing, as a private U.S. company, wouldn't and didn't. Another interpretation holds that Boeing's engineering-led organizational culture, which always sprang for a challenge, had shifted after the company's acquisition of McDonnell-Douglas in 1997 to a financial-control one; Boeing's managers didn't foresee much profit for the superjumbo.[17]

Another perspective, offered by Gordon Bethune, CEO of Continental Airlines, who previously was the program manager for Boeing's 737 and 757 aircraft models, is certainly the most intriguing. Bethune was quoted as saying that the reason why Boeing didn't commit to the super jumbos was because they had always wanted to go for speed, not for bulk.[18] Boeing, according to Bethune, waited till Airbus had made its commitment to bulk, and then announced its plans for speed when it was sure that Airbus, given the size of commitment it had made to the super-jumbo, would be in no position to shift toward developing a superfast plane. We don't know for sure whether there was a "strategic resource diversion" tactic by Boeing in its competition with Airbus Industrie or who between the two will eventually win, but this is certainly a plausible explanation for Boeing's on-again, off-again interest in the superjumbo.

The Army Forces Alexander to Head for Home

Back in the ancient world, after defeating Porus, Alexander continued to invade a few small princely states around the Jhelum River, as well as other tributaries of the Indus. There was little incentive for any of these states to resist Alexander's encroachments. Most surrendered and became part of his growing empire. Those that didn't give in faced annihilation or an expensive denouement.

The Macedonians were getting very tired, however, and there was much hand wringing in the ranks. Although the Indians would lose, they would do so only after exacting a heavy toll on the Macedonians. By the time they reached the River Hyphasis (today's Beas), his generals were to prevail upon him to turn back. They feared the roving Indian mercenaries, who would fight for anyone willing to pay their price, and they feared the armies of the large kingdoms that lay beyond the Hyphasis.

In a highly emotional speech, on behalf of the army, his general Coenus, who had led one of the key flanking maneuvers at the Battle of the Hydaspes, pleaded with Alexander to return home. Many men were dead, many had settled down in the lands conquered, but the ones on the campaign were overwhelmed with a desire to return home, Coenus said. If Alexander wanted to conquer the lands beyond the Hyphasis, he should raise a new army, and seeing the members of the old return to their homes in glory and in wealth, volunteers would sign up freely and easily for such an army. But now was the time to return home, see one's family, and set the affairs of Greece right.[19]

Like Achilles' famous sulk in the Trojan War, Alexander, hearing Coenus' words, went into his tent and pouted for three days. After that he came out and agreed to head home, but not before making a General MacArthur–like promise about returning someday. He divided his army into brigades and ordered them to build a dozen altars on the banks of the Hyphasis to serve as monuments of his expedition. Then, adding all the land so far conquered to the dominion of Porus, he set off toward the Hydaspes. In a few weeks Coenus mysteriously died.

Instead of retracing his steps through territories he had already conquered, Alexander set off toward the Gedrosian Desert, which, like the march of Napoleon's Grande Armée back from Moscow, was to lead to mass starvation and hardship. Clearly, while Alexander was able to turn the tables on foe after foe, with a wide variety of deceptive strategic maneuvers, his own troops wanted no more of it. There was not much Alexander could do to change their minds about returning home, though the routes he would take were again deceptive in nature in that they weren't just leading him back home, but were helping him consolidate what he had conquered.

SUMMARY OF THEMES

1. Disperse to concentrate.

"The principles of war, not merely one principle," wrote Basil H. Liddell Hart, the English military strategist and commentator, "can be condensed into a single word—*concentration*. . . . The concentration of strength against weakness."[20] To be able to concentrate, Liddell Hart continued, one must be able to disperse the opponent's strength, which can only be brought about by a dispersion of one's own strengths. "Your dispersion, his dispersion, your concentration—such is the sequence, and each is a sequel."[21] The entire battle for Mount Aornos is one of calculated dispersions and decisive concentrations.

2. DISLOCATE AND EXPLOIT.

Everything that Alexander did on the banks of the Hydapses before launching the attack was designed to throw the enemy off its guard. He didn't attack when or where they most expected it; he attacked when and where they least expected it. He managed to dislocate the enemy's comfort zone by his element of surprise, but he was also well prepared to exploit that dislocation to its maximum advantage. Execution of strategic and tactical moves in war and business often misses the element of surprise, because everyone is so focused on executing against plan that very few opportunities for surprise ever present themselves; or even when they present themselves, no one has the needed preparation to exploit them.

3. ERRONEOUS SIGNALS.

Signaling is a tactic frequently employed in a strategy by firms to communicate intentions or exchange pricing and other information, which might lead to collusive behavior. In war, signaling is deployed as a feint to focus the other side's resources at a point where no attack is planned. Such resource diversion strategies, when thoughtfully employed, can lead to competitive advantage, as Ralston proved in the pet food market and Boeing probably has in the commercial jetliner market.

CHAPTER 10

ALEXANDER'S DEATH—AND LEGACY

ALEXANDER HAD DRAWN THE EASTERN LIMITS TO HIS EMPIRE AT THE River Hyphasis (Beas). It was now time to go home, or at least toward Babylon, in today's Iraq, which was emerging as the center of his empire — much of the Macedonian bureaucracy worked out of Babylon, and the city was where his main mint was based.

Instead of following the route he had taken to reach India, Alexander traveled south toward the Arabian Sea. On reaching the outskirts of modern-day Karachi, Pakistan, he decided to split his army into three divisions. In 325 B.C. one contingent of about 10,000 troops and a similar number of followers took the route through the Hindu Kush back toward a rendezvous point in the vicinity of today's port city of Bandar-e-Abbas in ancient Carmania (modern southern Iran). This contingent consisted mainly of battle-scarred and tired long-term veterans of the campaign, as well as all the heavy siege engines, and the newly acquired Indian war elephants, the panzer tanks of ancient warfare.

He also dispatched several divisions by ship along the Arabian Sea, under the leadership of his general Nearchus, with an agreed-upon meeting at the rendezvous point. Alexander had planned to traverse the arid and inhospitable Gedrosian Desert (the modern Makran Desert) that lay between India and southern Iran, along a coastal route, so as to ensure supplies for the fleet, which would anchor for the supplies at several predetermined points along the coast; but soon after stepping into the desert he was forced to abandon the plan. The army under his command had swelled to about 50,000 troops (depending on which source one wishes to believe) and camp followers numbered as many as 25,000. It was very clear that it was every person for himself—so acute was the food and water shortage in the desert. So as not to strip the coastal areas of food, thereby depriving the fleet of its main source of food, the army turned inland.

There was massive devastation as the army and the followers toiled through the sand under the hot October sun. Not till Napoleon's Grande Armée would make its disastrous advance and retreat to and from Moscow between July and November 1812 would an army face as daunting a challenge as Alexander faced in the sixty days it took him to cross the almost thousand-mile Gedrosian Desert. Many of the bare-hoofed horses and other pack animals, without food or water, collapsed in the sands. The army sliced up the dead animals and ate them. The stragglers faced even greater hardship, because by the time the army had had its food, there were few, if any, leftovers for them.

Even in this hardship, however, there were examples of exemplary personal leadership. Arrian recounts the story of some soldiers bringing Alexander the last remaining water in a helmet to quench his thirst. He had been leading at the front of the army by walking on the sand, not riding his horse, so that none of his soldiers would ever think that he had it easier than they. Alexander poured the water into the sand and said that their gesture had quenched his thirst—he wasn't willing to drink if his soldiers hadn't had any water first. "The entire army was reinvigorated to such a degree," wrote Arrian about the event "that one would have imagined that the water poured away by Alexander had furnished a draught to every man."[1]

It was near Bandar-e-Abbas that Alexander met up with the fleet commanded by Nearchus as well as the contingent led by Craterus, who had swept into southern Iran and collected as many supplies as he could, traveling through the towns and villages of Afghanistan's Helmand Valley and eastern Iran. They brought so much food and wine that some historians have written about a week-long binge of prodigious drinking, serious debauch, and uncontrolled revelry. The hardship of the desert was soon forgotten.

Fusion of Cultures

After the army was rested, it started on its journey toward Persepolis, the former summer capital of the Achaemenid kings, and then onward on the royal road to the winter capital of Susa. Just outside Persepolis was the town of Pasargadae—the ancient capital of the Achaemenids, where the founder of the Persian empire, Cyrus the Great, lay buried. Alexander, now that he was the ruler of all Asia, with a large Persian population under his sway, decided to make the ceremonial trip to the tomb to pay his respects to the Great King—as every foreign dignitary did at the Tomb of Lenin when the Soviet Union was alive. Alexander was aware of his place in the world—he now was ruler of Greeks, Macedonians, *and* Persians, among others—and a visit to Cyrus' tomb would sit well with his Persian subjects.

Dressed in Persian clothes, Alexander visited the tomb, which was reputed to hold not only a casket with the bones of the Great King but also expensive jewelry and other treasures. Alexander, curious for a look inside, ordered the seal broken, and on entering the tomb was horrified to see what it contained: a decrepit casket, a threadbare couch, and nothing more than dust and cobwebs. He instantly ordered an investigation and had the magi tortured to see if they knew the tomb robbers. Persians were obviously very pleased at the concern Alexander displayed toward their forbears and were also touched by the expressions of sensitivity he had begun to display toward their culture.

He had been at it for several years—at the funeral of Darius' wife Stateira, for example, he had performed every custom that Persians performed at the demise of a family member—but on the return journey through Persia he had taken to donning Persian clothes, wearing an upright tiara, which was only worn by a Persian monarch, and demanding adherence to Persian customs—including *proskynesis*—the custom of genuflection before a king. Persians believed their kings were direct descendants of their god, Ahura Mazda, and gave their kings the same respect that they reserved for their god. Macedonians, too, believed their kings were descended from the Olympian gods, but treated their kings as equals—acts like prostration were reserved only for their gods or dead heroes.[2] Macedonians were horrified when Alexander demanded their adherence to the Persian customs.

Driving Alexander's adoption of the Persian mores was an eagerness to position himself as the true and rightful successor of the Persian kings, not merely as a "transient conqueror."[3] He had not only taken to wearing the dress of Persian monarchs, but also inducted several Persian nobles, including the brother of Darius, into his advisory entourage.

At Susa, Alexander caught up with the children of Darius, whom he had left in the charge of Greek teachers. To fulfill the promise he had made to their late mother as well as grandmother, after their capture at the Battle of Issus, he decided to marry off Darius' two daughters. To make it a celebration of the unity of Macedonian and Persian societies, he also persuaded almost a hundred of his Macedonian generals and close counselors to take on Persian brides. To lead by example he married Stateira, the older daughter of Darius, as well as the daughter of a Persian noble, Artaxerxes III.[4] They were his second and third wives—he was already wed to the Sogdian (Uzbek) princess Roxanne, who was now pregnant.

Hephaistion wed Darius' younger daughter, Drypetis. All the counselors who took on Persian wives were richly rewarded. Many of his rank-and-file troops also took on Macedonian brides, and each of them was paid a dowry from the king's exchequer. The wedding celebrations lasted five days, and by the time the army left for Babylon in spring 324 B.C., vast settlements had been established for those wishing to leave the army and settle down to raise families. The army had also expanded by the infusion of 30,000 Persian volunteers who had been in months of training at a Macedonian military school in Persia.

In the summer of 324 B.C., a year after leaving India, the army staggered into Opis, just outside of Babylon. Resentment and dissension plagued the army ranks—partly due to the sheer fact that over a decade since crossing the Hellespont, their energy was sapped and their spirits dissipated; partly due to the fact that the people they had fought against—the Persians—were a growing and influential presence in their ranks.

At Opis, when Alexander decreed that all the old guard of the army were to be sent back to Macedonia, with suitable rewards for their service, an open mutiny broke out among those who were being sent back, as well as among those whom he planned to keep. Since the rebellion at the Hyphasis, when the troops did not wish to go any farther into India, there had been a growing sense of unease among the troops that the Macedonian army had lost its bearings. It wasn't a Macedonian army anymore, but that wasn't the major concern—after all, since the day they left Greece they had had many other nationalities in their ranks. Despite the variety of nationalities, the one thing that really curled their toes was taking orders, however insignificant, from the Persians, who were not only foreigners, but also, till recently, their sworn enemies. Moreover, the traditional bonds that tie troops together—similar backgrounds, shared experiences, hardships, and toil—were only superficially present in an army that was now as much Asian as it was European.

From the rank-and-file's perspective Alexander had also changed. He wasn't leading them on a fight against a clearly defined enemy anymore; he was pursuing some undefined goals toward unity of cultures and societies, which, from their perspective, meant genuflection before their king and, frequently, taking orders from members of the Persian nobility. Not only that, but his personal style had become highly autocratic—he loomed large and tall like a giant oak tree, but an oak tree that wouldn't allow any foliage to grow below it.

Alexander was revealing those same tactical leadership missteps that would bring down many leaders in the ensuing centuries. Take Britain's Oliver Cromwell and Margaret Thatcher, for example. Both, like Alexander, came in at uncertain points of their nation's history. Cromwell took over as the Lord Protector of England in 1653, after Parliament had made a sorry state of running the affairs of the nation. The primacy of Parliament, and England's experiment with republicanism, came about under Cromwell's leadership in the English Civil War, which finally ended with the public beheading of Charles I—the king of England and Scotland. Over three hundred years later, in 1979, Margaret Thatcher would sweep into office on the promise of ending Britain's long experiment with socialism, which had led to massive unemployment, taxes as high as 83 percent, deep labor and social, especially racial, unrest, and an overwhelming state machinery that was totally inept.

Yet the man who led the nation out of total chaos and the woman who brought Britain back from the status of a second-rate power on the verge of falling into a third-rate one, were deeply despised and resented toward the end of their careers. Like Alexander near the end of his reign, they had both lost touch with their nation's feelings, and they had both forgotten to communicate with people even though it was their ability to touch their people's hearts when they spoke that had brought them into power in the first place.[5]

Mohandas Karamchand Gandhi

We see Alexander, toward the end of his career, rapidly losing touch with the hopes and aspirations of the people who had helped him achieve so much in so short a time. Most around him did not share his enthusiasm for social and cultural unity among Macedonians, Greeks, Egyptians, Babylonians, Persians, and Indians, among others. Yet they went along with highly publicized mass weddings between Macedonians and other nationalities. Even his generals were reluctant to hold up the mirror to him and went along with such initiatives at integration, like the mass weddings — although most of them divorced their foreign spouses immediately after Alexander's death. Many Macedonians did not believe in his divinity and yet furthered his divine pretensions. Alexander's private beliefs and public actions had blurred so much so that they were the same.

The way a leader's private beliefs shape his public posture has been a little-studied area in the annals of leadership or management, and yet, so many leaders lose their legacy or at least leave behind tarnished ones because they are uncertain as to where to draw the line between their private beliefs and public actions. In Cromwell, for example, his Puritan lineage and millenary beliefs could make him appear to make decisions that seemed to his followers inspired by divine intervention, while at others he would go through "agonies of spiritual torment from which he would emerge only after weeks to pronounce one way or the other."[6] The unpredictability of the way Cromwell's private beliefs might affect a public decision always kept his followers on their toes.

The one leader from relatively modern times who not only used his private beliefs to shape his public actions, but also effectively blurred the line between the two so that there was no dissonance between private beliefs and public actions, was Mohandas Karamchand Gandhi. Most people's image of Gandhi is of a modest, loincloth-draped, skeletal Indian with a walking stick in his hand. It often, therefore, comes as a surprise to learn that Gandhi was born to a prosperous family sufficiently well off to send him to London to study law. It was in the stark contrast of living in London that Gandhi's personal beliefs and convictions, as well as his preferences, got solidified: about clothes (sparse and retro), food (vegetarian), and social interactions (limited).

After London, Gandhi spent twenty-one years in South Africa, between 1893 and 1914. It was there that he found that his private beliefs not only shaped the way he and his family lived, but were central to the public leadership he was to provide for gaining equality for the large Indian community in racially polarized South Africa. The Gandhi family in South Africa, financially prosperous from his thriving law practice, took to baking bread and whole-wheat biscuits from the flour that had been ground by family members using a hand-operated mill. Everyone in the Gandhi household took turns cranking the heavy iron wheels of the mill, because it instilled pride in "self-reliance"—which would, on his return to India, become an important plank in Gandhi's manifesto for freeing India from British rule.

"Self-reliance," "self-sufficiency," and "self-restraint," were important positions of Gandhi's leadership in seeking Indian independence. It was from these positions, and their ardent practice, that he derived the "moral authority" to coax his followers to also adopt such practices. There was also a consistency in his positions. He had a unique ability to perceive the implications of a conflict and take sides based on what was right rather than what was politically expedient—even when that meant abandoning the fight for India's independence (and encouraging his followers to fight alongside the British against a greater threat in the First and the Second World Wars) or joining the fight against South Africa's racially divisive structure (and supporting the British in the Zulu and the Boer wars). According to him Britain's fight in each one of these four specific situations was just—they were, in each case, wars against the assertion of racial supremacy, which could have led, and did lead in South Africa, to stifling racial oppression. In Gandhi's mind there was nothing more morally abhorrent than racial oppression in any of its forms—color, creed, or genealogical heritage. The exercise of his moral authority was unflinchingly consistent.

India's fight against Britain, the way he positioned it, was a fight against economic oppression. The political philosophy of "self-reliance" and "self-sufficiency" was fundamental to the objective of achieving freedom from Britain, and "self-restraint" a way of achieving it. It was this package—together with his "moral authority"—that made Gandhi such a formidable foe for anyone caught in the unfortunate position of negotiating with him. Winston Churchill, who could never figure out a way to negotiate with him because his positions were unflinching and nonnegotiable, ended up calling him unfortunate names like "seditious fakir." Even his close friends and associates, like India's first prime minister, Jawaharlal Nehru, would often be at a loss to get him to back down from a stand, even when backing down might ease the process of arriving at a solution.

On top of all these Gandhi possessed an exemplary sense of surprise and timing. No one could predict when he might pick up salt at a beach in India and launch a movement for the repeal of the highly exploitative Salt Act, which forbade Indians to buy salt from anywhere outside of a British-government-regulated store. Or, when his followers went on a rampage against policemen who had fired on an unarmed procession, Gandhi immediately denounced the killing of the policemen and went on a fast to seek penance for the horrible act his followers had committed. Through his personal sacrifices and actions, Gandhi knew, he could prevail on his followers to recognize and believe in the basic decency of the human spirit.

Unlike leaders like Thomas Jefferson, say, who combined a committed belief in democracy and independence for the United States, but privately believed, practiced, and furthered not only slavery (granted it was preemancipation times) but also a way of life of grandeur and good living that was at odds with the lifestyle of the people he was leading, Gandhi's political philosophy was that, to represent the cause of Indians, one needed to live as one of them—later in life he always declared himself when asked about what his profession was to be a "farmer" or "weaver," which were the professions of most poor Indians. Like Alexander, Gandhi believed that was the only way that he could lead.

Unlike Alexander the Great, though, Gandhi was highly reluctant and deeply wary of the public adulation his followers showered on him. He warned his followers that he would never want for them "to shake off the government's slavery to be slaves to me afterwards."7

The Death of Alexander

Back in Opis, hearing of his plans to put the old and injured Macedonians out to pasture, one soldier asked why he didn't send all the Macedonians back. There was loud agreement from the crowd. Another Macedonian sarcastically exclaimed that if he seemed so certain of his ability to wage war without their help, why he didn't go campaigning by himself with his "father"—referring to Zeus Ammon, whom Alexander had taken to referring to as his father, rather than Philip. There was loud laughter and expressions of glee from the crowd. They could accept—and had lived—with Alexander claiming to be a "descendent" of Zeus by way of Heracles, but calling himself "son of Zeus," when he was the son of mortal parents, was going too far in forcing one's divinity. The rebellion was acerbic, widespread, and possessed all the subtlety of the rampaging war elephants in the Battle of the Hydaspes.

But how much criticism is too much criticism? While in the past he had listened to criticism, and acted behind the scenes to quell any rebellion, this time he decided that there was no conceivable way he would tolerate such open criticism of his leadership—especially when the whacks were coming so swiftly and often. He ordered his generals to arrest several of the leaders of the rebellion and had them summarily executed.

He then got up on a platform, and with all the purposefulness of entering a fierce rhetorical brawl, yelled to the Macedonians:

> The purpose of my speech is not to stop you from returning home, for as far as I am concerned, you may return home whenever you please.
>
> The purpose of my speech is to reveal to you the kind of people you have now become and the gratitude with which you treat those who conferred such wealth and magnanimity on you.
>
> Before I touch on what I have done for you, let me begin with my father, Philip.
>
> My father found you as vagabonds and destitutes, clad in hides, feeding a few sheep on the sides of mountains.
>
> He found you fending off Illyrians, Triballians, and Thracians with little success.
>
> He gave you cloaks to wear instead of your hides. He brought you down from the mountains into the plains. But most of all he gave you courage—the courage to fight the barbaric people who were everywhere.
>
> No more did you rush into the nooks and crannies of your impenetrable mountain stronghold for safety. You stood your ground and fought for what was rightfully yours.
>
> He made you colonizers and enacted laws and customs that not only preserved your safety but brought about the dawn of a new age of culture and living.
>
> From slaves and impoverished subjects, he made you rulers of the lands not only of your own but also of the barbarians who had previously threatened you by ravaging your property and seizing your assets.

He made you rulers over the Thessalians, of whom you had always lived in deep and mortal fear. By victory over the Phocians he assured our access into Greece through roads that were broad and traversable rather than narrow and difficult.

He humbled the Athenians and the Thebans to such an extent—and I rendered to him my personal assistance in that campaign at Chaeronea—that instead of these nations repeatedly attacking Macedonia and you paying tribute to the former and living as vassals to the latter, they now rely on our personal assistance and intervention to ensure their security.

He thrust into the Peloponnese and, after securing control of their affairs, was elected as commander in chief of all Greece in the expedition against the Persians—a glory which he didn't attach to himself, but brought to the entire nation of Macedonia.

These were the advantages you received from him—great if examined by themselves but small in the light of what you received from me.

For even though I only inherited a few silver and gold goblets from Philip, I found myself laden with an empty treasury and Philip's massive debts. I borrowed on your behalf to lead an expedition from a country that couldn't support you and forthwith opened up a passage to the Hellespont across a dangerous sea, which the Persians controlled.

After overpowering the viceroys of Darius with our cavalry, we conquered Ionia, entire Aeolis, the Phrygias, and Lydia, and captured Miletus[8] in a siege.

All other nations voluntarily surrendered to us.

I granted you the privilege of appropriating the immense wealth found in each conquest.

The riches of Egypt and Cyrene,[9] which I acquired without a fight, have come to you. The wealth of Syria, Palestine, and Mesopotamia are yours; as are the riches of Babylon, Bactra,[10] and Susa.[11] The treasures of the Persians as well as the immense riches of the Indians are yours as well.

You are the viceroys, the generals, and the captains of this campaign.

I have taken nothing for myself besides this purple robe and the diadem. No one can point to any possession of mine other than what is in your possession or that which I guard for you.

And now that I want to send home those who are old and sick, who I believe will be the envy of everyone back home, you all wish to go.

Go, then, and tell the people back home that your king, who conquered the Persians and the Bactrians, who subjugated the Uxians, who crushed the Parthians, and who marched over the Caucasus and through the Persian Gates, and crossed the great rivers Oxus and Indus, which have never been crossed since Dionysus, who reached the mouth of the Ocean, and who marched through the Gedrosian Desert over which no army has ever crossed alive, go and tell the people back home that after all these struggles you left the man who led you through all these behind, and in the hands of the people he had conquered.

Maybe your report will endear you to them and make you a source of envy and admiration in the eyes of men and women and devout in the eyes of God.

Go back to Macedonia. Leave.[12]

After this speech Alexander went into his tent and did not emerge for two days.

The effect of the speech on the men was mesmerizing. They rushed toward the palace and waited for him to show himself, and said they wouldn't stir from their position till Alexander had come out to meet them. When he finally emerged, he was so touched by their lamentations that tears rolled from his eyes. A Companion officer stepped forward and said, "O King, what grieves us Macedonians the most is that you have already made some Persians your kinsmen—they have the honor of calling themselves 'Alexander's kinsmen'—and can salute you with a kiss, yet none of the Macedonian so far had enjoyed this honor."

"But," Alexander interrupted the officer, "all of you without exception I consider as my kinsmen, and from now on that is what I shall call you."[13] Everything was settled, and like the moment in a religious service when everyone turns to his neighbors, shakes hands, and utters, "Peace," all the troops shook hands, thumped backs, or embraced their comrades—whatever nationality they might be.

Alexander made sacrifices to the gods so that Macedonians and Asians would rule together in harmony. He mixed Macedonians and Asians together into divisions, and many land and sea exercises were carried out so all the men could learn to work effectively with one another. At Babylon he personally supervised the construction of a naval base, where

Macedonians, Babylonians, Indians, and Persians learned from and worked alongside the Phoenicians, the finest naval architects and shipbuilders of the ancient world, and after one of the feasts to celebrate the launch of their new base, he caught a fever after an evening of heavy drinking.

Even though the fever kept increasing, he went back to work at the naval base. By the third day, however, he was entirely bedridden. His soldiers awaited news outside his tent and, when they realized that his health was rapidly sinking, made a plea to enter the tent to bid him good-bye. As the troops filed by his bed, he was too weak to speak—but he returned their greetings and wished each of them well by a nod of his head, a wave of a hand, or the flicker of an eye.

His top generals gathered around him, concerned that there was no succession plan in place. When asked to whom he desired to leave his kingdom he obscurely said, "To the strongest." Alexander died on the fourth day of his fever, June 11, 323 B.C. He was thirty-two years old. There continues to be some debate among classical historians as to what caused Alexander's death, though several leading historians have pointed toward malaria.[14]

His body, embalmed for burial next to the Macedonian kings in Pella, began the long journey back to Macedonia, but along the way was spirited away by Ptolemy, one of his top generals, first to the Egyptian temple at Memphis and then to a site in Alexandria. His generals divided up the spoils among themselves: Ptolemy took Egypt, where he launched the Ptolemaic rule that lasted some three hundred years—ending with the reign of Cleopatra, the last of the Greek rulers of Egypt; Seleucus got most of Asia east of the Euphrates—an empire stretching from Syria all the way to the borders of India, which he ruled from Babylon. Seleucus gave away his Indian dominions to the first Indian emperor to ever unify that large country, Chandra Gupta Maurya. Lysimachus ruled over all of ancient Thrace—modern Bulgaria and Turkey. Alexander's general Antigonus "the One Eyed" ruled over Asia Minor—all of the region west of the Tarsus Mountains till the Hellespont and the entire regions east up to the River Euphrates.

Antipater, whom Alexander had left behind to rule Macedonia in his absence, inherited that as regent; but Antipater had grown old, and soon died. His son, Cassander, would rule Macedonia, separated out from the rest of the empire.[15]

There was much personal cost to Alexander's immediate family. When he died in Babylon, Alexander's wife Roxanne was pregnant with their child. A few months after his death she gave birth to a son, who was named Alexander IV. In the power struggle between his generals as to who would rule Macedonia, it was decreed that Antipater would rule as regent on behalf of Arrhidaeus, the oldest—but illegitimate—son of Philip by his Thessalian mistress as well as Alexander IV. But six years after Alexander's death, when Arrhidaeus' wife—Arrhidaeus suffered from severe epilepsy—staked his claim to sit on the throne of Macedonia, she and Arrhidaeus were very quickly killed (some historians contend by Alexander's mother, Olympias, who came out at the head of a small army from Epirus and had Arrhidaeus, his wife, and their security detail slaughtered).

When Alexander IV was in his early teens, Cassander, realizing that the boy was coming of age, had Roxanne and the boy imprisoned and then murdered. (Before one feels sorry for Roxanne, it might be useful to remember, if Plutarch is to be believed, that immediately after Alexander's death, she sent a forged letter to Darius' daughter Stateira, whom Alexander had married, inviting Stateira and her sister Drypetis to visit; soon after the sisters arrived, Roxanne had them murdered, their bodies dismembered and thrown into a well.) Even Alexander's illegitimate son by Barsine, Heracles, was not spared. Cassander, in return for appointing an old warrior as general, had him murder the sixteen-year-old boy. Around 309 B.C., a year after Heracles' murder, Alexander's sister, Cleopatra, his only sibling (at whose wedding Philip had been assassinated) would be murdered as well.[16]

The war between different groups of the Diadochis (the "Successors") would culminate in the Battle of Ipsus in 301 B.C., where a coalition of them would defeat another led by the then eighty-one-year-old Antigonus "the One Eyed" and his son Demetrius "the Taker of Cities." The Macedonian and Greek army, which had served under Alexander, was split into numerous clumps—some accompanied the Diadochis, while others became roving mercenaries, offering their services to the highest bidders. These empires, as the French philosopher Charles Louis de Secondat Baron de Montesquieu wrote of the disintegration of the Roman empire, were founded by arms and sustained by arms.[17]

Winston Churchill, writing in *The History of the English-Speaking Peoples*, said that the history of empires reveals how each strong ruler—metaphorically and literally—sows the seeds of a weak one to follow. We will never know if Alexander's sons—Alexander IV or Heracles—were strong or weak, but the generals who served under him certainly did not have a chance to shine prominently enough to lead the empire that they each had seized. Partly it was due to the brightness of Alexander's own leadership traits, which made everyone shine less brightly; partly it was due to the recognition that anyone who emerged as a clear successor would have been viewed as a threat to Alexander himself, and met with tragic consequences; and, of course, partly it was due to Alexander's young age, well before a powerful man would begin to consider succession issues. Underlying all these there was one other reason: that Alexander's leadership was the stuff of legends — making it tough for anyone, no matter how strong, to be remembered as his replacement. Who remembers who replaced Green Bay Packers coach Vince Lombardi (Phil Bengston did), or the Chicago Bears' George Halas (Jim Dooley)? History books are not kind to those who follow legendary leaders.

Alexander never mentored or developed any as a successor — because to do so would create a challenge to his supremacy. Indeed, toward the end of his rule, he frequently selected people for senior positions because of their loyalty or record of service toward him — not necessarily due to their ability to lead people or win battles. He killed Cleitus, who had spoken out against Alexander's embrace of Persian customs; Philotas, for his knowledge about an assassination plot; Parmenion, for no other reason than that he was Philotas' father, and Callisthenes, Aristotle's nephew and the Macedonian army's official biographer, for his outspokenness against Alexander's identifying himself as the son of Zeus. Aristotle himself, toward the end of Alexander's reign, had lost all respect for his protégé's ruling style and actions. "No one," he is reported to have said, "would voluntarily endure such a rule."

The First Emperor of China

In another part of the world, about a century after Alexander's death, a similar sort of unification as Alexander had enforced on the then-known world, was brought about in China, although there's no reason to suspect a connection between the two epochal events. This integration was the work of King Ying Zheng of the Qin (or Ch'in) dynasty, who unified the seven warring states that comprised the region that is today's modern China, and was called Qin Shihuang Di — in English, "the first emperor of the Qin dynasty," and gave China its modern name. After his death the Chinese empire disintegrated much as had the Macedonian empire after Alexander's death.

King Ying Zheng came to the throne of the Qin dynasty in 246 B.C. when he was only thirteen years old. His mother was the concubine of a rich merchant, who had installed his father on the Qin throne even though he had no royal lineage.

Zheng's first action as king was to go to war with the warlords who ruled over the local provinces on behalf of their rulers.[18] Everything was fair game in his quest for unification—like Alexander's father, Philip, Zheng resorted to alliances, marriages, trickery, bribery, assault, kidnappings, and assassinations. Finally, in 221 B.C., after twenty-five years of work, he succeeded in unifying an empire, which stretched all the way to the steppes of Tibet on the East, the vast deserts of Mongolia to the north, and to the South China Sea in the south.

To secure the borders millions of men were drafted—often without pay—into building roads and highways for the army to travel. Along the borders Zheng built a complex mélange of stone fortifications, crenellated watchtowers, and garrison stations,[19] which came to be known as the Great Wall of China. The wall was at many levels a perverse achievement. While it kept out the marauding Huns (but not the Mongols, whose advance was recognizable to many Chinese peasants toiling on their terraced fields from the telltale thundering of thousands of horses' hoofs), it also shut China off from the rest of the world. Except for the "Silk Route" that the Han dynasty, which succeeded the Qin, was to build, and for the trade route that Marco Polo was to open up about 1,500 years later, there were few roads or routes that led to China.

It is believed that as many men died building the Great Wall (Qin Shihuang Di built only ten miles of the wall in ten years) as there are stones in the nearly two-thousand-mile-long wall—making it not only one of the longest roads (on top of the wall from end to end runs a nine- to twelve-foot-wide road) but also the largest memorial in the world.

Canals were built to water the fields of the largely agrarian nation, and waterways connected towns and cities to the Yangtze River, opening up maritime commerce as well as routes for warships to travel. The greatest of Qin Shihuang Di's architectural contributions was the Great Tomb, discovered by archeologists in 1970, which is a fifty-six-square mile miniature city, complete with buildings, parks, gardens, and mercury-flowing rivers, and a 7,000-strong terra-cotta army to guard him in the afterlife. It is said that almost a million men toiled for over thirty years to construct Qin Shihuang Di's tomb.

China at that time was under the influence of two different philosophical and religious strains: One was the teaching of Confucius, who lived in the sixth-century B.C., about the time of the Buddha in India; the other was a legalistic framework that decried the highly moral "Do unto others as you do to yourself" tone of Confucianism. To further the process of systematization of the diverse legal systems that existed in the country, of the different dialects of the same language, of the methods of governance, and even such areas as meteorology and currency, he rid the country of Confucius' teachings, and subjected the followers of the religion to a harsh regimen of working on his construction projects. Books on Confucian edicts were burnt in public ceremonies.

Unlike Alexander, who aspired to protect different cultures and religions in his empire, Qin Shihuang Di was not ecumenical. He passed definitive and dictatorial edicts, which, while at one end systematizing weights and measures, laws, and the language, at another end sought to enforce a totalitarian and stifling conformist culture on the people of China. Thousands of people were moved across regions to create settlements here, communities there. An administrative system, based on deep decentralized machinery for tax collection, was built, and the emperor often boasted about the ability of the empire to take care of itself without an emperor to personally enforce any of the laws. Like Alexander he, too, believed in his own divinity and later in life sought the help of shamans and seers to communicate with the gods.

After Qin Shihuang Di mysteriously died in 210 B.C., China erupted into a state of civil war, which lasted several years till a poor peasant, named Liu Bang, entered into an alliance with a military general named Xiang Yu and launched the Han dynasty, which again took China back to its classical heritage, restored Confucianism as well as introduced Buddhism into the country, and restored a relatively benevolent monarchy, which, under different Chinese empires, lasted till 1911. Importantly, the Hans built the "Silk Road" connecting China to central Asia, India, Babylon, and Rome—though travel to and from China was regulated through the Great Wall. Like the Ptolemies in Egypt, who built the first library, the first museum, and the first lighthouse (in part due to Alexander's influence), the Hans built the first public school system in the world, the first seismograph, and the first compass.

The legacy of Qin Shihuang Di has remained highly controversial for most of the more than 2,000 years since his death. He was best known for launching the wealthy Chinese propensity to build opulent graves for their afterlives, in keeping with the Chinese saying about the three duties in life: "Build a house, bear a son, and dig a grave." It was only in the twentieth century that Mao Tse-dong and other leaders of the Communist movement restored his reputation as one of the greatest emperors of China. The Communists followed a similar approach toward the systematization of languages, culture, education, and administration that Qin Shihuang Di had unleashed in China two millennia before. But there is no denying, many scholars of Chinese history agree, that without Qin Shihuang Di's intervention and foresight about a unified China, as well as a common language to bind it, China would not have developed as a nation, or would at any rate have developed differently.

THE MIXED LEGACY OF ANDREW CARNEGIE

Andrew Carnegie, the man who would almost single-handedly create the steel industry in the United States, and in so doing become the world's richest man, was born into poverty in 1835, in Dunfermline, the ancient capital of Scotland, just north of Edinburgh. Young Andrew experienced a Dickensian life of abject poverty and squalor. The mills of Dunfermline, where he was employed as a bobbin boy, subjected its employees to a state of human degradation similar to what Charles Dickens only a few years before had experienced in the factories of London and was writing about at the time Andrew was growing up.

Dunfermline, once the home of the finest handmade damask linen, was a town that the industrial revolution decimated. The automated looms subjected the town's master weavers to a Micawberish lifestyle of shared lodgings and meager morsels—if they were lucky. Andrew's parents, who, in addition to weaving, were both part-time teachers, finally, after hearing about the better life in America, immigrated with Andrew to Pittsburgh in 1848. Pittsburgh in the nineteenth century was a squalid industrial town, where the black soot from its coal-fired ironworks would suffuse the hair and lungs of its poor residents. In Pittsburgh Carnegie began earning his living as a runner in the telegraph office of the Pennsylvania Railroad, where he learned the benefits of efficient operations: the more the trains ran, and the more they carried, the more the owners earned. So important was speed that if a train wrecked on the network, it was cheaper to burn the wagons, then find ways to displace them from the tracks and slowly retrieve their cargo. Because of his initiative and industriousness, he quickly rose up the ranks of the railroad, becoming an officer in the company.

Andrew Carnegie sorely missed the United Kingdom and made many visits back to his country of birth. It was on a visit to England that he noticed the transition the nation's industries were making from iron to steel, thanks to Henry Bessemer's furnace. He returned to Pittsburgh and the money he had made in the Pennsylvania Railroad he plowed into furnaces to smelt iron into steel. The molten steel would be molded into ingots, which would then be stretched, formed, or rolled into rails, pipes, beams, or sheets for the railroads, bridges, skyscrapers, and ships that the United States—and the world—needed. Carnegie was not only the man to lead the U.S. into the steel age, but he ran the most cost-effective steel mills in the world, where workers worked thirteen-hour days, 364 days a year (only July Fourth was off), at subsistence-level pay, under pressure to achieve high output and quality. If anyone fell behind his production targets, he was immediately fired. If there was even the hint of a strike, Carnegie's partner, Henry Clay Frick, resorted to whatever means were necessary—threats, bribes, physical violence—to "encourage" the workers to not strike.

Even though he worked his men very, very hard, and they lived in constant fear of retribution from Frick, Carnegie presented a benevolent face toward them. He connected with them in a way that Alexander did with his troops, always reaching out to them, talking to them, seeking their advice, and promoting their cause. So loud and open were his prolabor causes that many leading business leaders would take Carnegie aside for a tongue-lashing. But as far as he was concerned, he could be the good cop, and he had Frick to play the bad cop who took care of things. Not surprisingly, labor relations in Carnegie's steel mills were deceptively harmonious for the times, when everywhere else in the United States labor was organizing itself into unions, and unions were aggressively trying to delineate the scope of their influence. Frick, for example, owned several coalfields, and labor relations there were a different matter and emblematic of the times: strikes were rampant, scabs were employed—often from as far away as Eastern Europe—to replace those who were on strike, and violence between opposing forces of labor or between labor and factory guards were the order of the day.

Toward the end of the nineteenth century even Carnegie would not remain immune from labor unrest. It found its way to his first steel mill in Pittsburgh. Carnegie's approach was not to negotiate with his workers and, like Alexander sulking in his tent for several days when his troops revolted in Opis, instead head down to New York City and wait it out. He had enough eyes and ears among his employees (intelligence-gathering was a common practice of Carnegie) to know which way they would go — stay with peaceful demonstrations, stage walkouts, or resort to violence — and how long they could afford to stay away from their jobs. He knew, since there was nothing else to do in Pittsburgh, they needed their jobs back, and when union representative came to New York to negotiate the plant's reopening, he followed them back to Pittsburgh to talk to his employees directly about their grievances — rather than even appearing to negotiate with the union representatives.

He assured his workers that their jobs were safe, announced that "Mr. Carnegie takes no man's job," and invited them to return to work. The hold that the union had over these workers was broken, and Carnegie was cheered as a friend of labor. Two years later Carnegie dedicated a large library — much bigger than what the workers could ever have envisaged — for their own and their children's benefit. Like Alexander's conception of the first library in human history in Alexandria, Egypt, Carnegie's gesture was a first — it indicated a genuine interest by the company owner in furthering the welfare of his employees. It was not only stocked with thousands of books, but it was large enough to provide space for meeting rooms, a community center, and a fitness gym. Workers were in love with him.

Labor's love affair with Carnegie wouldn't last long, and in a few years unions again raised their (as far as Carnegie was concerned) ugly heads and demanded job security and the right to comfortable living standards. Rather than give in to the union's demands, Carnegie again instructed Frick to close the plants and wait out their demands. This time, though, the unions were better organized, and not only did the strike last a long time, but there was a distinct shift in the stance of the workers. Heretofore they had viewed themselves as mere employees in the steel plants; but now they had begun to believe that factories were as much their own as their owners'.

When the workers refused to move away from the factory properties, Frick invited 300 Pinkerton guards, a private security service that aided the expanding band of industrialists in fights against labor, to seize control of the factory. In a battle that was to last fourteen hours, watched by every soul in the nation through press coverage in every major newspaper, the guards not only lost but the workers and their families — even women and children — beat and stabbed three to death; though seven workers lost their lives as well. Carnegie, vacationing in the somnolent confines of a

Scottish loch, instructed Frick to let grass grow over the factories if need be, but not negotiate with the unions; workers were welcome to come in and negotiate for themselves as individuals.

Many union members, believing Carnegie was a friend of labor, frantically sent telegrams to him in Scotland, all of which went unanswered. Carnegie's factories were at the end of the nineteenth century the industrial backbone of the nation, and a strike at one of them was a matter of national emergency. Six days after the strike began the governor of Pennsylvania sent in the state militia to arrest many workers, and to open the plant, and Frick hired nonunionized workers to replace the strikers. Five days later the strike collapsed. Unions had again failed to assert authority in Carnegie's steel mills—and therefore in the steel industry—and wouldn't have any hold till the middle of the twentieth century. Every time there was an attempt at unionizing, Carnegie's intelligence-gathering system forewarned him and he would have the men banished from work in the industry forever—these actions from a man whose father, mother, and grandfather were loyal and active members of Britain's Chartist movement, a political group whose main objective was the improvement of worker rights.

By 1892, the Carnegie private partnership, valued at $25 million was turning out extraordinary returns for Andrew Carnegie and his partner Henry Frick—first a 50 percent return, then 100 percent, and eventually over 200 percent.[20] As he bought and merged other steel mills, he also developed what he referred to as "young geniuses"—bright middle managers, whom he elevated to senior management ranks to run the mills, and endowed with a slice of equity.[21] As in many partnership organizations, if the manager left for any reason he was forced to sell his stake back at the current book value. Thousands of clerks and entry-level managers were hired, trained, and developed by the company, and Pittsburgh became a middle-class boomtown with sprawling, leafy suburbs where the emergent steel-industry middle class lived, and even leafier exclusive enclaves where the éminence grises of the industry lived in walled estates. The lot of the workers, on the other hand, didn't improve a bit.

Under these managers the Carnegie's company flourished. Carnegie and Frick embarked on a massive productivity and efficiency improvement process, whereby they replaced old furnaces with more efficient ones. They even undertook the first large-scale initiative at vertical integration the world had seen, whereby they bought not only almost all the iron ore and coke resources they needed, but also the barges and rails transporting iron and coal for their mills. To improve the speed at which the trains could travel, Carnegie encouraged replacement of old tracks with steel tracks and his company helped pay for the upgrading of wooden railroad bridges over rivers with sturdy steel ones. Whenever there was a new technological breakthrough in steel making, Carnegie could be counted on to introduce that technology into his mills—as he did with the open-hearth furnace in the 1890s. Carnegie's steel output was not only the largest in the United States, but he even displaced Great Britain as the largest steel producer in the world.

Carnegie had always wanted to retire early and get the education that he had never received when young. His relationship with Frick was increasingly fraught with tension, and in 1900, when Frick tried to raise prices on the coke he supplied to the mills, it was the proverbial last straw that broke the camel's back. Carnegie wanted Frick out of the partnership, and Frick threatened not only to take Carnegie to the courts but also to wreak physical violence on him—Carnegie, at five feet two inches, was a small man. The ensuing legal battle, entitled "the Clash of the Steel Kings," was the equivalent of the O. J. Simpson trial of the last decade. The entire nation hung on to every salacious detail of the workings of the private partnership. Finally, Carnegie bought Frick out—not at book value as he had threatened—but at the respectable sum of just over $30 million.

Dark clouds were hovering on the horizon for Carnegie, however. The New York financier J. P. Morgan's United States Steel Corporation, which had been buying up finishing mills, where the steel produced by Carnegie's steel mills were cut, polished, and sent off to individual customers, was now moving upstream into the steel-making process by building furnaces. To pressure Carnegie into selling his steel mills, Morgan refused to buy steel from Carnegie for his finishing mills, and many Carnegie mills slowly ground to a halt. Carnegie pooh-poohed the Morgan challenge, but he didn't know that the chief executive he had hired to replace Frick, Charles Schwab—worried about the direction the Carnegie Steel Corporation was headed—was to approach Morgan, privately and secretly, to seek an offer for sale. Schwab also applied pressure on Carnegie through his mother, who had been heartbroken at her son's actions against the unions, and wanted Carnegie to get out of the business and apply himself to what he had always said he wanted to do: philanthropy. In 1901 the Carnegie Steel Corporation was sold to United States Steel Corporation for about $250 million.

The impact of U.S. Steel on the modern world is much like the impact the Diadochis—Alexander's successors—had on their world. On one hand, the company truly launched the era of managerial capitalism, where well-educated professionals from the nation's law and business schools—the ones who had followed a similar sort of course and curriculum development as Aristotle had in training Alexander—were hired and rose up the ranks. On the other hand, like the Diadochis, U.S. Steel faced its own problems and uncertainties—first of coordination and control as it went through the acquisition, absorption, and reorganization of steel plants brought into its fold, then from customers replacing steel with other tough but light materials like aluminum, then from technological developments and improved production techniques, which U.S. Steel's Japanese and European counterparts were using, and finally from cheaper and higher quality imports—primarily from Japan but also from Korea and Taiwan. In the 1980s, not only was the company, renamed USX, gasping to stay alive against tough competition from Japan and nimble players like Nucor, but also had to fight off a brutal takeover battle against leveraged-buyout artist Carl Icahn even as it slowly and steadily faded into ignominy. Like the history of the Diadochis, that of U.S. Steel is one of the leading "harvest" (rather than "build" or "grow") stories in business history.

Like Alexander's mark on the world, Carnegie's was deep and long lasting—though, like Alexander's, frequently criticized. Critics accused him of exerting undue influence over scientific and medical research or academic institutions. But the criticisms never deterred Carnegie. In his "Gospel of Wealth," Carnegie wrote, "The man who dies rich, dies disgraced," and he proceeded to give away what he called his "surplus wealth" for the "improvement of mankind" as fast as he possibly could. He gave away $350 million ($250 million from the sale and another $100 million of his personal wealth) to seven different trusts, each set up to benefit a distinct constituency. There were a few common targets that the trusts were designed to fund: educational, medical, and research institutions, libraries, and institutions that further the cause of global understanding and peace. Like the cities for which Alexander laid the foundations, which not only exist but thrive even today, the richly endowed trusts and financing mechanisms that Carnegie set up, such as the

Carnegie Endowment for International Peace and the Carnegie Corporation of New York, continue to provide much-needed financing to many important educational, cultural, scientific, medical, and social causes. Carnegie never forgot where he came from, and of the $62 million he gave away to three British trusts, one is specifically charged with the objective of improving educational institutions in the town of Dunfermline, where he was born.

Alexander's Unified World

Alexander's vision of one world where different cultures and societies would mingle and coexist with one another pretty much went up in smoke after his death. His dream was the creation of a Greco-Oriental empire, which would be ruled by a Greco-Oriental ruling class, and would be Greco-Oriental down to its very essence.[22] In the pursuit of his goals he had not only created a military training institution for inculcating Asians in the Macedonian art of war, given senior-level responsibilities to Asians in the military and in the governance of the empire, but he had also begun to prepare thousands of Asians for civil service jobs in his empire. His vision, unfortunately, gave way under the Diadochis to a Greco-Macedonian rule, comprised of people who essentially were of the same stock, spoke the same language, and practiced the same religion, and could never comprehend the multicultural ethos that they had inherited. Michael I. Rostovtzeff, one of the greatest classical historians, describes this post-Alexander, Greco-Macedonian rule over the world (commonly called "the Hellenistic Period") as "a peculiar phenomenon, unique of its kind in the evolution of mankind."[23]

In the nations and provinces under the Greco-Macedonian rule the native population remained as alien and isolated as they had been before the arrival of the Macedonians. The Ptolemies of Egypt led a life of distanced grandeur every now and then taking boat rides down the Nile and waving to their native Egyptian subjects, who largely remained as poor as they had been before. Exceptions were those native Egyptians who helped advance the Ptolemies' vast commercial interests: that is, those who loaded and unloaded ships at the port in Alexandria, transported grain, textiles, and oil, or labored as construction workers on the public projects—the roads, canals, and buildings.

So singularly focused were the Ptolemies on commerce that Ptolemaic Egypt has often been described as a stellar example of the practice of modern capitalistic principles in ancient times. One Macedonian governor in Egypt even introduced the notion of arbitrage trading—tipped off about an enlarging famine in Greece, he intervened in the Egyptian grain market to immediately corner it, and sold it back to the Greeks, who were already the main customers of the grain, at inflated prices.

Although the Ptolemies did a roaring trade out of the new world, it is important for us to remind ourselves, as Rostovtzeff once said, that Alexander was no Columbus.[24] Alexander didn't discover a new world or even a trade route. There had always existed brisk trade between the Persians and the Greeks, and several centuries before Alexander, the Persians had constructed the Royal Road from the Persian empire's eastern end to Sardis in the western end—guaranteeing safe passage for traders and merchants from East Asia to Europe.

Although he wasn't a Columbus, Alexander did present a compelling vision for conquering Persia and lands beyond. He also, in the process of achieving that vision, opened up vast markets for Greek goods in Asia, which turned the balance of trade that had historically been negatively oriented against the Greeks (since they imported all their grains and other essentials from Asia) to a formidably positive one.

Unfortunately for Alexander, the Diadochis had no such vision. They were the undeserving beneficiaries of an amazing stroke of misfortune for Alexander and his family, and a massive stroke of luck for them. Their entire objective was managing what they had seized in the breakup of Alexander's empire for their personal benefit. They couldn't think in terms of the legacies of the worlds they now ruled. They were men—and and later men and women—driven only by their personal legacies—that is, the legacies they would leave behind for their children and grandchildren, but not the legacies of the people they ruled. They turned the open passage between Asia and Europe from a route that had been used to trade *with the world* into a route to trade (from their capitals in faraway lands) *with Greece*. While Alexander pursued a vision of discovering new vistas, exploring new lands, and assimilating different cultures, the Diadochis inevitably focused on Greece. Imagine the fur trade in the U.S. just after Lewis and Clark's expedition in the early nineteenth century had opened up the route to the West. What if John Jacob Astor, and the other American and Canadian fur traders, had conducted their trade only with the East Coast of the United States?

Even their respective armies were drawn not from local nationals but from Greece and Macedonia. Unlike Alexander, who sent home large contingents of Macedonian and Greek soldiers, replaced them with local men, and united his Greek and native forces together into a unified army, the Diadochis relied on clumps of unemployed Macedonian and Greek mercenaries, whose services they purchased on an open market.

So Hellenocentric were the Diadochis and the Greek bourgeoisie that surrounded them that they could see little or any use for other models of governance that were beginning to develop during the Hellenistic Period. Take Polybius, for example, the greatest chronicler of Rome's constitution, who shaped the way many political philosophers like Montesquieu viewed the world and the way the Founding Fathers conceived of and constructed the constitution of the United States. Probably the greatest Greek historian of the Hellenistic age (almost a latter-day Thucydides), he had a lot to say about the Roman constitution, especially the way the separation of powers among the consuls, the Senate, and the assemblies had kept the others' power and influence checked and finely balanced.

Polybius had been held a hostage in Rome for seventeen years, between 167 and 151 B.C., so he had a chance to closely observe the workings of the Roman political and governance structure. Yet, while granting that "the Romans in less than fifty-three years have succeeded in subjugating nearly the whole inhabited world to their sole government—a unique thing in history," Polybius' Hellenocentric superiority could never allow him to appreciate that the Romans had managed to create a constitution that had never existed before. He dismissed the rules underlying the governance of Rome's constitution as no different from those that governed the rapidly declining Hellenistic monarchies.[25]

Ruling from within the confines of their opulent palaces, it was not surprising that none of the Diadochis made an iota of dent on the social or economic lives of their subjects. Indeed, as soon as Alexander was dead, every one of the Companions, down to the last man, rid themselves of their non-Greek or non-Macedonian wives. Some of the Diadochis had little interest in investing in their empires—they were purely interested in exploiting them. In Egypt, for example, in their three hundred years of rule, the Ptolemies added two other towns to Alexandria, but that was it.

Some of the other Diadochis, like the Seleucids and the Antigoneads, added many new towns and cities. Indeed, of the eighty or so cities that are supposed to have been created by Alexander, no more than a dozen or so were his creation; the rest were created by these Diadochis, many named after him so they could continue to exploit the myth that surrounded him. Unfortunately these new towns and cities were used to attract only Greeks and Macedonians to settle.

One area in which the Hellenistic Period continued to make important contributions even after Alexander's death was in art and culture. The pursuit of art and culture was so prolific and so profound that not till the Italian Renaissance in the early fourteenth century would the world witness anything similar in the varied types and sheer scale of contributions. One of the areas where art flourished was in the eastern edges of the Seleucid empire, where thousands of Greek artisans joined the men from Alexander's army who had settled here. Even today there survive many monasteries, sculptures, artifacts, images, and coins from that era, which attest to the comingling of cultures. The Buddha's statues in this area are often depicted in Greek or Roman motifs, and coins frequently are found to feature Greek script on one side and Sanskrit on the other.

Many of these Greeks even converted to the local religions, some embracing Buddhism, others Hinduism. Indeed, one of the last of the Greek rulers of the region, Menander, who converted to Buddhism, even had a Sanskrit name, Milind. His long Socratic dialogue to assess the benefits of the conversion with a Buddhist missionary, "The Questions of Milind," remains one of the enduring and important texts of Buddhism. For almost five hundred years after his death Alexander's vision continued to influence this remote part of the world—the eastern end of Iran, Afghanistan, Uzbekistan, Tajikistan, Uzbekistan, and western India—while the world he had come from disintegrated into the Roman empire.

Egypt, with Rome's help, would conquer most of west Asia. But Egypt's hegemony would end with the suicide of her last Macedonian monarch, Cleopatra. With the help of her husband, the Roman general Mark Antony, she was close to realizing her dream of unifying the world again as Alexander the Great had done, but Mark Antony's crushing naval defeat at the hands of Octavian, the brother of his divorced and disgraced Roman wife, Octavia, at Actium in the fall of 31 B.C. almost three hundred years after Alexander's death, put a stop to that.[26]

Greece and Macedonia would be under Roman rule till the fourth century A.D., then pass on to Byzantium, and thereafter, in the fifteenth century, become part of the Ottoman empire. Greece and Macedonia would become independent as sovereign nations only in the nineteenth century.

Cleopatra and the End of the Hellenistic Period

In his novel *Immortality* Czech writer Milan Kundera writes of man's longing to leave behind an enduring legacy. Such a legacy would make him immortal, because, despite inevitable death, he would live in the hearts and minds of men.[27] It is this deep yearning for a legacy that made Cleopatra smuggle an asp (a deadly Egyptian cobra) in a basket of figs to her bed, because death by snakebite was assumed by the Egyptians to lead to immortality of the divine kind—of the soul.

We don't know whether Cleopatra achieved immortality in the after-life, but she did achieve immortality—unfortunately, as a femme fatale who cunningly used her beauty to snare first Julius Caesar (while she was married to her younger brother Ptolemy XIV) and then, after Caesar's death, his close friend Mark Antony. A remarkable coincidence was that it was Caesar's nephew and Antony's brother-in-law, C. Julius Caesar Octavius, at age thirty-two (exactly the age at which Alexander died), who brought an end to the chaos that reigned in Rome after Caesar's death and secured the Mediterranean by defeating the forces of Cleopatra and Antony at Actium.

On August 29, 30 B.C., Octavian stood before the embalmed body of Alexander, which lay in state in Alexandria, and declared that with the death of Cleopatra, the entire Hellenistic Period was now officially dead. (This was "Stunde Null," the German phrase that describes that moment in history when the Second World War ended.) In less than three years the Roman Senate would confer on him the title of Imperator Caesar Augustus, a religious term that not only stood for emperor but also implied superhuman powers,[28] and Augustus Caesar, the first Roman emperor, through his sickly but long life, would realize many of the precepts for a unified world that Alexander had set out to fulfill.

Once the Diadochis were all gone, attention returned to the life and legacy of Alexander the Great. Numerous histories were written. Diodorus of Sicily, considered to be an uncritical compiler of information from many sources, wrote one of the first. Plutarch followed almost 120 years after Diodorus with his biographies of forty-six Roman and Greek lives in which the heroes couldn't be more heroic and the devils more devilish. Arrian followed almost a half century after Plutarch and is considered to have done the best job of clarifying, interpreting, and integrating the sources. But it is certainly the case that Alexander's legacy depends on who examines or defines it.

As Kundera wrote, immortality often leads not to a glorious legacy as planned but to a ridiculous one where one is remembered not for acts of courage and benevolence but for embarrassing and unfortunate blips and deviations. Consider Christopher Columbus' legacy as an example. Up until recently, most American schoolchildren merrily chanted the rhyme "In fourteen hundred and ninety-two, Columbus sailed the ocean blue." But just before the celebrations of the five hundredth anniversary of his voyage, as *Newsweek* columnist Meg Greenfield wrote, "The great navigator got hit in the face with a custard pie."[29] Greenfield wrote that "his legacy was revised from one of courage, imagination, and diligence," to an "assortment of villainies that include genocide, racism, and heedless rape and ruin of the environment."[30]

Alexander's legacy, too, has gone through a revisionist phase. Until a few years ago he was most remembered for his vision of unifying the world, for acting on that vision at a time when the might of the Persian empire stacked the odds high against him, for achieving more than what he had promised, for furthering a world view of cultural and social coexistence, and for building institutions, nations, and cities that still survive today. He could have just hoarded and exploited the wealth for his personal benefit. In the unflinching pursuit of his ambition he certainly made mistakes and often ruthlessly pursued the enlargement of his empire or his personal convictions. Thousands of lives were lost. Some historians have preferred to focus on these blips entirely and remember him as a power hungry megalomaniac, destroyer of many great civilizations, marauder extraordinaire, a rapacious autocrat, and a mass killer.

Whatever end of Alexander's legacy one wishes to focus on, what he did right or what he got wrong, there is no doubt that his actions and decisions, his strategies and tactics, and his leadership qualities and vision will always serve as guideposts and beacon to all those who wish to build institutions, however large or small, personal or professional, and his understanding and appreciation of different cultures helps clarify the ambiguities and uncertainties of the world we live in today. It does require studying his character and achievements with some skepticism and going beyond what a classicist, biographer, or historian might have to offer—or at least understanding that there are many interpretations.

Alexander did achieve immortality as an individual who went where no one before had had the courage to go, to do what no one had done before, and achieved his objectives in a fashion that not only served him well but has also provided guideposts for generations after. He did it in an era when history seemed to present a stark choice between democratic humanism—albeit imperfect—of Greece or the totalitarianism of Persia. The story of Alexander the Great will always serve as a bright sun to anyone willing to cut through the fog of critical propaganda or through the dark clouds of derision about him. Every age will interpret and reinterpret him through the social and moral positions of that age, and each interpretation will say as much about us as about him. There is no denying, however, that after 2,500 years of such interpretations he continues to inspire us in what we do today.

SUMMARY OF THEMES

1. No clear succession plan.

One of the fundamental challenges of succession planning in business and political organizations, as it is in the rule of nations, is that very few organizations ever make contingency plans for the loss of their leader. The history of Alexander the Great's death and the loss of the empire by his successors serves as a telling testimony to the ramifications of not being prepared for the loss of a leader.

2. Promoting loyalists over talent.

Although the Companions were highly capable leaders, Alexander never mentored or developed any as a successor—because to do so would create a challenge to his supremacy. Indeed, toward the end of his rule, he frequently selected people for senior positions because of their loyalty or record of service toward him, not necessarily their ability to lead people or win battles. Too often the legacy of a strong leader is an organization without sufficient leadership capacity to fill the void left behind by the departing leader.

3. Quashing criticism leads to conformity.

The Companions, who had started off as colleagues and equals of Alexander, after the assassinations of Parmenion and his son Philotas, stopped challenging Alexander's approaches, plans, and decisions. Toward the end of his reign there was reluctance to "rock the boat," and all the senior generals and governors pretty much went ahead with whatever Alexander said or wanted.

4. PRIVATE VALUES, PUBLIC ACTIONS.

Alexander lost the script on those specific qualities that had brought him so much success in the first place. His private values and public actions became one and he never thought about how his private beliefs affected those whom he had led so far, who might not share those same beliefs.

5. LACK OF STEWARDSHIP.

Everyone associated with Alexander became incredibly wealthy—beyond his or her wildest expectations. On the other hand, his successors never bolstered the political and military institutions that first Philip and then Alexander had worked so hard to create. Partly, that blame lies with his successors, but also part of it lies with Alexander himself. He was so focused on integrating and unifying the world that he paid little attention to building those very institutions that had made it possible for the Macedonians to conquer almost the entire known world.

SELECTED BIBLIOGRAPHY

Adcock, F. E. *The Greek and Macedonian Art of War*. Berkeley and Los Angeles: University of California Press, 1957.

Allison, Graham T. *Essence of Decision: Explaining the Cuban Missile Crisis*. Boston: Little Brown, 1971.

Ambrose, Stephen E. *D-Day, June 6, 1944: The Climactic Battle of World War II*. New York: Simon & Schuster, 1994.

Argyris, Chris. *Flawed Advice and the Management Trap: How Managers Can Know When They're Getting Good Advice and When They're Not*. Oxford: Oxford University Press, 2000.

——. *Knowledge for Action: A Guide to Overcoming Barriers to Organizational Change*. San Francisco: Jossey-Bass, 1993.

Aristotle. *The Politics of Aristotle*, trans. Peter L. Phillips Simpson. Chapel Hill: University of North Carolina Press, 1997; *The Politics of Aristotle*, ed. and trans. Ernest Barker. Oxford: Oxford University Press, 1946; and *The Politics*, trans. T. A. Sinclair and Trevor J. Saunders London: Penguin Books, 1981.

Armstrong, Karen. *Holy War: The Crusades and Their Impact on Today's World*. New York: Random House, 1988.

Arrian. *Anabasis of Alexander*, trans. P. A. Brunt. Cambridge, MA: Harvard University Press, 1983.

Badian, Ernst. *Studies in Greek and Roman History*. Oxford: Basil Blackwell, 1964.

Barr-Sharrar, B., and E. N. Borza. *Macedonia and Greece in Late Classical and Early Hellenistic Times*. (Studies in History of Art, Vol. 10) Washington: National Gallery of Art, 1982.

Barzun, Jacques. *From Dawn to Decadence: 500 Years of Western Cultural Life*. New York: HarperCollins, 2000.

Beard, Mary. *The Parthenon*. London: Profile Books, 2002.

Beatty, Jack, ed. *Colossus: How the Corporation Changed America*. New York: Broadway Books, 2001.

———. *The World According to Peter Drucker: The Life and Work of the World's Greatest Management Thinker*. New York: The Free Press, 1998.

Boorstin, Daniel J. *The Creators: A History of Heroes of the Imagination*. New York: Random House, 1992.

Boot, Max. *The Savage Wars of Peace: Small Wars and the Rise of American Power*. New York: Basic Books, 2002.

Boritt, Gabor S., ed. *Jefferson Davis's Generals*. Oxford: Oxford University Press, 1999.

Borza, Eugene N. *In the Shadow of Olympus: The Emergence of Macedon*. Princeton, NJ: Princeton University Press, 1990.

Bosworth, A. B., *Alexander and the East: The Tragedy of Triumph*. Oxford: Oxford University Press, 1996.

———. *Conquest and Empire: The Reign of Alexander the Great*. Cambridge: Cambridge University Press, 1988.

Bosworth, A. B., and E. J. Baynham, ed. *Alexander the Great in Fact and Fiction*. Oxford: Oxford University Press, 2000.

Bradley, Ben. *A Good Life: Newspapering and Other Adventures*. New York: Simon & Schuster, 1995.

Burckhardt, Jacob. *The Greeks and Greek Civilization*, ed. Oswyn Murray and trans. Sheila Stern. New York: St. Martin's, 1999.

Burkert, Walter. *Ancient Mystery Cults*. Cambridge, MA: Harvard University Press, 1987.

Burns, James MacGregor. *Leadership*. New York: Harper and Row, 1978.

———. *Roosevelt: The Lion and the Fox*. New York: Harcourt Brace, 1956.

Campbell, Joseph, with Bill Moyers. *The Power of Myth*. New York: Random House, 1988.

Carney, Elizabeth. *Women and Monarchy in Macedonia*. Norman, OK: University of Oklahoma Press, 2000.

Caro, Robert A. *Master of the Senate: The Years of Lyndon Johnson*. New York: Alfred A. Knopf, 2002.

Cartledge, Paul. *Ancient Greece: Cambridge Illustrated History*. Cambridge: Cambridge University Press, 1998.

Cawkwell, George L. *Philip of Macedon*. London: Faber and Faber, 1978.

Chandler, Alfred D. Jr., *Strategy and Structure: Chapters in the History of the American Industrial Enterprise*. Cambridge, MA: MIT Press, 1962.

———. *The Visible Hand: The Managerial Revolution in American Business*. Cambridge, MA: Harvard University Press, 1980.

Chandler, David G. *The Military Maxims of Napoleon*, trans. Lieutenant-General Sir George C. D'Aguilar. London: Greenhill, 1987.

Churchill, Winston. *A History of the English-Speaking People*, Vol. 1–4. London: Cassell, 1956.

———. *The Second World War*, Vol. 1–6. London: Cassell, 1948–1954.

Clausewitz, Carl von. *On War*, ed. and trans. Michael Howard and Peter Paret. Princeton, NJ: Princeton University Press, 1976.

Clayton, Tim, and Phil Craig. *Finest Hour: The Battle of Britain*. New York: Simon & Schuster, 1999.

Collingwood, R. G. *The Idea of History*. Oxford: Clarendon Press, 1993.

Collins, James C. and Jerry I. Porras. *Built to Last: Successful Habits of Visionary Companies.* New York: Harper Business, 1994.

Crankshaw, Edward. *The Fall of the House of Habsburg.* London: Longmans, Green, 1963.

Cusumano, Michael A., and David B. Yoffie. *Competing on Internet Times: Lessons from Netscape and its Battle with Microsoft.* New York: Free Press, 1998.

Das, Gurcharan. *India Unbound.* London: Profile Books, 2002.

Davis, Paul K. *100 Decisive Battles: From Ancient Times to the Present.* Oxford: Oxford University Press, 1999.

Diodorus Siculus. *Library of History*, trans. C. Bradford Welles. Cambridge, MA: Harvard University Press, 1963.

Dixon, Norman. *On the Psychology of Military Incompetence.* London: Random House, 1976.

Dodge, Theodore Ayrault. *Alexander.* Boston, MA: Houghton Mifflin, 1890.

Drucker, Peter F. *The Age of Discontinuity: Guidelines to Our Changing Society.* London: Heinemann, 1969.

——. *The Changing World of the Executive.* London: Heinemann, 1982.

——. *The Practice of Management.* London: Butterworth-Heinemann, 1955.

Eccles, Robert G., and Nitin Nohria, with James D. Berkley. *Beyond the Hype: Rediscovering the Essence of Management.* Boston: Harvard Business School Press, 1992.

Engels, Donald W. *Alexander the Great and the Logistics of the Macedonian Army.* Berkeley and Los Angeles: University of California Press, 1978.

Ellis, Joseph. *Founding Brothers: The Revolutionary Generation.* New York: Random House, 2000.

Errington, R. Malcolm. *A History of Macedonia*, trans. Catherine Errington. Berkeley and Los Angeles: University of California Press, 1990.

Finley, M. I. *Democracy Ancient & Modern.* New Brunswick, NJ: Rutgers University Press, 1985.

Fischer, David Hackett. *Historians' Fallacies: Toward a Logic of Historical Thought.* New York: Harper & Row, 1970.

Fischer, Louis. *The Life of Mahatma Gandhi.* New York: Harper & Row, 1950.

Fox, Robin Lane. *Alexander the Great.* London: Allen Lane, 1973.

Frankel, Max. *The Times of My Life and My Life with the Times.* New York: Random House, 1999.

Fraser, P. M. *Cities of Alexander the Great.* Oxford: Oxford University Press, 1996.

Fuller, J.F.C. *The Generalship of Alexander the Great.* New Brunswick, NJ: Rutgers University Press, 1960.

——. *Julius Caesar: Man, Soldier, and Tyrant.* New Brunswick, NJ: Rutgers University Press, 1965.

——. *Military History of the Western World, Vol. 1–3.* New Brunswick, NJ: Rutgers University Press, 1955–1961.

Gardner, John W. *Excellence.* New York: W. W. Norton, 1984.

——. *On Leadership.* New York: Free Press, 1990.

——. *Self-Renewal: The Individual and the Innovative Society.* New York: W. W. Norton, 1981.

Ghemawat, Pankaj. *Commitment: The Dynamic of Strategy*. New York: The Free Press, 1991.

Gilbert, Martin. *First World War*. London: Weidenfeld & Nicolson, 1994.

Graham, Katherine. *Personal History*. New York: Alfred A. Knopf, 1997.

Grant, Michael. *The Classical Greeks*. London: Weidenfeld & Nicolson, 1989.

Grant, Ulysses S. *Personal Memoirs*. New York: C. L. Webster, 1885.

Graves, Robert. *The Greek Myths*. New York: George Braziller, 1957.

Green, Peter. *Alexander of Macedon, 356–323 B.C.: A Historical Biography*. Berkeley and Los Angeles: University of California Press, 1991.

——. *Alexander to Actium: The Historical Evolution of the Hellenistic Age*. Berkeley and Los Angeles: University of California Press, 1990.

Hamilton, Edith. *The Echo of Greece*. New York: W. W. Norton, 1957.

——.*The Greek Way*. New York: W. W. Norton, 1930.

——. *Mythology*. Boston: Little Brown, 1942.

Hammond, N.G.L. *Alexander the Great: King, Commander and Statesman*. London: Bristol Classical Press, 1989.

——. *The Genius of Alexander the Great*. London: Gerald Duckworth, 1997.

Hanson, Victor Davis. *The Wars of the Ancient Greeks: And Their Invention of Western Military Culture*. London: Cassell, 1999.

——. *The Soul of Battle: From Ancient Times to the Present Day, How Three Great Liberators Vanquished Tyranny*. New York: The Free Press, 1999.

——. *The Western Way of War: Infantry Battle in Classical Greece*. New York: Alfred A. Knopf, 1989.

Herman, Arthur. *How the Scots Invented the Modern World*. New York: Crown, 2001.

Hesketh, Roger. *Fortitude: The D-Day Deception Campaign*. New York: Overlook Press, 2000.

Hibbert, Christopher. *Nelson: A Personal History*. London: Viking, 1994.

——. *Wellington: A Personal History*. London: HarperCollins, 1997.

Hobsbawm, Eric, and Terence Ranger, ed. *The Invention of Tradition*. Cambridge, MA: Cambridge University Press, 1983.

Homer. *The Iliad*, trans. Robert Fagles. Introduction and notes by Bernard Knox. New York: Penguin, 1990.

Horne, Alistair with David Montgomery. *How Far from Austerlitz? Napoleon 1805–1815*. London: Macmillan, 1996.

——. *The Lonely Leader: Monty 1944–1945*. London: Macmillan, 1994.

Howard, Sir Michael. *Strategic Deception in the Second World War. British Intelligence Operations Against the German High Command*. New York: Norton, 1990.

Huntington, Samuel P. *The Clash of Civilizations and the Remaking of World Order*. New York: Simon & Schuster, 1996.

——. *Political Order in Changing Societies*. New Haven, CT: Yale University Press, 1968.

Jardine, Lisa. *Worldly Gods: A New History of Renaissance*. London: Macmillan, 1996.

Jenkins, Roy. *Churchill: A Biography*. New York: Farrar, Straus and Giroux, 2001.

Johnson, Paul. *The Renaissance: A Short History*. New York: Random House, 2000.

Jones, Archer. *The Art of War in the Western World*. Oxford: Oxford University Press, 1987.

Kagan, Donald. *On the Origins of War and the Preservation of Peace.* New York: Doubleday, 1995.

Kaplan, Robert D. *Warrior Politics: Why Leadership Demands a Pagan Ethos.* New York: Random House, 2002.

Katzenbach, Jon R., and Douglas K. Smith. *The Wisdom of Teams: Creating the High-Performance Organization.* Boston, MA: Harvard Business School Press, 1993.

Keay, John. *The Honorable Company: A History of the English East India Company.* London: HarperCollins, 1991.

———. *India: A History.* London: HarperCollins, 2000.

Keegan, John. *The First World War.* London: Hutchinson, 1998.

———. *A History of Warfare.* London: Hutchinson, 1993.

———. *The Mask of Command.* London: Penguin Books, 1987.

———. *War and Our World.* London: Hutchinson, 1998.

Kennedy, Paul, ed. *Grand Strategies in War and Peace.* New Haven, CT: Yale University Press, 1991.

Kershaw, Ian. *The "Hitler Myth": Image and Reality in the Third Reich.* Oxford: Oxford University Press, 1987.

———. *Hitler 1889–1936: Hubris.* London: Allen Lane, 1998.

———. *Hitler 1936–1945: Nemesis.* London: Allen Lane, 2000.

Klingman, William K. *Abraham Lincoln and the Road to Emancipation: 1861–1865.* New York: Penguin Putnam, 2001.

Kundera, Milan. *Immortality,* trans. Peter Kussi. New York: HarperPerennial, 1992.

Landes, David S. *The Wealth and Poverty of Nations.* New York: Norton, 1998.

Liddell Hart, B. H. *History of the Second World War.* New York: Putnam, 1971.

———. *Strategy.* London: Faber & Faber, 1954.

Lourie, Richard. *Sakharov: A Biography.* Hanover, NH: Brandeis University Press, 2002.

Luttwak, Edward N. *The Grand Strategy of the Roman Empire: From the First Century A.D. to the Third.* Baltimore, MD: Johns Hopkins University Press, 1976.

Macaulay, Thomas Babington. The *History of England.* London: Longman, Brown, Green, and Longmans, 1849.

Machiavelli, Niccolò. *The Prince,* trans. George Bull. London: Penguin Books, 1961.

Manville, Philip Brook. *The Origins of Citizenship in Ancient Athens.* Princeton, NJ: Princeton University Press, 1990.

Martin, Thomas R. *Ancient Greece: From Prehistoric to Hellenistic Times.* New Haven, CT: Yale University Press.

Mason, Philip. *The Men Who Ruled India.* Kolkata, India: Rupa, 1985.

Melchert, Norman. *The Great Conversation.* New York: McGraw-Hill, 1991.

McCullough, David. *John Adams.* New York: Simon & Schuster, 2001.

McKeon, Richard. *Introduction to Aristotle.* New York: The Modern Library, 1947.

McLynn, Frank. *Napoleon: A Biography.* London: Jonathan Cape, 1997.

Middlekauff, Robert. *The Glorious Cause: The American Revolution, 1763–1789.* Oxford: Oxford University Press, 1982.

Miller, Perry. *Errand into the Wilderness.* Cambridge, MA: Harvard University Press, 1984.

Milton, Giles. *Big Chief Elizabeth: How England's Adventurers Gambled and Won the New World.* London: Hodder & Stoughton, 2000.

Mitford, Nancy. *Frederick the Great.* London: Hamish Hamilton, 1970.

Montesquieu. *Considerations on the Causes of the Greatness of the Romans and Their Decline,* trans. with Introduction and Notes by David Lowenthal. New York: The Free Press, 1965.

Montgomery of Alamein, Field Marshal Viscount. *A Concise History of Warfare.* London: William Collins, 1968.

Morris, Edmund. *Theodore Rex.* New York: Random House, 2001.

Nalebuff, Barry J., and Adam M. Brandenburger. *Co-Opetition.* London: Harper-Collins, 1996.

Napoleon. *How to Make War.* New York: Ediciones La Calavera, 1998.

Neustadt, Ray, and Ernie May. *Thinking in Time: The Uses of History for Decision Makers.* New York: The Free Press, 1986.

Nohria, Nitin, Davis Dyer, and Frederick Dalzell. *Changing Fortunes: Remaking the Industrial Corporation.* New York: John Wiley, 2002.

Norwich, John Julius. *Shakespeare's Kings.* London: Penguin Books, 1999.

Ohmae, Kenichi. *The Mind of the Strategist: The Art of Japanese Business.* New York: McGraw-Hill, 1982.

Pagden, Anthony. *People and Empires: A Short History of European Migration, Exploration, and Conquest from Greece to the Present.* New York: Random House, 2001.

Pagonis, Lt. Gen. William G., with Jeffrey L. Cruikshank. *Moving Mountains: Lessons in Leadership and Logistics from the Gulf War.* Boston, MA: Harvard Business School Press, 1992.

Pakenham, Thomas. *The Boer War.* London: Weidenfeld & Nicolson, 1979.

Peters, Thomas J., and Robert H. Waterman Jr. *In Search of Excellence: Lessons from America's Best-Run Companies.* New York: HarperCollins, 1982.

Plutarch. *Lives,* trans. Bernadotte Perrin. Cambridge, MA: Harvard University Press, 1928.

———. *The Age of Alexander: Nine Greek Lives,* trans. Ian Scott-Kilvert. New York: Penguin, 1973.

Polybius. *The Rise of the Roman Empire,* trans. Ian Scott-Kilvert. New York: Penguin, 1979.

Porter, Glenn. *The Rise of Big Business: 1860–1920.* Wheeling, IL: Harlan Davidson, 1992.

Porter, Michael E. *Competitive Advantage: Creating and Sustaining Superior Performance.* New York: The Free Press, 1985.

———. *Competitive Strategy: Techniques for Analyzing Industries and Competitors.* New York: Free Press, 1980.

Potter, John. *The Antiquities of Greece.* London: J. Nicholson, 1715.

Pratt, Fletcher. *The Battles That Changed History.* New York: Doubleday, 1956.

Quinn, James Brian. *Strategies for Change: Logical Incrementalism.* Homewood, IL: Richard D. Irwin, 1990.

Ray, John. *Reflections of Osiris: Lives from Ancient Egypt.* London: Profile, 2001.

Rostovtzeff, Michael. *The Social and Economic History of the Hellenistic World.* Oxford: Oxford University Press, 1941.

Rufus, Quintus Curtius. *The History of Alexander*, trans. John Yardley. New York: Penguin Books, 1984.

Sage, Michael M. *Warfare in Ancient Greece: A Sourcebook.* London: Routledge, 1996.

Schom, Alan. *Napoleon Bonaparte.* New York: HarperPerennial, 1997.

Schön, Donald A. *Educating the Reflective Practitioner.* San Francisco: Jossey-Bass, 1987.

———. *The Reflective Practitioner: How Professionals Think in Action.* New York: Basic Books, 1983.

Selbourne, David. *The Principle of Duty.* London: Sinclair-Stevenson, 1994.

Stalk, George Jr., and Thomas M. Hout. *Competing Against Time: How Time-Based Competition Is Reshaping Global Markets.* New York: The Free Press, 1990.

Stark, Freya. *Alexander's Path.* London: John Murray, 1958.

Starkey, David. *Elizabeth: Apprenticeship.* London: Chatto & Windus, 2000.

Starr, Chester G. *A History of the Ancient World.* Oxford and New York: Oxford University Press, 1965.

Strassler, Robert B., ed. *The Landmark Thucydides: A Comprehensive Guide to the Peloponnesian War.* New York: Simon & Schuster, 1996.

Strouse, Jean. *Morgan: American Financier.* New York: Random House, 1999.

Sun Tzu. *The Art of War*, trans. S. B. Griffith. Oxford: Oxford University Press, 1963.

Thapar, Romila. *A History of India*, Vol. 1. London: Penguin Books, 1966.

Thomas, Hugh. *The Conquest of Mexico.* London: Random House, 1993.

Thompson, Julian. *The Lifeblood of War: Logistics in Armed Conflict.* London: Brassey's, 1991.

Titamayenis, T. T. *History of Greece: From the Earliest Times to the Present.* New York: D. Appleton, 1883.

Tuchman, Barbara W. *Stillwell and the American Experience in China, 1911–45.* New York: Macmillan, 1970.

Tushman, Michael L., Charles O'Reilly, and David A. Nadler, ed. *The Management of Organizations: Strategies, Tactics, Analyses.* New York: Harper & Row, 1989.

U.S. Marine Corps. *Warfighting.* New York: Doubleday, 1994.

Van Creveld, Martin. *Command in War.* Cambridge, MA, and London: Harvard University Press, 1985.

———. *Supplying War: Logistics from Wallenstein to Patton.* Cambridge, MA: Cambridge University Press, 1977.

———. *The Transformation of War: The Most Radical Re-interpretation of Armed Conflict since Clausewitz.* New York: The Free Press, 1991.

Vernant, Jean-Pierre. *The Universe, the Gods, and the Mortals: Ancient Greek Myths*, trans. Linda Asher. London: Profile, 2001.

Warsh, David. *Economic Principles: Masters and Mavericks of Modern Economics.* New York: The Free Press, 1993.

Weigley, Russell F. *The Age of Battles: The Quest for Decisive Warfare from Breitenfeld to Waterloo.* Bloomington and Indianapolis, IN: Indiana University Press, 1991.

Weir, Alison. *The Life of Elizabeth I.* New York: Random House, 1998.

Wilcken, Ulrich. *Alexander the Great*, trans. G. C. Richards, with an introduction by E. N. Borza. New York: W. W. Norton, 1967.

Wills, Garry. *Lincoln at Gettysburg: The Words That Remade America*. New York: Simon & Schuster, 1992.

——. *Saint Augustine*. New York: Penguin Putnam, 1999.

Womack, James P., Daniel T. Jones, and Daniel Roos. *The Machine That Changed the World*. New York: Macmillan, 1990.

Wood, Michael. *In the Footsteps of Alexander the Great: A Journey from Greece to Asia*. London: BBC Books, 1997.

Wood, W. J. *Civil War Generalship: The Art of Command*. Westport, CT: Greenwood Press, 1997.

Woodward, Bob. *The Commanders*. New York: Simon & Schuster, 1991.

Worthington, Ian, ed. *Ventures into Greek History: Essays in Honor of N.G.L. Hammond*. Oxford: Oxford University Press, 1994.

Zinn, Howard. *A People's History of the United States: 1492–Present*. New York: HarperCollins, 1980.

ENDNOTES

INTRODUCTION

1. Lisa Jardine, *Worldly Gods: A New History of the Renaissance* (London: Macmillan, 1996), pp. 67–68.

2. Ken Auletta, "The Lost Tycoon," *The New Yorker*, April 23 and 30, 2001, p. 151.

3. Steven J. Ott, ed., *Classic Readings in Organizational Behavior* (Belmont, CA: Brooks/Cole Publishing Company, 1989), p. 10.

4. Theodore Ayrault Dodge, *Alexander* (Boston, MA: Da Capo Press, 1996), p. 153.

5. Geoffrey Parker, ed. *Cambridge Illustrated History: Warfare* (Cambridge, MA: Cambridge University Press, 1995), pp. 36–37.

6. Thomas R. Martin, *Ancient Greece: From Prehistoric to Hellenistic Times* (New Haven, CT and London: Yale University Press), Orations 9.31, p. 188.

7. Quintus Curtius Rufus, *The History of Alexander*, trans. John Yardley (London: Penguin Books, 1984), Book Four, Section 7, Line 31.

8. Borza, Eugene N. *In the Shadow of Olympus: The Emergence of Macedon*, (Princeton, NJ: Princeton University Press, 1990), p. 282, contends though that there was little in the way of a cultural footprint that the Macedonians would leave behind, it was their effective use of military power for which they would be most remembered.

CHAPTER 1
IN THE PRESENCE OF GREATNESS

1. Homer, *The Iliad,* trans. Robert Fagles with introduction and notes by Bernard Knox (New York: Penguin Books, 1990), Book 6-570, p. 211.

2. Plutarch, *The Age of Alexander,* trans. Ian Scott-Kilvert (London: Penguin Books, 1973), p. 254.

3. Peter Green, *Alexander of Macedon, 356–323 B.C.: A Historical Biography* (Berkeley, CA, Los Angeles, CA, London: The University of California Press, 1991), p. 15.

4. Plutarch, p. 254.

5. Quoted from J. M. Edmonds, *Elegy and Iambus with the Anacreontea II* (New York: G. P. Putnam's Sons, 1931), p. 175.

6. Based on the John Jay Osborne Jr. novel of the same name.

7. The lines from Eliot read: "Where is the life we have lost in living! Where is the wisdom we have lost in knowledge! Where is the knowledge we have lost in information!"

8. David Leonhardt, "A Matter of Degree? Not for Consultants" (*The New York Times,* October 1, 2000), Section 3, p. 1.

9. Norman Melchert, *The Great Conversation, Volume 1: Pre-Socratics through Descartes,* 4th Edition (New York: McGraw-Hill, 2002), p. 159.

10. Ibid.

11. Aristotle, *Nichomean Ethics,* trans. W. D. Ross, Book 2, Section 1. Quoted from "Introduction to Aristotle," ed. Richard McKeon (New York: The Modern Library, 1947), p. 331.

12. Ibid.

13. Barbara W. Tuchman, *Stilwell and the American Experience in China, 1911–45* (New York: Bantam Books, 1970), p. 155.

14. Ibid.

15. Bruce Catton, "The Generalship of Ulysses S. Grant," from Grady McWhinney, ed., *Grant, Lee, Lincoln and the Radicals: Essays on Civil War Leadership* (Baton Rouge, LA: Louisiana State University Press), p. 6.

16. Ibid.

17. Barbara W. Tuchman, p. 155.

18. Forrest C. Pogue, *George C. Marshall: Global Commander,* U.S. Air Force Academy Harmon Memorial Lecture # 10, 1968.

19. Alden M. Hayashi, "When to Trust Your Gut," *Harvard Business Review,* February 2001, pp. 59–65.

20. An interview with Professor C. Roland Christensen that originally appeared

in 1985, *Graduate Management Admissions Council Spring/Summer 2000 Selections*, Vol. 16, No. 2, p. 4,349.

CHAPTER 2
THE DAWN OF STRATEGY

1. A. B. Bosworth, *Conquest and Empire: The Reign of Alexander the Great* (Cambridge: Cambridge University Press, 1988), p. 12.

2. Michael E. Porter, "What Is Strategy?" *Harvard Business Review*, November–December, 1996, p. 70.

3. Lionel Giles' description for Sun Tzu's Chinese word. Giles, a curator of books in the British Museum, was one of the earliest translators of Sun Tzu's *The Art of War* in English, when in 1910 he did it as a gift for his brother who was a soldier in the British Army in the hope that the text, written 2,400 years ago, might provide some lessons to the soldier of "today"—"today" being the eve of the First World War.

4. Chester G. Starr, *A History of the Ancient World* (New York and Oxford: Oxford University Press, 1991), p. 370.

5. J.F.C. Fuller, *Julius Caesar: Man, Soldier, and Tyrant* (Reading, MA: Da Capo Press), p. 86

6. Stephen E. Ambrose, *D-Day, June 6, 1944: The Climactic Battle of World War II* (New York: Simon & Schuster, 1994), p. 74

7. Ibid.

8. Martin Van Creveld, *Command in War* (Cambridge, MA, and London: Harvard University Press, 1985), p. 20.

9. Peter Green, *Alexander of Macedon, 356–323 B.C.—A Historical Biography* (Berkeley and Los Angeles, CA, London: University of California Press, 1991)

10. Paul K. Davis, *100 Decisive Battles—from Ancient Times to the Present* (Oxford: Oxford University Press, 1999), p. 29.

11. George Stalk Jr., Philip Evans, and Lawrence E. Shulman, "Competing on Capabilities: The New Rules of Corporate Strategy," *Harvard Business Review*, March–April, 1992.

12. Kenneth R. Andrews, *The Concept of Corporate Strategy* (New York: Dow Jones–Irwin, 1971, and Richard D. Irwin, Inc., 1980 and 1987), p. 22.

13. Barbara Tuchman, *Stilwell and the American Experience in China, 1911–45* (New York: Bantam Books), p. 56.

14. George Stalk Jr. and Thomas M. Hout, *Competing Against Time: How Time-Based Competition Is Reshaping Global Markets* (New York: The Free Press, 1990), p. 58.

15. Jonathan Fahey, "Love into Money," *Forbes*, January 7, 2002, p. 60.

16. Michael E. Porter, "What Is Strategy?" *Harvard Business Review*, p. 69.

17. Ibid.

18. James Brian Quinn, *Strategies for Change: Logical Incrementalism* (Homewood, Ill: Richard D. Irwin Inc, 1980), p. 158.

19. Ibid.

CHAPTER 3
THE MEN WHO COULD BE KING

1. Lisa Endlich, *Goldman Sachs: The Culture of Success* (New York: Touchstone Books, 2000), p. 69.

2. Plutarch, *The Age of Alexander*, trans. Ian Scott-Kilvert (London: Penguin Books, 1973), p. 261.

3. Ibid.

4. David McCullough, *John Adams* (New York: Simon & Schuster, 2001), p. 408.

5. David Starkey, *Elizabeth* (London: Chatto & Windus, 2000) p. 222.

6. Katharine Graham, *Personal History* (New York: Alfred P. Knopf, 1997) p. 341.

7. Janet Lowe, *Warren Buffett Speaks: Wit and Wisdom from the World's Greatest Investor* (New York: John Wiley & Sons, Inc., 1997), p. 70.

8. Alison Weir, *The Life of Elizabeth I* (New York: Ballantine Books, 1998), p. 43.

9. Weir, p. 44.

10. Ibid.

11. Joseph J. Ellis, *Founding Brothers: The Revolutionary Generation* (New York: Alfred P. Knopf, 2001) p. 124.

CHAPTER 4
SETTING THE TONE OF HIS REIGN

1. J.F.C. Fuller, *The Generalship of Alexander the Great* (Reading, MA: Da Capo Press, a member of the Perseus Books Group; originally published by Rutgers University Press, New Brunswick, NJ, 1960) p. 81.

2. Ibid.

3. *The Nation*, Editorial, Vol. 260, No. 16. April 24, 1995, p. 545.

4. Patrick J. Maney, "Hundred Days' Standard Long Outmoded," *The State* (Columbia, SC), Editorial, April 28, 2001, p. 11.

5. Ibid.

6. Ibid.

7. Ibid.

8. Walter Lippmann, *New York Herald Tribune*, January 8, 1932; quoted in Herbert Mitgang's *New York Times Book Review*, titled "The Crusader in the Unseen Wheelchair: A New Life of FDR" (*The New York Times*, March 31, 1990), Section 1, p. 17—a review of Frank Freidel's "Franklin D. Roosevelt: A Rendezvous with Destiny" (Little Brown, 1990).

9. James A. Barnes, "The First 100 Days Are Often Hectic," *The National Journal*, November 12, 1988, Vol. 20, No. 46, p. 2,840.

10. Henry F. Graff, "In the Van of History," *Newsweek*, May 3, 1993, p. 39.

11. Joel Swerdlow, "How to Handle the First Hundred Days; Words of Wisdom for Jimmy Carter from President Adviser-Survivors of Honeymoons Gone By," *Washington Post*, January 9, 1977, p. 10.

12. Philip Johnston, "Verdict on Blair's 100 Days," *The Daily Telegraph*, August 9, 1997, p. 4.

13. Gerard Baker, "Perspectives: A hundred days and the FDR factor—Roosevelt's first three months began a fad. Now it's Bush's turn," *Financial Times* (London), April 28, 2001, p. 3.

14. Richard E. Neustadt, "The Contemporary Presidency: The Presidential Hundred Days—An Overview," *Presidential Studies Quarterly*, March 1, 2001, No. 1, Vol. 31, p. 121.

15. Stephen Hess, "First Impressions: A Look Back at Five Presidential Transitions," *Brookings Review*, Spring 2001, Vol. 2, No. 4.

16. Ibid.

17. Ibid.

18. Betsy Morris, "He's Smart. He's Not Nice. He's Saving Big Blue," *Fortune*, April 14, 1997, p. 68.

19. David Kirkpatrick, "Lou Gerstner's First 30 Days," *Fortune*, May 31, 1993, p. 57.

20. Betsy Morris, p. 68.

21. William J. Broad, "Fumes and Visions Were Not a Myth for Oracle at Delphi," *The New York Times*, March 19, 2002, Section F, p. 1.

CHAPTER 5
SACRED COWS, GILDED SHIELDS, AND A TURK'S-HEAD KNOT

1. Hugh Thomas, *The Conquest of Mexico* (London: Hutchinson, 1993), pp. 222–223.

2. Ibid.

3. These numbers are the best estimation from a variety of sources: Arrian (30,000 infantry and 5,000 cavalry), Diodorus and Justin (32,000 infantry and 4,500 cavalry), Plutarch (30,000–43,000 infantry and 4,000–5,000 cavalry).

4. Andrew Douglas, John O. Burtis, and Kristine L. Pond-Burtis, "Myth and Leadership Vision: Rhetorical Manifestations of Cultural Force," *Journal of Leadership Studies*, No. 4, Vol. 7, p. 55.

5. *The Economist*, "Do you Sincerely Want to Go Crazy?" January 19, 2002, p. 69.

6. Diodorus Siculus, trans. C. Bradford Welles, Book XVII (Cambridge, MA: Harvard University Press; London: William Heinemann Ltd., Loeb Classical Library, 1963), p. 167.

7. Ibid.

8. Wills, p. 34.

9. James Philbin, "A Contratrian View of the Great Emancipator," *The Washington Times*, February 12, 2000, p. B3.

10. Wills, p. 38.

11. Adapted from Arrian, *Anabasis of Alexander*, trans. E. J. Chinnock (London: George Bell and Sons, 1893), Book I, 11–16.

12. Paul K. Davis, *100 Decisive Battles: From Ancient Times to the Present* (Oxford and New York: Oxford University Press, 1999), p. 158.

13. Buster Olney, "New York Yankee Mystique as They Once Again Are Taking Part in Baseball's World Series," *Weekend All Things Considered*, National Public Radio, October 27, 2001.

14. Arrian, *Anabasis of Alexander*, trans. P. A. Brunt (London and Cambridge, MA: Harvard University Press, 1976), p. 131.

15. Michael Wood, *In the Footsteps of Alexander the Great* (London: BBC Books, 1997), p. 49.

16. Werner Burkert, "Ancient Mystery Cults" (Cambridge, MA: Harvard University Press, 1987.)

17. Hugh Trevor-Roper, "The Invention of Tradition: The Highland Tradition of Scotland," from Eric Hobsbawm and Terence Ranger, ed. *"The Invention of Tradition"* (Cambridge: Cambridge University Press, 1983), p. 15.

18. Ibid.

19. Winston Churchill, June 4, 1940, speech before the House of Commons.

20. Gavin Bell, "Myths and Miracles of Darkest Hour," *The Scotsman*, June 3, 2000, p. 9.

CHAPTER 6
SEVEN DISTINCT LEADERSHIP STYLES

1. David W. Oldach, Robert E. Richard, Eugene N. Borza, and R. Michael Benitez, "A Mysterious Death," *The New England Journal of Medicine*, 38: 1,764–1,769, June 11, 1998 and Eugene N. Borza, "Malaria in Alexander's Army," *Ancient History Bulletin*, Vol 1.2, 1987, pp. 36–38.

2. Arrian, *The Anabasis of Alexander*, Book II, trans. Edward James Chinook (London: George Bell & Sons, 1893), p. 76.

3. Fernando Bartolomé, "Nobody Trusts the Boss Completely—Now What?" *Harvard Business Review*, March–April, 1989, pp. 135–142.

4. Andy Server, "It's a Saga that Brings Together Bill Gates, Bernie Ebbers, and Bill Miller—and even Warren Buffett," *Fortune*, July 22, 2002, pp. 131–142.

5. Jomini, *Precis de l'art de la guerre*, p. 333, as quoted in F. E. Adcock, "The Greek and Macedonian Art of War" (Berkeley and Los Angeles, CA: University of California Press, 1957), p. 69.

6. Peter Green, *Alexander of Macedon, 356–323 B.C.: A Historical Biography* (Berkeley and Los Angeles, CA: The University of California Press, 1991) p. 227.

7. This speech is primarily based on Arrian's *The Anabasis of Alexander*, Book II, trans. Edward James Chinook (London: George Bell & Sons, 1893), p. 82, and secondarily on two other translations of Arrian titles: *The Campaigns of Alexander* by Aubrey De Sélincourt (London: Penguin Books, 1971), p. 112, and by P. A. Brunt (Cambridge, MA and London: Harvard University Press, 1976), pp. 145–147.

8. Peter Green, *Alexander of Macedon, 356–323 B.C: A Historical Biography* (Berkeley and Los Angeles, CA: University of California Press, 1991), p. 230.

9. Lord Montgomery of Alamein, *A Concise History of Warfare* (Hertfordshire, UK: Wordsworth Books, 2000), p. 18.

10. Martin Fletcher, "In Memory of the Fallen," *The Times*, March 4, 2002, p. 4.

11. William "Gus" Pagonis with Jeffrey L. Cruikshank, *Moving Mountains: Lessons in Leadership and Logistics from the Gulf War* (Boston, MA: Harvard Business School Press, 1992), pp. 158–197.

12. J.F.C. Fuller, *The Generalship of Alexander the Great* (Boston, MA: Da Capo Press, 1960), p. 155.

13. Arrian, *Anabasis of Alexander*, Book II, trans. Edward James Chinook (London: George Bell & Sons, 1893) p. 96.

14. Ibid.

15. Arrian, *The Campaigns of Alexander*, trans. Aubrey De Sélincourt (London: Penguin Books, 1971) p. 123.

16. Michael Wood, *In the Footsteps of Alexander the Great* (London: BBC Books, 1997), p. 67.

17. Arrian, *The Campaigns of Alexander*, trans. Aubrey De Sélincourt, (London: Penguin Books, 1971), p. 281.

18. Arline B. Tehan, "The Father of a Nation: Going Beyond Myth, Biography Captures Mandela in His Humanness, Greatness," *The Hartford Courant*, January 16, 2000, p. G3 — Book review of Anthony Sampson's *Mandela: The Authorized Biography* (New York: Knopf, 1999).

19. Nadine Gordimer, *Burger's Daughter* (New York: Viking Penguin, 1980).

20. Arrian, *Anabasis of Alexander*, Book II, trans. Edward James Chinook (London: George Bell & Sons, 1893), p. 103.

21. Ulysses S. Grant, *Personal Memoirs*, New York: Penguin Putnam, 1999, p. xix.

22. Quintus Curtius Rufus, *The History of Alexander*, trans. John Yardley (London: Penguin Books, 1984), p. 62.

23. Rufus, p. 151.

24. Michael Useem's *Leading Up: How to Lead Your Boss So You Both Win* (New York: Crown, 2001). Chapter 1 provides an interesting look at McClellan as well as other Civil War generals' leadership capabilities.

25. The lines from Euripedes' *Andromache* run: "Oh, how perverse customs are in Greece! When the army sets up trophies over an enemy, people do not regard this as the deed of those who have done the work. Instead the general receives the honor" — from Euripedes, *Andromache*, ed. and trans. David Kovacs, Loeb Classical Library (London and Cambridge, MA: Harvard University Press, 1995), p. 337.

26. See his highly readable *The Soul of Battle: From Ancient Times to the Present Day, How Three Great Liberators Vanquished Tyranny* (New York: The Free Press, 1999).

27. Thomas C. Schelling, *Arms and Influence* (New Haven, CT: Yale University Press, 1966) p. 2.

28. It is said that Prime Minister Winston Churchill knew as much as two days before the raid over Coventry, through an intelligence source named "Ultra" that Coventry would be bombed. Many today believe, as have several of the key participants in the decision-making with Churchill, who went on to write books about it, that Churchill decided to not evacuate the city because doing so would have tipped the Germans off about the British government's access to an agent in the highest levels of the German government.

29. Shawn Tully, "The Jamie Dimon Show," *Fortune*, July 22, 2002, pp. 88–96.

30. Ronald R. Sims and Johannes Brinkmann, "Leaders as Role Models: The

Case of John Gutfreund at Solomon Brothers," *Journal of Business Ethics*, Vol. 35, No. 4, pp. 327–339.

31. Ibid.

CHAPTER 7
A GLOBAL STRATEGY TO UNIFY THE WORLD

1. Sawhney, Mohanbir S., "Leveraged High-Variety Strategies: From Portfolio Thinking to Platform Thinking," *Journal of the Academy of Marketing Science*, Winter 1998, Vol. 26, No. 1, pp. 54–61.

2. Huw V. Bowen, "400 Years of the East India Company," *History Today*, July 2000.

3. Emma Rothschild, "The Politics of Globalization circa 1773," *OECD Observer*, September 1, 2001, p. 12.

4. J.F.C. Fuller, *The Generalship of Alexander the Great* (New Brunswick, NJ: Rutgers University Press, 1960; republished by Da Capo Press Inc., a member of the Perseus Group), p. 103.

5. N.G.L. Hammond, *Alexander the Great: King, Commander, and Statesman* (London: Bristol Classical Press, 3rd Edition, 1980), p. 123.

6. P. M. Fraser's *Cities of Alexander the Great* (Oxford: Clarendon Press, 1996) lists about a dozen cities genuinely having been found by him, including: Alexandria, Egypt; Herat and Kandahar, Afghanistan; Khojend, Tajikistan; Boukephala, outside of Rawalpindi, Pakistan; and Naisan, Iran.

7. Ibid, p. 130.

8. Gurcharan Das, *India Unbound* (London: Profile Books, 2002), p. 117.

9. Nanette Byrnes, Dean Foust, Stephanie Anderson, William C. Symonds, and Joseph Weber, "Brands in a Bind," *Business Week*, August 28, 2000.

10. *Encyclopaedia Britannica*, Vol. 1, p. 766.

11. Ken Auletta, "The Howell Doctrine," *The New Yorker*, June 10, 2002, p. 68.

12. Diodorus Siculus, Books XXI–XXXII (Cambridge, MA, and London: Harvard and Heinemann), trans. F. R. Walton, p. 95.

13. Ibid, p. 85.

14. Arrian, *The Campaigns of Alexander* (London: Penguin Books), trans. Aubrey de Selincourt, 1958; revised, with new introduction and notes by J. R. Hamilton, 1971, p. 163.

15. Ibid.

CHAPTER 8
"TEETH VERSUS TAIL" — LOGISTICS STRATEGY

1. Andrè, ed., *Le Testament Politique du Cardinal de Richelieu* (Paris: 1947), p. 480.

2. A. B. Bosworth, *Conquest and Empire: The Reign of Alexander the Great* (Cambridge: Cambridge University Press, 1988), p. 99, and Arrian, *Anabasis of Alexander*, Book III, 5–25, trans. P. A. Brunt (Cambridge, MA: Harvard University Press, Loeb Classical Library, 1976), p. 311.

3. Engels, p. 71.

4. Quintus Curtius Rufus, *The History of Alexander*, trans. John Yardley (London: Penguin Books, 1984), Book 6, 14–17, p. 129.

5. James P. Womack, Daniel T. Jones, Daniel Roos, *The Machine That Changed The World* (New York: Macmillan, 1990), p. 160.

6. Ibid.

7. Faith Keenan, "The Marines Learn New Tactics — from Wal-Mart," *Business Week*, December 24, 2001.

8. James W. Crawley, "Supplying the War Machine: Pentagon's intricate 10,000-mile pipeline keeps fighting forces equipped and ready," *The San Diego Union-Tribune*, December 30, 2001, p. A1.

9. Larry Goodson, "Simple Strategies to Win Afghan War," *The Irish Times*, September 24, 2001, p. 16.

10. Donald W. Engels, *Alexander the Great and the Logistics of the Macedonian Army* (Berkeley and Los Angeles, CA: University of California Press, 1978), p. 73.

11. Ibid, p. 72.

12. Engels, p. 91.

13. Michael Wood, *In the Footsteps of Alexander the Great* (London: BBC Books, 1997), p. 136.

14. Donald W. Engels, *Alexander the Great and the Logistics of the Macedonian Army* (Berkeley and Los Angeles, CA: University of California Press, 1978), p. 21.

15. Lt. Gen. William G. Pagonis with Jeffrey L. Cruikshank, *Moving Mountains: Lessons in Leadership and Logistics from the Gulf War* (Cambridge, MA: Harvard Business School Press, 1992), p. 63.

16. Lee Smith, "Lessons from the Gulf," *Fortune*, January 28, 1991, p. 86.

17. Lt. Gen. William G. Pagonis, with Jeffrey L. Cruikshank, *Moving Mountains: Lessons in Leadership and Logistics from the Gulf War* (Cambridge, MA: Harvard Business School Press, 1992), p. 147.

18. Ibid, p. 118.

19. Graham Sharman, "The Rediscovery of Logistics," *Harvard Business Review*, September–October, 1984, p. 71.

20. Wood, p. 144.

21. Ibid.

CHAPTER 9
THE ART OF DECEPTIVE STRATEGY

1. Hugh Thomas, *The Conquest of Mexico* (London: Random House, 1993), p. 5.

2. A. B. Bosworth and E. J. Baynham, ed., *Alexander the Great in Fact and Fiction* (Oxford: Oxford University Press, 2000) contains an interesting chapter by Brian Bosworth titled "A Tale of Two Empires: Hernán Cortés and Alexander the Great," which delineates the similarities and differences in the imperialistic approaches of both men.

3. N.G.L. Hammond, *Alexander the Great: King, Commander & Statesman* (London: Chatto & Windus, 1980 and Bristol Classical Paperbacks, 1989), p. 198.

4. Sun Tzu, *The Art of War* (Oxford: Oxford University Press, 1963), trans. S. B. Griffith, p. 93.

5. Rita Gunther McGrath, Ming-Jer Chen, Ian C. MacMillan, "Multimarket maneuvering in uncertain spheres of influence: Resource diversion strategies," *Academy of Management Review*, October 1998, Vol. 23, No. 4, p. 724.

6. Tim Hindle, "Why Honesty Is the Best Policy," *The Economist*, March 9–15, 2002, Survey, p. 9

7. A. B. Bosworth, *Alexander and the East: The Tragedy of Triumph* (Oxford: Oxford University Press, 1995), p. 71.

8. Michael Howard, *Strategic Deception in the Second World War: British Intelligence Operations Against the German High Command* (London and New York: Norton, 1990), p. 115.

9. Winston Churchill, *The Second World War*, Vol 5, *Closing the Ring* (London: Cassell, 1952), p. 338.

10. Howard, p. 128.

11. Roger Hesketh, *Fortitude: The D-Day Deception Campaign* (New York: Overlook Press, 2000), p. 194.

12. J.F.C. Fuller, *The Generalship of Alexander the Great* (Reading, MA: Da Capo Press, 1960), p. 47.

13. Historians have long debated how, who, and where did the breakaway cavalry charge happen, but by and large there is agreement that it did happen.

14. Lionel Giles trans. Sun Tzu's *Art of War*, 1910.

15. "Towards the Wild Blue Yonder—Boeing v Airbus," *The Economist*, April 27, 2002.

16. Benjamin C. Esty and Pankaj Ghemawat, *Airbus vs. Boeing in Super jumbos: A Case of Failed Preemption*, Harvard Business School Working Paper 02-061, Aug. 3, 2001 (revised Feb 14, 2002).

17. Ibid.

18. Matthew Brelis, "Faster vs. Bigger," *The Boston Globe*, May 6, 2001, p. C7.

19. Arrian, *The Anabasis of Alexander*, trans. Edward James Chinnock (London: George Bell & Sons, 1893), Book V, p. 290.

20. Basil H. Liddell-Hart, "*Strategy*," 2nd Edition (London: Faber & Faber, 1954, 1967; Meridian Books, 1991), p. 334.

21. Ibid.

CHAPTER 10
ALEXANDER'S DEATH — AND LEGACY

1. Arrian, *The Anabasis of Alexander*, trans. E. J. Chinnock (London: George Bell and Sons, 1893), Book VI, Chapter XXVI, p. 333.

2. Ian Worthington, "How Great was Alexander?" *The Ancient History Bulletin*, Volume 13.2, 1999, pp. 39–55.

3. A. B. Bosworth, *Conquest and Empire — The Reign of Alexander the Great* (Cambridge: Cambridge University Press, 1988), p. 99.

4. Bosworth, p. 156.

5. Therese Raphael, "An English Lesson for France's President," *The Wall Street Journal*, June 13, 2002, p. A16.

6. Roy Strong, *The Story of Britain* (London: Oman Productions Ltd., 1996), p. 271.

7. Curt Schleier, "Organizer Mohandas Gandhi: Persistence Helped Him Lead India to Independence," *Investor's Business Daily*, April 20, 2001, p. 2.

8. All regions in Anatolia (in today's Turkey)

9. Libya

10. In today's Afghanistan, Uzbekistan, and Tajikistan

11. In southwestern Iran

12. This speech has been adapted from Arrian, *The Anabasis of Alexander*, trans. E. J. Chinnock (London: George Bell and Sons, 1893), Book VII, Chapter IX and X, pp. 356–360.

13. Arrian, p. 362.

14. Among them Eugene N. Borza (see "Some Observations on Malaria and the Ecology of Central Macedonia in Antiquity," *American Journal of Ancient History*, 4th Issue, pp. 102–104).

15. A. B. Bosworth, *Conquest and Empire—The Reign of Alexander the Great* (Cambridge: Cambridge University Press, 1988), p. 174.

16. Peter Green, *Alexander to Actium: The Historical Evolution of the Hellenistic Age* (Berkeley and Los Angeles, CA: University of California Press, 1990), pp. 28–29.

17. Montesquieu, *Considerations on the Causes of the Greatness of the Romans and their Decline*, trans., with introduction and notes, by David Lowenthal (New York: The Free Press, 1965; Hackett 1999), p. 170.

18. Chester G. Starr, *A History of the Ancient World* (New York and Oxford: Oxford University Press, 1991, 1983, 1974, 1965), p. 174.

19. *The New Encyclopedia Britannica*, Volume 16, p. 74.

20. Nohria, Nitin, Dyer, Davis, and Dalzell, Frederick, *Changing Fortunes: Remaking the Industrial Corporation* (New York: John Wiley, 2002), p. 165.

21. Nohria, p. 164.

22. Michael I. Rostovtzeff, "The Hellenistic World and Its Economic Development," Presidential address delivered before the American Historical Association at Chattanooga on December 28, 1935, reprinted in *American Historical Review*, 41:2, January 1936, pp. 231–52.

23. Michael I. Rostovtzeff, *Hellenistic World: The Social and Economic History of the Hellenistic World* (Oxford: Oxford University Press, 1941), Volume 2.

24. Ibid.

25. Peter Green, p. 282.

26. Peter Green, p. 679.

27. Milan Kundera, *Immortality*, trans. Peter Kussi (New York: Grove Press Inc., 1991), p. 48.

28. Chester Starr, pp. 547–571

29. Meg Greenfield, "Goodbye, Columbus," *Newsweek*, February 15, 1999, p. A29.

30. Ibid.

INDEX

I

ABOUT THE AUTHOR

P artha Bose is marketing director of Allen & Overy, one of the largest law firms in the world, with nearly five thousand professionals in twenty-six offices around the globe. Until March 2003, he was chief marketing officer and partner of the Monitor Group, an international strategy advisory firm, and has previously been a partner at McKinsey & Company and editor in chief of *The McKinsey Quarterly*.

Partha holds a Bachelor of Engineering degree from the MS University in Baroda, India, a Master of Science from Columbia University's Graduate School of Journalism, and a Master of Business Administration from the Massachusetts Institute of Technology's Sloan School of Management. He has been a recipient of the India Abroad—Columbia University fellowship and the *Sloan Management Review* fellowship. While at Sloan, he served as an editor of the *Sloan Management Review*.

Partha makes his home in Boston and London. When not chasing his kids around the lawns or the soccer field, he enjoys playing tennis, browsing at antiquarian bookshops, or watching the Chelsea Football Club play in the English Premiership League.